1KBW on Financial Provision for Children

1KBW on Financial Provision for Children

The Honourable Mr Justice Harrison

Katherine Kelsey
Laura Moys
Charlotte Hartley
Thomas Dance
Max Turnell
Elle Tait

Bloomsbury Professional
LONDON • DUBLIN • EDINBURGH • NEW YORK • NEW DELHI • SYDNEY

BLOOMSBURY PROFESSIONAL

Bloomsbury Publishing Plc

50 Bedford Square, London WC1B 3DP, UK

1385 Broadway, New York, NY 10018, USA

Bloomsbury Publishing Ireland Limited

Bloomsbury Publishing Ireland Limited, 29 Earlsfort Terrace, Dublin 2, D02 AY28, Ireland

First published in Great Britain 2025

1

British Library Cataloguing-in-Publication Data

A catalogue record for this book is available from the British Library.

ISBN: PB: 978 1 52653 083 7
ePDF: 978 1 52653 085 1
ePub: 978 1 52653 084 4

Typeset by Compuscript Ltd, Shannon
Printed and bound by CPI Group (UK) Ltd, Croydon, CR0 4YY

MIX
Paper | Supporting responsible forestry
FSC® C013604

For product safety related questions contact productsafety@bloomsbury.com

To find out more about our authors and books visit www.bloomsburyprofessional.com. Here you will find extracts, author information, details of forthcoming events and the option to sign up for our newsletters

Preface

This book is intended to be a comprehensive guide to the law relating to financial provision for children. The work is aimed at practitioners in this field and we have focused upon practice and procedure wherever possible. We hope that it will also be useful to others who have an interest in this important area of family law.

Child maintenance in purely domestic cases is usually now dealt with by the Child Maintenance Service (CMS) rather than the courts. We have included a chapter about the CMS, explaining how the formula is applied and the scope which exists to depart from it. The majority of the book relates to applications which can be made to the court and the considerations which apply to the different forms of financial provision which it is possible to seek.

Our collective experience has been that this is an area of practice on the increase, which is perhaps a reflection of the changing demographics in society. It is certainly a topic which specialist family lawyers encounter on a regular basis.

We are indebted to many people who have supported us throughout our careers. We would like to pay particular tribute to the late James Turner KC. He was one of the most distinguished barristers at the family Bar and his untimely death in 2025 has been a great loss to 1KBW and the family law world in general. He is much missed as a friend and colleague.

As ever, we would also like to extend our gratitude and thanks to the outstanding publishing team at Bloomsbury for their expertise and the help and support they have given us with this work.

RH, KK, LM, CH, TD, MT and ET
July 2025

Contents

Table of Statutes

Table of Statutory Instruments

Table of European Legislation

CONVENTIONS

REGULATIONS

Table of Cases

D

E

F

G

H

X

Y

Z

CHAPTER 1

Introduction

1.1 The purpose of providing financial remedies for children is to alleviate the consequences which they may suffer as a result of the breakdown of their parents' relationship.

1.2 In cases where the parents are married or civil partners, it is unusual for the court to consider claims for capital on behalf of the children. Their capital needs are usually subsumed within the claims made by the parents themselves. Child maintenance in such cases is often a relatively small component of the overall financial remedy package agreed by the parents or ordered by the court.

1.3 In cases which do not involve marriages or civil partnerships, a parent has no right to pursue claims against their separated partner on their own behalf. They are limited to pursuing claims on behalf of the children. Any award made 'on behalf of the children' may comprise the entirety or the majority of the financial resources which will support the children and their carer during the children's minority.

1.4 On the face of it, the Children Act 1989 ('CA 1989'), Sch 1 gives the court unrestricted powers to make orders for the payment of lump sums or the transfer or settlement of property to an applicant, so long as such orders are made 'for the benefit of a child'. The courts, however, have been very clear in specifying that orders intended to make provision for housing must, save in cases involving a child with long-term needs arising from a disability, have effect only until soon after the relevant child finishes their tertiary education[1].

1.5 The consequence of this approach is that there is a dramatic difference between the outcome for applicants with children who have been married or within a civil partnership and those who have not been married or civil partners. An economically vulnerable married applicant with a child may well recover housing for life if their former spouse is sufficiently wealthy to allow for this, however short the marriage. By contrast, an unmarried parent cannot make a claim for housing provision beyond the child's years of dependence, however long their relationship may have endured.

1.6 A compelling case can be made that the current system is unfair. It has a disproportionately negative impact upon women and is arguably, therefore, discriminatory. It leaves many women (in particular) in a precarious financial

1 See, for example, *DN v UD* [2021] EWCA Civ 1947, [2022] Fam 289, [2022] 2 WLR 1047, [2022] 2 FLR 308.

position once the period of the child's dependency comes to an end. In big money cases, orders are often made which result in female carers going overnight from a position whereby they enjoy the benefit of a substantial six-figure child maintenance award and luxurious housing to one where their income and home is suddenly removed from them. So far as the authors of this book are aware, there has been no research into the impact which such a consequence has on the applicants or the children whose interests the orders are intended to serve. It is easy to envisage that some children may suffer indirectly from the strain placed upon a caring parent who knows that their financial security is time-limited and nearing its end.

1.7 If there is to be a change in the law, it will probably have to come from Parliament although there does exist a need for the Supreme Court to review the manner in which the CA 1989, Sch 1 is interpreted by the courts. The purpose of this book is not to campaign for a change in the law, but to describe the law as it stands.

1.8 The book has been divided into chapters dealing with discrete topics. The primary focus of the book is on applications to court. **Chapter 3**, however, deals with the potential remedies available through the Child Maintenance Service ('CMS'), pursuant to the Child Support Act 1991. The CMS has exclusive jurisdiction over child maintenance in the majority of cases; before pursuing such an application to court, practitioners must ensure that their client falls within one of the exceptions. Applications for maintenance in cases where the courts do have jurisdiction are considered in **Chapter 12**. Applications for variation are addressed in **Chapter 14**.

1.9 **Chapter 4** addresses the question of jurisdiction at an international level and considers in detail the concepts of 'habitual residence' and 'domicile' which are a central feature of the rules of jurisdiction.

1.10 **Chapters 2, 5 and 7** contain a degree of overlap but are intended to fulfil different functions. **Chapter 2** contains a summary overview of the main three statutes pursuant to which applications for child maintenance may be made. The focus of **Chapter 5** is on the different applicants who may bring a claim under different regimes and the potential respondents to such claims. **Chapter 7** addresses more widely the procedure involved in making a claim.

1.11 In a number of cases, applications for the benefit of a child are made alongside civil claims in relation to a property in which both parties may have a beneficial interest. The issues raised by such related claims are considered in **Chapter 6**.

1.12 Interim provision is addressed in **Chapters 8 and 9**, the latter of which focuses exclusively on applications for legal services funding. Such applications are often of crucial importance in circumstances where it is rare for an applicant to be eligible for legal aid. The question of costs is different from applications for legal funding and is considered in **Chapter 16**.

1.13 **Chapters 10 and 11** are both concerned with claims for capital: the former with housing claims (which are often the most significant issue in a case) and the latter for claims with other forms of capital.

1.14 The question of enforcement could occupy an entire book. Some of the available enforcement remedies have been covered in detail by the authors in *1KBW on Enforcement in Financial Remedies Proceedings*. **Chapter 15** of this book addresses more concisely issues of enforcement which may arise in the context of claims for financial provision for children.

1.15 This book is intended to be a user-friendly guide for practitioners although it is hoped that it may also be of interest to academics and students of family law. As has been done with previous titles in the '1KBW on' series, the authors have sought to illustrate the legal principles addressed with graphics and case summaries.

CHAPTER 2

Overview of Statutory Regimes

Content at a glance:

INTRODUCTION

2.1 This chapter is intended to provide a high-level summary of the different statutory regimes available to seek financial remedies for children through the courts. Applications to the Child Maintenance Service are governed by the Child Support Act 1991 and are dealt with in **Chapter 3**.

2.2 The statutes considered in this Chapter are:

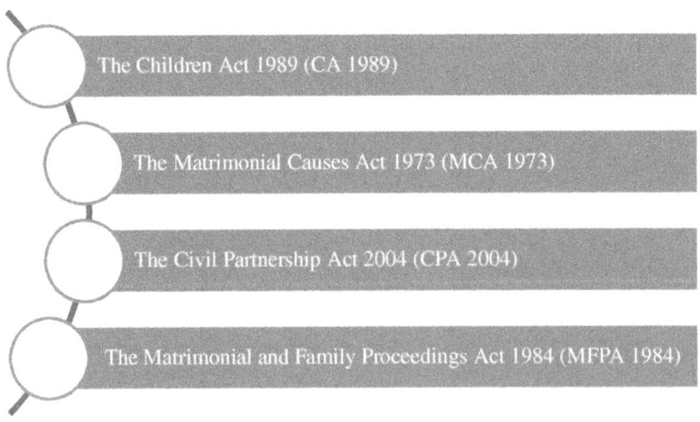

2.3 Each of those statutes contains different provisions through which it is possible to apply to court for financial remedies for a child. Which route will be most appropriate is likely to depend primarily upon the status of the parties. Practitioners should first consider the following preliminary questions:

- Are or were the parties married?
- If married, are there proceedings for divorce, judicial separation or nullity or will such proceedings be brought?
- If divorced etc, was this as a result of proceedings in an overseas jurisdiction?
- Are or were the parties civil partners?
- If civil partners, are there proceedings for dissolution, legal separation or nullity or will such proceedings be brought?
- If the civil partnership has been dissolved etc, was this as a result of proceedings in an overseas jurisdiction?

SUMMARY OF PROCEDURAL ROUTES FOR SEEKING FINANCIAL REMEDIES FOR A CHILD

2.4 The following summarises the main procedural routes through which applications can be made, depending on the status of the parties (NB in the diagram, references to divorce include marriages subject to annulment and judicial separation; references to dissolved civil partnership include those subject to annulment or legal separation):

CA 1989, Sch 1, para 1	• All parents
CA 1989, Sch 1, para 2	• Adult children
MCA 1973, s 27	• Married parents (no proceedings) • Failure to maintain
MCA 1973, ss 23–24	• Married parents (proceedings) • Divorced etc parents (divorce in E & W)
MCA 1973, s 22	• Married parents (proceedings) • Interim orders
CPA 2004, Sch 5, Pt 9	• Civil partners (no proceedings) • Failure to maintain
CPA 2004, Sch 5, Pts 1 & 2	• Civil partners (proceedings) • Civil partnership dissolved etc (dissolution in E & W)
CPA 2004, Sch 5, para 38	• Civil partners (proceedings) • Interim orders
MFPA 1984, Pt III	• Divorced etc parents (overseas divorce) • Leave of court required
MFPA 1984, s 14	• Divorced etc parents (overseas divorce) • Interim orders (leave of court required)
CPA 2004, Sch 7	• Former civil partners (dissolution etc overseas) • Leave of court required
CPA 2004, Sch 7, para 5	• Former civil partners (dissolution etc overseas) • Interim orders (leave of court required)

2.5 Under each of the four statutes the court has the power to make the following orders to or for the benefit of a child:

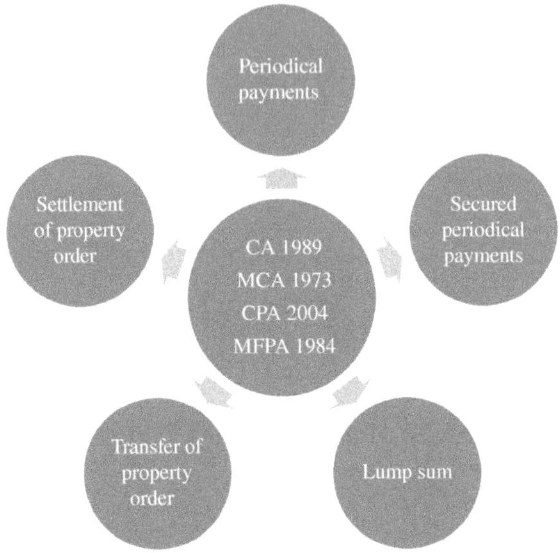

2.6 Where the only orders sought by an applicant are for the benefit of a child, proceedings are typically brought under CA 1989, Sch 1, even if the parties are or have been married or civil partners. Practitioners should, however, bear in mind that the powers of the court are more extensive under MCA 1973, CPA 2004 and MFPA 1984 than they are under CA 1989.

2.7 Under CA 1989 the court does not have the power to vary a nuptial settlement (in a case involving a marriage) or a 'relevant' settlement (in cases involving civil partnerships). Such settlements can be varied for the benefit of a child pursuant to respectively MCA 1973, s 24 or CPA 2004, Sch 5, para 7. The power also exists (with the leave of the court) in proceedings brought following an overseas divorce, judicial separation or annulment, or where a civil partnership has been dissolved or made subject to legal separation or annulment by means of proceedings overseas: see MFPA 1984 and CPA 2004, Sch 7, para 9[1].

2.8 Under CA 1989, Sch 1 the court is restricted to making just one transfer of property or settlement of property order against the same respondent in respect of the same child: see CA 1989, Sch 1, para 1(5)(b). An equivalent restriction is not contained in MCA 1973, CPA 2004 or MFPA 1984[2].

1 See also **Chapter 11** at **11.12**.
2 See also **Chapter 11** at **11.7–11.11**.

2.9 The position is illustrated by the following diagram:

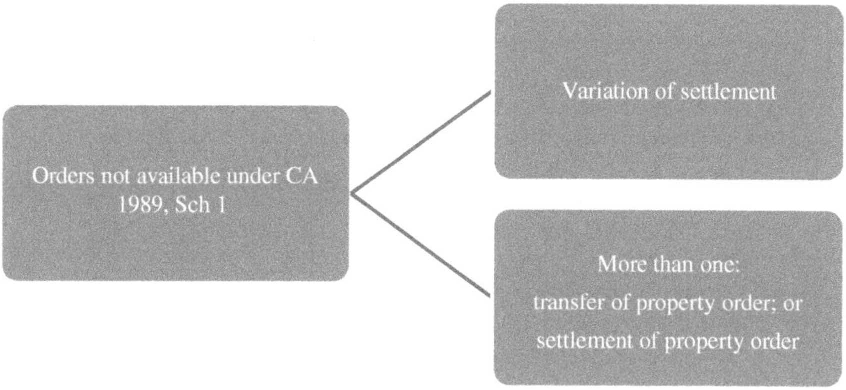

2.10 Under CA 1989, Sch 1 there is a difference between the orders which can be sought by a parent for the benefit of a child and those which can be sought directly by an adult child. An adult child is entitled to seek the following orders against one or both of their parents:

- periodical payments;
- lump sum.

There is no power, however, to make the following orders in favour of an adult child under CA 1989, Sch 1, para 2:

- secured periodical payments;
- property adjustment orders.

2.11 There is also a difference in the class of children entitled to benefit from orders made under CA 1989, Sch1 between: (i) applications made by a parent (or others) for the benefit of a child pursuant to CA 1989, Sch 1, para 1; and (ii) applications made by an adult child under CA 1989, Sch 1, para 2. In cases where the parents are or have been married or civil partners, an applicant is entitled to seek orders for relief against a parent to or for the benefit of 'a child of the family'; by contrast, an adult child is only entitled to seek orders against their legal parent: see CA 1989, Sch 1, para 16(2)[3].

KEY PROVISIONS OF CHILDREN ACT 1989, SCH 1

2.12 The following table contains a summary of the key provisions of CA 1989, Sch 1:

3 See also **Chapter 5** at **5.15–5.18**.

Children Act 1989, Sch 1: summary of key provisions	
Para	**Provisions**
1	**Applications by parents, guardians, special guardians and holders of 'lives with' orders** **(1) and (2)** On an application by a parent, guardian or special guardian or a person with a 'lives with' order[4] in their favour, the court can make one or more of the following orders to or for the benefit of a child: • periodical payments; • secured periodical payments; • lump sum; • settlement of property; • transfer of property. **(3)** The powers conferred by para 1 can be exercised at any time. **(4)** Periodical payments and secured periodical payments can be varied. **(5)** The court can make multiple orders for periodical payments, secured periodical payments and lump sums if the child has not reached the age of 18. The court can only make one settlement of property order or transfer of property order against the same person in respect of the same child. **(6), (6A) and (7)** The court can exercise its powers of its own motion when it makes varies or discharges a special guardianship order or a 'lives with' order or when the child is a ward of court.
2	**Applications by adult children** **(1) and (2)** On an application by an adult child who is, will be, or would be receiving education or training[5] or where there are special circumstances[6] the court can make one or more of the following orders against either or both of the parents[7]: • periodical payments; • lump sum. **(3) and (4)** No application/order if periodical payments order in force before adult child turned 18 or if parents living together in same household. **(5)** Periodical payments variable. **(8)** More than one order can be made.
3	**Terms of periodical payments and secured periodical payment orders made on applications by parents, etc** **(1) and (2)** An order under para 1 may begin on date of application or later date but: (a) shall not in the first instance extend beyond the child's seventeenth birthday unless the court thinks 'it is right' to specify a later date; and (b) shall not extend beyond the child's eighteenth birthday unless the child is, will be or would be receiving education or training[8] or there exist 'special circumstances'[9].

4 CA 1989, s 8.
5 See **Chapter 13**.
6 See **Chapter 13**.
7 Orders can only be made against the child's legal parents; it is not possible for a 'child of the family' to seek orders under CA 1989, Sch 1, para 2: see CA 1989, Sch 1, para 16.
8 See **Chapter 13**.
9 See **Chapter 13**.

	(3) and (4) Periodical payments cease to have effect on death of payor or if payor and payee parents live together for more than six months.
4	**Relevant criteria for making orders** **(1)** In exercising its powers under paras 1 and 2, the court shall have regard to all the circumstances including: (a) the income, earning capacity, property and other financial resources which each relevant person[10] has or is likely to have in the foreseeable future; (b) the financial needs, obligations and responsibilities which each relevant person[11] has or is likely to have in the foreseeable future; (c) the financial needs of the child; (d) the income, earning capacity (if any), property and other financial resources of the child; (e) any physical or mental disability of the child; (f) the manner in which the child was being, or was expected to be, educated or trained. **(2)** Where a para 1 order is sought against a person not the mother or father[12] of the child the court shall also have regard to: (a) whether that person had assumed responsibility for the maintenance of the child and, if so, the extent to which and basis on which they assumed that responsibility and the length of the period during which they met that responsibility; (b) whether they did so knowing that the child was not their child; (c) the liability of any other person to maintain the child.
5	**Supplemental provisions relating to lump sums** **(1)** Lump sums under para 1 can be made to meet expenses or liabilities incurred in connection with the child's birth or reasonably incurred before the making of the order. **(3)** On varying or discharging periodical payments the court can make a lump sum order. **(5) and (6)** Lump sums may be payable by instalments, which are variable.
6	**Variation applications** **(1)** On an application to vary/discharge periodical payments the court must have regard to all the circumstances of the case including any change in the para 4 factors. **(2)** The court has the power to suspend temporarily periodical payments and to revive suspended payments. **(3)** The court can vary from any specified date no earlier than the date of the application. **(4)** A variation application can be made by the child, after the age of 16. **(5)** A child aged 16+ but not yet 18 can apply to revive an order which has ceased to have effect at age 16.

10 See CA 1989, Sch 1, para 4(4).
11 See CA 1989, Sch 1, para 4(4).
12 References to 'father' include a woman who is a parent under Human Fertilisation and Embryology Act 2008, ss 42 or 43: see CA 1989, Sch 1, para 4(5).

6A	**Enforcement power on a variation application** On a variation application the family court can exercise its powers under the Maintenance Enforcement Act 1991, s 1(4) and (4A) if satisfied that payment has not been made in accordance with the order; but only if the payor was ordinarily resident in England and Wales at the time the original order was made.
7	**Variation after death of payor** **(1), (2), (6) and (6A)** After the death of the payor, their personal representatives are included among the persons who can apply to vary/discharge an order for secured periodical payments. Save with the leave of the court, a variation application must be made within six months of the date on which representation in regard to the estate of the deceased parent is first taken out. **(3)** Personal representatives cannot be liable for estate distributions after six months of the date of representation on the ground that they ought to have considered the possibility that the court might permit a variation application by the person entitled to payments. **(6)** On a variation application after the death of the payor, the circumstances which the court must take into account include changed circumstances resulting from the death.
9	**Interim orders** The court has the power to make an order for interim periodical payments from such date as may be specified no earlier than the date of the application.
10	**Power to vary maintenance agreements** The court can make an order varying or revoking any financial arrangements contained in a maintenance agreement as may appear just having regard to all the circumstances if it is satisfied that: (a) by reason of a change in circumstances in the light of which the financial arrangements were concluded the agreement should be altered; or (b) the agreement does not contain proper financial arrangements for the child.
11	**Altering maintenance agreements after death** The court can alter a maintenance agreement which provides for payment after the death of one of the parties, following the death of that party. Save with leave of the court an application must be made within six months of the day on which representation is taken out with regard to the estate of the deceased.
12	**Requirement to notify change of address** A person liable to make payments under an order made pursuant to CA 1989, Sch 1 must give notice of any change of address to such person (if any) as may be specified in the order. Failure to do so is a criminal offence.
13	**Referral to conveyancing counsel of the court** Where an order is made for secured periodical payments or for the transfer or settlement of property the court can direct that the matter be referred to conveyancing counsel of the court to settle an instrument to be executed by the parties.
14	**Jurisdiction** **(1)** The court has jurisdiction[13] under para 1 if any of the following are habitually resident in England and Wales on the date of the application: (a) a parent; (b) a guardian or special guardian; (c) a person in whose favour there is a 'lives with' order; (d) the child.

13 For jurisdiction, see **Chapter 4**.

	(2) The court has jurisdiction under para 2 if the adult child or the parent against whom the order is sought is habitually resident or domiciled in England and Wales on the date of the application.
16	**Interpretation** Provisions for the interpretation of 'child', 'parent' and 'maintenance calculation'.

KEY PROVISIONS OF MATRIMONIAL CAUSES ACT 1973

2.13 The following table contains a summary of the key provisions of MCA 1973 relating to financial remedies for a child:

Matrimonial Causes Act 1973: summary of key financial remedy provisions for a child	
Section	**Provisions**
21	**Definition of financial provision orders and property adjustment orders** **(1) Financial provision orders** include the following orders in favour of a child of the family: • periodical payments; • secured periodical payments; • lump sum. **(2) Property adjustment orders** include the following orders: • transfer of property; • settlement of property; • variation of settlement.
22	**Maintenance pending suit** On application for divorce, nullity or judicial separation, the court can make an order for maintenance pending suit as the court thinks reasonable, beginning no earlier than the date of the application and ending on the date of determination of the suit.
22ZA	**Legal services payment orders** In proceedings for divorce etc[14], the court can make orders requiring one party to pay the other an amount for the purpose of enabling the applicant to obtain legal services[15].
22ZB	**Criteria for making or varying legal services payment order** **(1)** When considering whether to make or vary a legal services order under MCA 1973, s 22ZA the court must have regard to: (a) the income, earning capacity, property and other financial resources which each of the applicant and the paying party has or is likely to have in the foreseeable future; (b) the financial needs, obligations and responsibilities which each of the applicant and the paying party has or is likely to have in the foreseeable future;

14 Includes proceedings for nullity and judicial separation.
15 For legal services costs allowances see **Chapter 9**.

	(c) the subject matter of the proceedings, including the matters in issue within them; (d) whether the paying party is legally represented in the proceedings; (e) any steps taken by the applicant to avoid all or part of the proceedings, whether by proposing or considering mediation or otherwise; (f) the applicant's conduct in relation to the proceedings; (g) any amount owed by the applicant to the paying party in respect of costs in the proceedings or other proceedings to which both the applicant and the paying party are or were parties; and (h) the effect of the order or variation on the paying party. **(2)** Earning capacity includes any increase it is reasonable to expect the person to take to steps to acquire. **(3)** For the purposes of (1)(h) the court must have regard, in particular, to whether the order is likely to: (a) cause undue hardship to the paying party; or (b) prevent the paying party from obtaining legal services for the purposes of the proceedings.
23	**Financial provision orders** **(1)** On making a divorce etc[16] order or at any time thereafter (before or after the order if made final) the court can make the following financial provision orders for the benefit of a child of the family: • periodical payments to or for the benefit of a child of the family; • secured periodical payments to or for the benefit of a child of the family; • lump sum to or for the benefit of a child of the family. This is subject to restrictions in MCA 1973, s 29(1) and (3) on making orders in favour of children who have attained the age of 18. **(2)(a)** The court can make interim financial provision orders in favour of a child. **(2)(b)** Where the divorce etc proceedings are dismissed the court can make orders in favour of a child forthwith or within a reasonable period after the dismissal. **(3)(a)** A lump sum can be ordered to meet liabilities or expenses reasonably incurred by the applicant in maintaining herself or a child of the family before the application. **(3)(b)** A lump sum in favour of a child can be ordered to meet liabilities or expenses reasonably incurred by or for the benefit of that child before the application. **(3)(c)** The court can order a lump sum to be paid by instalments and for the instalments to be secured. **(4)** The power of the court to make orders in favour of a child is exercisable from time to time and more than one order can be made. **(5)** Financial provision orders in divorce and nullity proceedings cannot take effect until the divorce or nullity order is final. **(6)** The court can order interest in respect of lump sums which are deferred or payable by instalments.

16 Includes an order for nullity and judicial separation.

24	**Property adjustment orders** **(1)** On making a divorce etc[17] order or at any time thereafter (before or after the order if made final) the court can make the following property adjustment orders for the benefit of a child of the family: • transfer of property; • settlement of property; • variation of nuptial settlement. This is subject to restrictions in MCA 1973, s 29(1) and (3) on making orders in favour of children who have attained the age of 18. **(3)** Property adjustment orders cannot take effect until the divorce etc is final.
24A	**Orders for sale** **(1)** On making a secured periodical payments order, a lump sum order or property adjustment order or at any time thereafter the court has the power to order the sale of such property as may be specified in the order in which either or both parties has a beneficial interest in possession or reversion. **(2)** An order for sale can include supplementary or consequential provisions including as to payment from the proceeds of sale and provision requiring the property to be offered for sale to a person or class of persons. **(3)** Orders for sale cannot take effect until the divorce etc is final. **(4)** Where a third party has a beneficial interest in the relevant property, before ordering a sale, it is the duty of the court to allow the person to make representations and the court must have regard to such representations as may be made.
25	**Criteria for making financial provision orders, property adjustment orders and orders for sale** **(1)** In deciding whether to exercise its powers to make financial provision orders, property adjustment orders or orders for sale the court must have regard to all the circumstances of the case, first consideration being given to the welfare while a minor of a child of the family under the age of 18. **(2) and (3)** As regards orders to or for the benefit of a child, the court must have particular regard to: (2)(a) the income, earning capacity, property and other financial resources which each of the parties to the marriage has or is likely to have in the foreseeable future, including in the case of earning capacity any increase in that capacity which it would in the opinion of the court be reasonable to expect a party to the marriage to take steps to acquire; (2)(b) the financial needs, obligations and responsibilities which each of the parties to the marriage has or is likely to have in the foreseeable future; (2)(c) the standard of living enjoyed by the family before the breakdown of the marriage; (2)(e) any physical or mental disability of either of the parties to the marriage; (3)(a) the financial needs of the child; (3)(b) the income, earning capacity (if any), property and other financial resources of the child;

17 Includes an order for nullity and judicial separation.

	(3)(c) any physical or mental disability of the child; (3)(d) the manner in which the child was being and in which the parties to the marriage expected the child to be educated or trained; **(4)** Where the child of the family in question is not the child of the paying party the court must also have regard to: (a) whether that party assumed any responsibility for the child's maintenance, and, if so, to the extent to which, and the basis upon which, that party assumed such responsibility and to the length of time for which that party discharged such responsibility; (b) whether in assuming and discharging such responsibility that party did so knowing that the child was not his or her own; (c) the liability of any other person to maintain the child.
26	**Commencement of proceedings** Financial proceedings may be begun at any time after the presentation of the application for divorce etc[18].
27	**Failure to maintain** **(1) and (6)** Either party to a marriage can apply for the following orders to or for the benefit of a child of the family on the ground that the other party has … (b) failed to provide, or make a proper contribution towards, reasonable maintenance for the benefit of the child: • periodical payments; • secured periodical payments; • lump sum order. **(2)** The court cannot entertain an application unless one of the following jurisdictional grounds is satisfied on the date of the application: (a) either party is domiciled in England and Wales; (b) the applicant has been habitually resident in England and Wales for a year ending with that date; (c) the respondent is resident there. **(2A)** Where the Hague Child Maintenance Convention[19], Art 18[20] applies, the court cannot entertain the application unless permitted by that Article. **(3A) and (3B)** Where an application is made in relation to a child, the court shall have regard to all the circumstances of the case including the factors under MCA 1973, s 25 which apply in relation to orders sought to or for the benefit of a child (see above), as modified by (3B). **(5)** The court can make interim orders.

18 Includes nullity and judicial separation.

19 The Convention on the International Recovery of Child Support and Other Forms of Family Maintenance concluded on 23 November 2007 at The Hague.

20 Article 18 provides that where a decision is made in a Contracting State where the creditor is habitually resident, as long as the creditor remains habitually resident there proceedings to modify the decision or make a new decision cannot be brought in any other Contracting State. This is subject to various exceptions in Article 18(2) (see further **Chapter 4**).

29	**Restrictions on making orders in favour of adult children** **(1) and (3)** No financial provision order and no transfer of property order shall be made in favour of a child who has attained the age of 18 unless the child is, will be or would be undergoing education or training[21] or there exist special circumstances[22]. **(2) and (3)** Periodical payments or secured periodical payments for a child may begin on the date of the application (or later) but shall not in the first instance extend beyond the birthday after the child attains the upper limit of compulsory school age and in any event not beyond the age of 18 unless the child is, will be or would be undergoing education or training[23] or there exist special circumstances[24]. **(4)** Periodical payments cease to have effect on the death of the payor save in relation to arrears at the date of death.
30	**Referral to conveyancing counsel of the court** Where the court makes a financial provision order requiring payments to be secured or a property adjustment order, the court can direct that the matter be referred to conveyancing counsel of the court to settle an instrument to be executed by the parties.
31	**Variation, discharge, suspension and revival** **(1) and (2)** The court can vary, discharge, suspend or revive the following orders to or for the benefit of a child: • interim maintenance orders; • periodical payments; • secured periodical payments; • lump sums which are payable by instalments or deferred; • settlement of property orders and variation of settlement orders made on or after a judicial separation order (but only on an application for recission of the judicial separation order or for dissolution of the marriage: **(4)**); • orders for sale. **(2A)** The court can remit arrears of maintenance. **(2B)** The court cannot vary deferred lump sums after the death of either party. **(3)** The powers under this section can also be exercised in relation to any instrument executed pursuant to a variable order. **(6)** Where the payor of secured periodical payments dies, a variation/discharge application can be made by the payee or their personal representatives, but save with leave of the court, no such application can be made more than six months after the date of death. **(7)** The court shall have regard to all the circumstances of the case, first consideration being given to the welfare while a minor of any child of the family who has not attained the age of 18, and the circumstances of the case shall include any change in any of the matters to which the court was required to have regard

21 See **Chapter 13**.
22 See **Chapter 13**.
23 See **Chapter 13**.
24 See **Chapter 13**.

	when making the order to which the application relates; relevant circumstances also include changed circumstances resulting from the deal of the payor. **(8) and (9)** Personal representatives cannot be liable for estate distributions after six months of the date of representation on the ground that they ought to have considered the possibility that the court might permit a variation application by the person entitled to payments.
32	**Arrears more than 12 months' old** Arrears of maintenance arising more than 12 months before the date of the application cannot be enforced without the leave of the court.
33	**Orders for repayment of excess payments** The court can order repayment of excessive sums paid pursuant to a maintenance order where there has been a change of circumstances including following the death of the payor.

KEY PROVISIONS OF CIVIL PARTNERSHIP ACT 2004, SCH 5

2.14 The following table contains a summary of the key provisions of CPA 2004, Sch 5 relating to financial remedies for a child:

Civil Partnership Act 2005, Sch 5: summary of key financial remedy provisions for a child	
Para	**Provisions**
1, 2	**Financial provision orders** On making a dissolution, nullity or separation order or at any time thereafter the court can make the following financial provision orders for the benefit of a child of the family: • periodical payments to or for the benefit of a child of the family; • secured periodical payments to or for the benefit of a child of the family; • lump sum to or for the benefit of a child of the family. The power is exercisable 'at any time' and more than one order can be made in favour of a child.
3	**Supplementary powers relating to lump sums** **(1)** A lump sum can be ordered to meet liabilities or expenses reasonably incurred by the applicant in maintaining herself or a child of the family before the application. **(2)** A lump sum in favour of a child can be ordered to meet liabilities or expenses reasonably incurred by or for the benefit of that child before the application. **(3)** The court can order a lump sum to be paid by instalments and for the instalments to be secured. **(5)** The court can order interest in respect of lump sums which are deferred or payable by instalments.
4, 8, 12	**Financial remedies take effect when dissolution or nullity orders are final** Financial provision orders, property adjustment orders and orders for sale of property made in dissolution or nullity proceedings cannot take effect until the dissolution or nullity order is final.

5	**Restrictions on power to make orders in favour of adult children** The power to make financial provision orders in favour of children is subject to restrictions in CPA 2004, Sch 5, para 49(1) and (5) on making orders in favour of children who have attained the age of 18.
6, 7	**Property adjustment orders** On making a dissolution etc[25] order or at any time thereafter the court can make the following property adjustment orders for the benefit of a child of the family: • transfer of property; • settlement of property; • variation of nuptial settlement.
9	**Restrictions on power to make orders in favour of adult children** The power to make financial provision orders in favour of children is subject to restrictions in CPA 2004, Sch 5, para 49(1) and (5) on making orders in favour of children who have attained the age of 18.
10, 11	**Orders for sale** **10 and 11(1)** On making a secured periodical payments order, a lump sum order or property adjustment order or at any time afterwards the court has the power to order the sale of such property as may be specified in the order in which either or both parties has a beneficial interest in possession or reversion. **11(2) and (3)** An order for sale can include supplementary or consequential provisions including as to payment from the proceeds of sale and provision requiring the property to be offered for sale to a person or class of persons.
13	**Orders for sale to secure periodical payments ceasing to have effect** A sale of property order with a provision requiring the proceeds to be used to secure periodical payments ceases to have effect on the death of the payor or the payee marrying or forming a civil partnership.
14	**Third parties with beneficial interests** Where a third party has a beneficial interest in the relevant property, before ordering a sale, the court must allow the person to make representations and have regard to such representations as may be made.
20	**General criteria for making financial provision orders, property adjustment orders and orders for sale** In deciding whether to make a financial provision order, property adjustment order or order for sale and if so in what way the court must have regard to all the circumstances of the case, giving first consideration to the welfare, while under 18, of any child of the family who has not reached 18.
21, 22	**Specific criteria for making financial provision orders, property adjustment orders and orders for sale where orders sought in favour of a child** As to the exercise of the court's powers in favour of a child, the court must in particular have regard to: **21(2)(a)** the income, earning capacity, property and other financial resources which each civil partner has or is likely to have in the foreseeable future, including in the case of earning capacity any increase in that capacity which it would in the opinion of the court be reasonable to expect a civil partner to take steps to acquire;

25 Includes an order for nullity and separation.

	21(2)(b) the financial needs, obligations and responsibilities which each civil partner has or is likely to have in the foreseeable future; **21(2)(c)** the standard of living enjoyed by the family before the breakdown of the marriage; **21(2)(e)** any physical or mental disability of either civil partner; **22(2)(a)** the financial needs of the child; **22(2)(b)** the income, earning capacity (if any), property and other financial resources of the child; **22(2)(c)** any physical or mental disability of the child; **22(2)(d)** the manner in which the child was being and in which the civil partners expected the child to be educated or trained; **22(3)** Where the child of the family in question is not the child of the paying party the court must also have regard to: (a) whether that party assumed any responsibility for the child's maintenance, and, (b) if so, to the extent to which, and the basis upon which, that party assumed such responsibility and to the length of time for which that party discharged such responsibility; (c) whether in assuming and discharging such responsibility that party did so knowing that the child was not his or her own; (d) the liability of any other person to maintain the child.
38	**Interim maintenance** On an application for a dissolution[26] etc the court can make an order requiring each civil partner to make for the other's interim maintenance such periodical payments as it considers reasonable beginning no earlier than the date of the application and ending on the date on which the proceedings are determined.
38A	**Legal services payment orders** In proceedings for a dissolution etc[27], the court can make orders requiring one party to pay the other an amount for the purpose of enabling the applicant to obtain legal services[28].
38B	**Criteria for making or varying legal services payment order** **(1)** When considering whether to make or vary a legal services order under CPA 2004, Sch 5, para 38A the court must have regard to: (a) the income, earning capacity, property and other financial resources which each of the applicant and the paying party has or is likely to have in the foreseeable future; (b) the financial needs, obligations and responsibilities which each of the applicant and the paying party has or is likely to have in the foreseeable future; (c) the subject matter of the proceedings, including the matters in issue within them; (d) whether the paying party is legally represented in the proceedings;

26 Includes proceedings for nullity and separation.
27 Includes proceedings for nullity and separation.
28 For legal services costs allowances see **Chapter 9**.

	(e) any steps taken by the applicant to avoid all or part of the proceedings, whether by proposing or considering mediation or otherwise; (f) the applicant's conduct in relation to the proceedings; (g) any amount owed by the applicant to the paying party in respect of costs in the proceedings or other proceedings to which both the applicant and the paying party are or were parties; and (h) the effect of the order or variation on the paying party. **(2)** Earning capacity includes any increase it is reasonable to expect the person to take to steps to acquire. **(3)** For the purposes of (1)(h) the court must have regard, in particular, to whether the order is likely to: (a) cause undue hardship to the paying party; or (b) prevent the paying party from obtaining legal services for the purposes of the proceedings.
39, 41	**Failure to maintain** Either civil partner can apply for the following orders to or for the benefit of a child of the family on the ground that the other party has … (b) failed to provide, or make a proper contribution towards, reasonable maintenance for the benefit of the child: • periodical payments; • secured periodical payments; • lump sum order. **39(2)** The court cannot entertain an application unless one of the following jurisdictional grounds is satisfied on the date of the application: (a) either party is domiciled in England and Wales; (b) the applicant has been habitually resident in England and Wales for a year ending with that date; (c) the respondent is resident there. **39(2A)** Where the Hague Child Maintenance Convention[29], Art 18[30] applies, the court cannot entertain the application unless permitted by that Article. **39(3)** The court can make interim orders.
44	**Criteria to be applied in relation to failure to maintain application for orders in favour of a child** **(2), (3) and (4)** Where an application is made in relation to a child, the court shall have regard to all the circumstances of the case including the factors under CPA 2004, Sch 5, para 21(2) which apply in relation to orders sought to or for the benefit of a child (see above), as modified by para 44(4).
45	**Restrictions on making orders in favour of adult children** The power to make orders in favour of a child is subject to restrictions in para 49 on making orders in favour of children who have reached 18.

29 The Convention on the International Recovery of Child Support and Other Forms of Family Maintenance concluded on 23 November 2007 at The Hague.

30 Article 18 provides that where a decision is made in a Contracting State where the creditor is habitually resident, as long as the creditor remains habitually resident there proceedings to modify the decision or make a new decision cannot be brought in any other Contracting State. This is subject to various exceptions in Article 18(2) (see further **Chapter 4**).

49	**Restrictions on making orders in favour of adult children** **(1) and (5)** No financial provision order, transfer of property order or failure to maintain order shall be made in favour of a child who has attained the age of 18 unless the child is, will be or would be undergoing education or training[31] or there exist special circumstances[32]. **(2), (3) and (4)** Periodical payments or secured periodical payments for a child may begin on the date of the application (or later) but shall not in the first instance extend beyond the birthday after the child attains the upper limit of compulsory school age and in any event not beyond the age of 18 unless the child is, will be or would be undergoing education or training[33] or there exist special circumstances[34]. **(6)** Periodical payments cease to have effect on the death of the payor save in relation to arrears at the date of death.
50, 51	**Variation, discharge, suspension and revival** The court can vary, discharge, suspend or revive the following orders to or for the benefit of a child: • interim maintenance orders; • periodical payments; • secured periodical payments; • lump sums which are payable by instalments or deferred; • settlement of property orders and variation of settlement orders made on or after a judicial separation order (but only on an application for recission of the judicial separation order or for dissolution of the marriage: (para 56)); • orders for sale.
52	**Remission of arrears** The court can remit arrears of maintenance.
59	**Criteria to be applied on application for variation etc** **(1) and (2)** The court shall have regard to all the circumstances of the case, first consideration being given to the welfare while a minor of any child of the family who has not attained the age of 18, and the circumstances of the case shall include any change in any of the matters to which the court was required to have regard when making the order to which the application relates; **(6)** Relevant circumstances also include changed circumstances resulting from the death of the payor.
60	**Variation of secured periodical payments after death of payor** **(2) and (3)** Where the payor of secured periodical payments dies, a variation/discharge application can be made by the payee or their personal representatives, but save with leave of the court, no such application can be made more than six months after the date of death. **(4)** Personal representatives cannot be liable for estate distributions after six months of the date of representation on the ground that they ought to have considered the possibility that the court might permit a variation application by the person entitled to payments.

31 See **Chapter 13**.
32 See **Chapter 13**.
33 See **Chapter 13**.
34 See **Chapter 13**.

63	**Arrears more than 12 months' old** Arrears of maintenance arising more than 12 months before the date of the application cannot be enforced without the leave of the court.
64	**Orders for repayment of excess payments** The court can order repayment of excessive sums paid pursuant to a maintenance order where there has been a change of circumstances including following the death of the payor.

CHAPTER 3

Maintenance for Children via the Child Maintenance Service

Content at a glance:

Introduction

Eligibility and the jurisdiction of the CMS

Making an application to the CMS

Calculating child maintenance

Paternity disputes

Applications for variation and revision of assessments

Appeals

Collecting payments

Enforcement

INTRODUCTION

3.1 Since April 1993 when the Child Support Act 1991 ('CSA 1991') came into force, for the majority of separated parents the calculation, collection, and enforcement of claims for child maintenance are dealt with administratively via (what is now known as) the Child Maintenance Service ('CMS') rather than through the family court. Applications to the court for chid maintenance are considered in **Chapter 12**.

3.2 In the last three decades there have been a number of different statutory schemes underpinning the calculation of child maintenance in operation at different times. This chapter deals with the scheme – sometimes referred to as the 'third scheme' – which was introduced from December 2012 and has been in full force since 26 November 2013.

3.3 The CMS website (https://www.gov.uk/child-maintenance-service) describes the assessment of child maintenance as being a decision about:

> '… how your child's living costs will be paid when one of the parents does not live with the child. It's made when you've separated from the other parent or if you've never been in a relationship'.

3.4 That simple government definition highlights certain key features of the scheme:

- both parents have a duty to maintain their child ('how your child's living costs will be paid …');
- the structure of the scheme assumes the child lives (mainly) with one parent or person (the 'resident' parent or 'person with care') and that the other parent does not 'live' with the child or lives with them for a minority of the time compared with the parent with care ('the non-resident parent');
- an obligation to pay child maintenance is not based on the nature of the former relationship between the child's parents; in other words, there is no requirement for parents to have been married or to have cohabited or even to have been in a relationship at all for an assessment of child maintenance to be made.

3.5 The description also echoes the statutory 'duty to maintain' a child which is described at CSA 1991, s 1 as follows (emphasis added):

Child Support Act 1991, s 1

(1) For the purposes of this Act, **each parent** of a **qualifying child** is responsible for maintaining him.

(2) For the purposes of this Act, a **non-resident parent** shall be taken to have met his responsibility to maintain any qualifying child of his by making periodical payments of maintenance with respect to the child of such amount, and at such intervals, as may be determined in accordance with the provisions of this Act.

(3) Where a **maintenance calculation** made under this Act requires the making of periodical payments, it shall be the **duty of the non-resident parent with respect to whom the calculation was made to make those payments**.

3.6 In this chapter we will look at:

(1) eligibility for CMS assessed maintenance;

(2) how the quantum of child maintenance is assessed by the CMS; and

(3) the options available if you are not happy with a maintenance calculation or need to enforce payments of child maintenance.

The calculation, collection, and enforcement of child maintenance is a complex area which is worthy of its own dedicated textbook. The following is intended as a practical overview.

ELIGIBILITY AND THE JURISDICTION OF THE CMS

3.7 The CMS (as opposed to the family court) has jurisdiction to make a calculation of maintenance **where**:

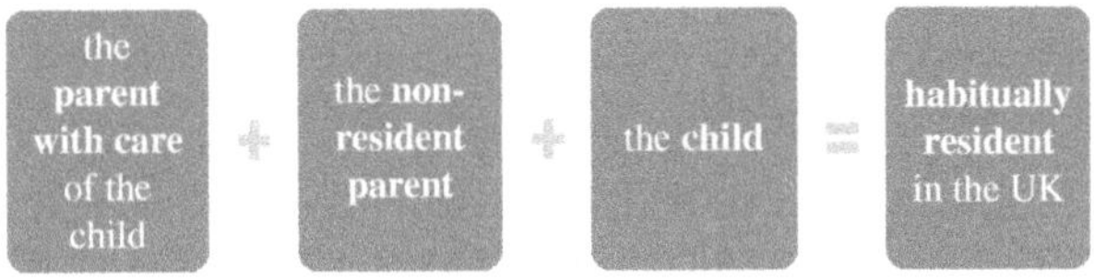

OR:

where the parent with care and the child are habitually resident in the United Kingdom and the **non-resident parent** is habitually resident overseas *but is a member of* the **Diplomatic or Overseas Civil Services**, **Armed Forces** *or* the employee of a **company registered in the United Kingdom**.

Definition of 'qualifying child'

3.8 In order to be eligible for a CMS calculation, the 'child' (CSA 1991, s 55(1)) must be:

- under 16; **or**
- between 16 and 20 but in either education or training (such that they would qualify for receipt of child benefit)[1].

If the 'child' is undertaking paid work or has ever been married or in a civil partnership (including a *void* marriage), they will not qualify as a 'child' for CMS purposes (CSA 1991, ss 55(2) and (3)).

In addition, either **one or both** of the child's parents must be a **'non-resident parent'**.

1 Child Support Maintenance Calculation Regulations 2012 (SI 2012/2677), reg 76 as amended.

Definition of 'non-resident parent'

3.9 As set out at CSA 1991, s 3(2) a parent falls within the definition of a 'non-resident parent' if:

(a) that parent is not living in the same household with the child; and

(b) the child has his home with a person who is, in relation to him, a person with care.

Definition of 'person with care'

3.10 Section 3(3) of the CSA 1991 provides (emphasis added):

> **Child Support Act 1991, s 3(3)**
>
> A person is a 'person with care', in relation to any child, if he is a person—
>
> (a) with whom the child has his **home**;
>
> (b) who usually provides day to day care for the child (**whether exclusively or in conjunction with any other person**); and
>
> (c) who does not fall within a prescribed category of person.

3.11 The CSA 1991 expressly provides for there to be more than one 'person with care' in relation to the same qualifying child: s 3(5).

It is important to note that a **local authority** or a person (such as a foster carer) with whom the child has been placed by the local authority (for example where a child has been voluntarily accommodated under the Children Act 1989 ('CA 1989'), s 20 or has been placed with a foster carer under an interim care order) **does not qualify as a person with care**.

Exclusive jurisdiction

3.12 It was and remains a key feature of the CSA 1991 that the CMS and not the family court should have jurisdiction to assess and enforce child maintenance in the vast majority of cases.

Where the jurisdictional and eligibility criteria for a CMS maintenance assessment are met, the CMS has **exclusive jurisdiction** and a parent cannot choose to opt out of the scheme and apply to the family court instead: CSA 1991, s 8(3).

This prohibition exists *even if* the formula/methodology underpinning a CMS calculation (considered at para 3.17 onwards below) would result in an assessment that no child maintenance should be paid by the non-resident parent at all.

3.13 Conversely, where the jurisdictional/eligibility conditions are **not** met (for example because the non-resident parent is habitually resident overseas), it may be possible to apply to the court for child maintenance[2].

3.14 The exceptions to the general rule by which the CMS has jurisdiction are summarised in the following diagram.

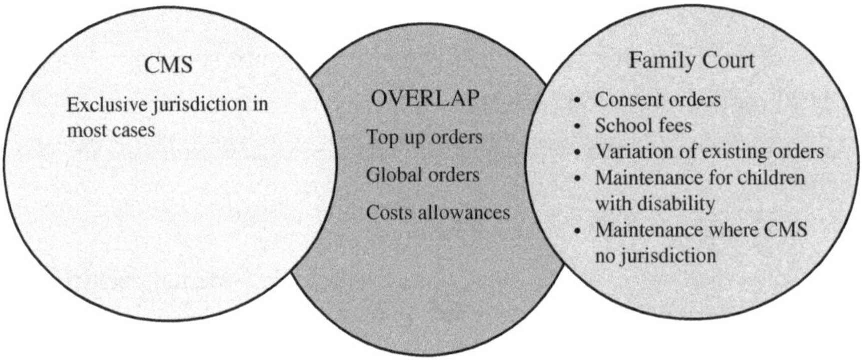

3.15 The family court retains jurisdiction to determine applications for:

- school fees/educational expenses – CSA 1991, s 8(7);
- child maintenance for children with a disability, provided that the maintenance is for 'some or all of any expenses referable to the child's disability' – CSA 1991, s 8(8); see *C v F*[3];
- the variation of an existing child maintenance order made by a court *provided there has not been an application made to the CMS for a maintenance calculation* – CSA 1991, s 8(3A); see *V v V (Child Maintenance)*[4];
- orders under s 8(5) of the CSA 1991 allowing the court to make an order by consent if it repeats the terms of a written agreement. In practice this means that the family court can continue to make *consent* orders for child periodical payments. However, there are important caveats:
  - if the consent order was made **before 3 March 2003** the family court retains jurisdiction to vary the order and that jurisdiction cannot be 'ousted'

2 See **3.14** below and **Chapter 12**.
3 [1999] 1 FCR 39, [1998] 2 FLR 1.
4 [2001] 2 FLR 799.

by a parent making a later application to the CMS for a calculation. On an application, however, the court can expressly revoke the court order to enable a CMS application to be made;

– if the consent order was made **on or after 3 March 2003 either party to the order can apply to the CMS after a period of 12 months from the date on which the order was made**. Once a CMS application is made, the order will be automatically discharged and replaced by the CMS assessment;

- so-called '*Segal*' orders, where the court makes a 'global' order setting out the combined obligation for periodical payments for both the spouse and the child(ren) of the family drafted in such a way as to vary automatically – pound for pound – with any sum assessed to be payable under a CMS maintenance calculation[5]. Global orders cannot be used as a 'device' to get around the restriction imposed by CSA 1991, s 8 and so to be valid they must contain a substantial element of *spousal* maintenance: *Dorney-Kingdom v Dorney-Kingdom*[6];
- 'top-up' maintenance orders. Where a non-resident parent's annual gross income *exceeds* the maximum sum for which the current child support legislation provides – currently £156,000 gross a year – the court has jurisdiction to order that parent to pay additional maintenance designed to 'top up' the existing CMS calculation – CSA 1991, s 8(6). For a top-up maintenance order to be made the CMS must have *already* made what is called a 'maximum assessment' (ie where the payer is assessed as having income of at least £156,000 pa gross) and the court must furthermore decide that it is 'appropriate' for the non-resident parent to make additional payments: *Dickson v Rennie*[7]. *Dickson v Rennie* does not go as far as to say that a party must wait *until* the maximum assessment calculation is in force *before* issuing their application for top-up maintenance, and there are good reasons why a party may wish to seize the court's jurisdiction sooner rather than later (for example because applications for top-up maintenance in the case of unmarried couples made by a parent using CA 1989, Sch 1 must be made *before* the date on which the child turns 18 even if the 18 year old is in education[8]);

5 For Segal orders in the context of interim provision see **Chapter 8** at **8.16–8.19**.
6 [2000] 3 FCR 20, [2000] 2 FLR 855; for a case summary of *Dorney-Kingdom* see **Chapter 8** at **8.17**.
7 [2014] EWHC 4036 (Fam), [2015] 2 FLR 978.
8 Provided that the application has been *issued* before the child's 18th birthday the court retains jurisdiction to make the order itself *after* the child has turned 18, provided that the provisions of CA 1989, Sch 1, para 3 are satisfied: *DN v UD* [2021] EWCA Civ 1947, [2022] Fam 289, [2022] 2 WLR 1047, [2022] 2 FLR 308.

- orders *against* the parent with care. By virtue of CSA 1991, s 8(10) in theory a non-resident parent can apply to the court for a maintenance order *against* a parent with care, although it is hard to conceive of many situations in which this is likely to occur in practice. An example might be where a less well-off non-resident parent is obliged to pay maintenance to a wealthy parent with care under the CMS formula (which leaves no real room for discretion) in circumstances where the CMS calculation has affected their overall household income to such an extent they struggle to meet the reasonable needs of the child on the occasions when the child spends time with them. There is a potential tension between the language of CSA 1991, s 8(10) and the way in which the CMS deals with fully equal shared care arrangements (see **3.31** below and *N v C (Financial Provision: Schedule 1 Claims Dismissal)*[9]);
- applications for costs allowance orders by way of a lump sum: *CF v KM (financial provision for child: costs of legal proceedings)*[10].

MAKING AN APPLICATION TO THE CMS

3.16 Applications for child maintenance in most cases can be made online with the current website address being: https://www.gov.uk/child-maintenance-service/how-to-apply.

For parents who are not the *biological* parent of the qualifying child, or where the child is in local authority care for some of the time, a telephone application is required instead (the current number is 0800 171 2345 and calls are said to be free from UK landlines and mobiles).

CALCULATING CHILD MAINTENANCE

3.17 Unlike assessments of maintenance by the family court, in which judges have a wide, welfare-focussed discretion, CMS assessments are essentially formulaic and maintenance is calculated by reference to a (complex) prescribed set of rules that focus on the circumstances of the paying party.

3.18 There are six steps carried out by the CMS to establish how much child maintenance the paying parent should pay[11]:

9 [2013] EWHC 399 (Fam).
10 [2010] EWHC 1754 (Fam), [2011] 1 FLR 208.
11 For further detail see the Child Support Maintenance Calculation Regulations 2012 (SI 2012/2677).

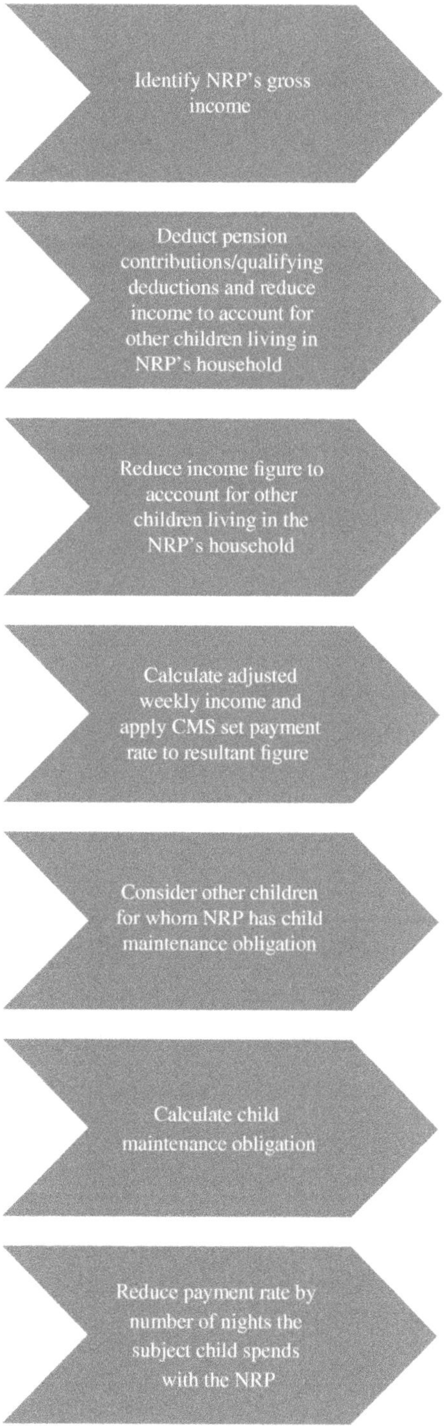
Identify NRP's gross income
Deduct pension contributions/qualifying deductions and reduce income to account for other children living in NRP's household
Reduce income figure to acccount for other children living in the NRP's household
Calculate adjusted weekly income and apply CMS set payment rate to resultant figure
Consider other children for whom NRP has child maintenance obligation
Calculate child maintenance obligation
Reduce payment rate by number of nights the subject child spends with the NRP

Step 1 – working out the payer's income

3.19 This is ordinarily done using information obtained **directly** from HMRC such as a P60 or the payer's last annual tax return. For the purpose of establishing the level of income the CMS ignores tax credits, student grants, and receipt of loans. If it has not been possible to obtain information from HMRC, or there is a 25% variance between the last HMRC figures and the payer's current income, then a figure for current income is used, obtained **from the non-resident parent** directly. Pension contributions are left out of account when calculating gross income at stage 1.

Step 2 – considering other factors that affect income

3.20 At this second stage the CMS deducts pension contributions along with making an adjustment to the payer's notional gross income figure where there are other 'relevant other children' living in the payer's household (for example, where the payer has formed a new relationship and the children from that relationship now live with him).

Meaning of 'relevant other child'

For the purpose of the formula, a 'relevant other child' means a child **in the household of the non-resident parent**. The significance of relevant other children is that their presence in the non-resident parent's household results in a **reduction of weekly income** to be calculated **before** the child support maintenance rate is applied.

Where there are relevant other children in the payer's household, the assessable gross weekly income is reduced as follows:

- by 11% where there is one relevant other child;
- by 14% where there are two relevant other children;
- by 16% where there are three or more relevant other children.

Step 3 – arriving at the weekly income figure

3.21 Having considered steps (1) and (2) above to work out the payer's annual gross income, this figure is then converted into a weekly amount after which one of the following five set rates applies:

Gross weekly income	Applicable rate	Weekly amount to be paid
Unknown/payer did not provide	Default	£38 for 1 child, £51 for 2 children, £64 for 3 or more children

Below £7 or for payers in certain categories such as parents who are themselves children, prisoners, 16 and 17 year olds receiving certain benefits, and those in full-time education	Nil	£0
£7–£100 or for those in receipt of certain state benefits including pension credit	Flat	£7
£100.01–£199.99	Reduced	The flat rate of £7 plus an uplift calculated by reference to a CMS formula. The amount is calculated as follows: **Flat rate (£7) + (A × T)** where— A is the amount of the non-resident parent's gross weekly income; and T is the percentage determined in accordance with a table set out in the regulation (SI 2012/2677).
£200–£3000	Basic	The formula for basic rate assessments applies. An initial rate is applied to the first £800 pw gross income with an additional tapered amount applying to income in excess of £800 (but capped at £3,000 pw).

Step 4 – considering whether the payer has child maintenance obligations for other children

3.22 At this stage, the CMS will take into account the number of children the paying parent has **to pay child maintenance for**.

Step 5 – working out the maintenance obligation

3.23 Based on all of the information from the first four steps, the CMS then decides the weekly amount to be paid. This is done in two stages. First, the CMS calculates the 'basic rate' of maintenance. Second, if the payer's assessed income exceeds £800 per week, a further calculation is carried out (the 'basic plus' rate) in respect of the additional weekly income.

How is the basic rate of child maintenance calculated?

3.24 Before any further deductions are applied, the percentage of gross weekly income up to £800 per week which is payable as child support maintenance is:

(a) 12% where there is one qualifying child;

(b) 16% where there are two qualifying children;

(c) 19% where there are three or more qualifying children.

How is the basic plus rate calculated?

3.25 Where there is gross income over £800 per week any excess of gross income over that amount is assessed as payable at the following rates:

(a) 9% of the excess where there is one qualifying child;

(b) 12% of the excess where there are two qualifying children;

(c) 15% of the excess where there are three or more qualifying children.

Step 6 – Reducing the maintenance obligation because of shared care

3.26 Where the qualifying child spends **at least 52 nights per year overnight** with the paying parent a percentage reduction is then made to the amount of child maintenance they would otherwise be required to pay, based on the number of nights a year that the child stays with them.

3.27 The reduction to the weekly amount the non-resident parent is required to pay is as follows:

Number of overnight stays each year	Reduction to child maintenance for each child
52 to 103 nights	14.29%
104 to 155 nights	28.57%
156 to 174 nights	42.86%
175 nights or more	50%, plus an extra £7 a week reduction

Fully shared care

3.28 It is well understood in the context of CA 1989, s 8 child arrangements disputes that a child can 'live with' both parents for unequal amounts of time (for example 'living with' one parent on alternate weekends and for half of all holidays, and 'living with' the other parent the remainder of the time). A 'share care' arrangement in the context of CA 1989, s 8 applications has a different meaning from the specific way that 'share care' is referred to and factored into CMS decision making.

3.29 For the purpose of the CMS, 'shared care' simply means spending time with the non-resident parent for 52 nights or more. This is because the scheme operates on the basis that the paying parent is a 'non-resident parent'.

3.30 Where the qualifying child's care is shared precisely **equally** between parents (for example, in the case of a week on/week off arrangement) there is no parent who comes within the definition of a non-resident parent and so **no child maintenance is payable**.

3.31 The upshot is that a non-resident parent who has the child overnight with them for 175 nights will pay 50% of the child maintenance they would otherwise have been liable to pay, whereas a parent who has the child for 183 nights (ie for just eight nights more) will be assessed as having no maintenance liability at all.

3.32 The unfortunate unintended effect of this position is that (as is sadly not uncommon in child arrangements disputes) parents can be disincentivised from reaching agreement because of the effect on a CMS calculation and, therefore, the amount they are either assessed as being required to pay or entitled to receive.

Determining disputes between parents about the extent of shared care

3.33 Where the applicant for CMS maintenance is in receipt of child benefit for the qualifying child, they will be assumed to be the 'parent with care' providing care to the child to a greater extent than any other person, unless evidence is provided to the contrary[12].

3.34 Under the Child Support Maintenance Calculation Regulations 2012, SI 2012/2677, reg 46(2) CMS decision makers must determine the number of nights for which a non-resident parent is '**expected**' to have the care of the qualifying child overnight in a twelve-month period starting with the 'effective date' (which is the date on which written notification is sent to the non-resident parent).

3.35 The word 'expected' reflects the fact that many maintenance calculations will be carried out when part of the period is in the future and the actual position in terms of child arrangements is not known. Unsurprisingly, this can lead to disputes between parents.

3.36 To reach a decision about the extent of shared care, the CMS will take into account any court order or written agreement reached between the parties regarding contact arrangements. Where there is no agreement or court order, the CMS must consider whether '... a pattern of shared care has already been established over the past 12 months ...' (SI 2012/2677, reg 46(4)(b)).

3.37 A court order will, in most cases, settle any argument about the number of nights a child is expected to spend time with the non-resident parent. Where, however, a court order or written agreement about child arrangements is in place *but the reality on the ground differs from what was ordered* the CMS

12 Child Support Maintenance Calculation Regulations (SI 2012/2677), reg 50(3).

decision-maker is entitled to look at the reality of the expected arrangements for the child: *EA v Secretary of State for Work and Pensions*[13].

3.38

Case summary: *EA v Secretary of State for Work and Pensions*[14]

Facts:

A child arrangements order provided for F to have substantial contact with the child. Contact broke down to the extent that F no longer had sufficient contact to entitle him to a shared care reduction in chid maintenance.

The First-tier Tribunal took into account the circumstances that had arisen since the order was made in setting F's maintenance obligation.

F appealed.

Held by the Upper Tribunal:

FTT decision upheld. It was not bound by the child arrangements order and was entitled to consider the factual situation which had arisen since.

PATERNITY DISPUTES

3.39 Section 26(2) of the CSA 1991 empowers the CMS to presume paternity in certain circumstances listed in full in that section including where the child is habitually resident in England and Wales and the alleged father is registered as the father on the child's birth certificate.

3.40 Section 27 of the CSA 1991 enables either the Secretary of State[15] or the parent with care to apply to the magistrates' court, county court or High Court for a declaration under the Family Law Act 1986, s 55A that the alleged father is the father of the child.

DNA testing is governed by the provisions of the Family Law Reform Act 1969 ('FLRA 1969'), s 20. The Ministry of Justice is responsible for maintaining a list of accredited bodies to carry out court-directed tests for parentage. DNA testing directed by the court pursuant to FLRA 1969, s 20 may only be carried out by an accredited testing agency[16].

13 [2019] UKUT 149 (AAC).
14 [2019] UKUT 149 (AAC).
15 For Work and Pensions.
16 Family Law Reform Act 1969, s 20(1A).

APPLICATIONS FOR VARIATION AND REVISION OF ASSESSMENTS

3.41 If either the paying parent or the receiving parent is unhappy with the initial CMS decision they can apply for a 'variation' of that decision, but the grounds for variation are limited. Some of the more common situations in which a variation may be sought are described below (see also **Chapter 14** at **14.29** onwards). It is possible also for parents to initiate other processes to change the amount of assessments known as 'revision', 'supersession' and 'appeal'. The following table summarises these.

Action	When it is used
Revision (also known as Mandatory Reconsideration)	The amount was calculated using the wrong information. For example, where the CMS has: • made a mistake about the number of children the paying parent pays maintenance for; • used incorrect income figures; • not included all the days the parent receiving payments or the paying parent care for the child; • if the paying parent has not disclosed all their earnings.
Supersession	Either parent's circumstances have changed since the child maintenance was calculated. A new calculation may be needed because: • there has been a change in financial circumstances; • the contact or living arrangements for the child have changed; eg if the number of nights the child stays with the paying parent has changed.
Variation	The parent receiving payments wants additional information about the paying parent's finances to be taken into account: • the parent receiving payments believes the paying parent has income other than wages or self-employed earnings, or unearned income from capital worth over £2,500 a year; • the parent receiving payments wants other information or circumstances to be taken into account; • they can ask the CMS to look at the paying parent's income that may not have been included in the original CMS calculation; • the CMS can be asked to take into account income or circumstances that it has not already considered; • the parent receiving payments believes that the paying parent's income is higher than they have declared to the CMS; • the parent receiving payments might suspect that the paying parent is using self-employment or payment by dividend to make their salary income look artificially low. The paying parent wants additional information about their financial commitments to be taken into account, including in relation to contact costs, costs relating to a disability, boarding school fees, certain debts and mortgage costs.

Appeal	The parent receiving payments wants to challenge a decision made by the CMS, such as a decision to refuse their request for a revision. A refusal to a request for a supersession or variation can also be appealed but a revision request must be made first.

Application for variation by non-resident parent

3.42 **A non-resident parent** may qualify for a variation where they have a financial obligation for:

- regular contact costs, including travel costs, accommodation costs where reasonable and the costs of an accompanying other person where reasonable (SI 2012/2677, reg 63) (but note that a parent cannot ask for additional expenses to be taken into account if their gross income is already less than £7 per week);
- costs attributable to a long-term illness or disability of a relevant child (SI 2012/2677, reg 64);
- the maintenance element of boarding school fees (if shared with another person the amount to be taken into account is reduced pro rata). Where it is not possible readily to distinguish between the educational element of school fees and the maintenance element, the CMS decision maker determines what element of the total school fees bill relates to maintenance, up to a maximum of 35% of the total bill. This ground of variation enables a maximum reduction of 50% in the calculation of the non-resident parent's notional gross weekly income (SI 2012/2677, reg 66);
- the payment of prior debts (but only in certain very specific circumstances for which see SI 2012/2677, reg 65);
- The payment of mortgages, loans or insurance payments made **directly in relation to a home where the parent with care and child still lives**, and only if the non-resident parent **retains no interest in that home** (SI 2012/2677, reg 67).

Application for variation by parent with care

3.43 The three grounds for a variation by a parent who is receiving payments are:

Unearned income	• This includes all other types of taxable income from assets such as rental income from property, savings, shares or other investments. • The parent receiving payments must be able to show that the total value of this unearned income is at least £2,500 per year. • Information about company shareholders can be found on the share register of the company, a public document held by the company registrar and at Companies House.

Earned income	This can be used when the paying parent is paying maintenance at a 'nil' or 'flat' rate, but the parent receiving payments believes they have a gross weekly income of £100 or more from employment, self-employment or a pension.
Diversion of income	This can be used when the paying parent can control their own income so they appear less well off than they are. This category often applies when the paying parent is self-employed or runs their own business. Examples of when this can be used are: • they employ a relative and pay them more than their job is worth; • they make excessive contributions to their pension, leaving themselves with less income; • they have a business which makes substantial profits but they are not paying themselves a dividend; • they have given an interest in their business to a new partner or a relative.

It can be hard successfully to apply for a variation because the CMS will expect the parent receiving payments to prove the facts. The CMS will not usually carry out a detailed investigation itself. If the parent receiving payments does not achieve the outcome they want, or the CMS does not investigate, they can ask for a mandatory reconsideration and then appeal.

Additional income

3.44 A **parent with care** may invite the CMS to vary the assessment decision by considering **additional income** earned by the non-resident parent, both in terms of the payer's *actual* and *deemed* income resources. This ground for variation applies where:

- the non-resident parent has **unearned** income of £2,500 pa or more – for example, income from property or dividends, including dividends from a company where the non-resident parent is a shareholder; or
- the non-resident parent has assets (other than their primary residence) with an aggregate value in excess of £31,250. A notional income of 8% arising on the value of those assets will be added to gross weekly income; or
- the non-resident parent is assessed as paying a nil or flat rate, but the CMS is satisfied that there is additional income of £100 or more per week.

Diversion of income

3.45 It may also be possible to vary an assessment if the parent with care is able to demonstrate that the non-resident parent is able to control, directly or indirectly, the amount of income available to them and there is evidence that the income has been *diverted* – SI 2012/2677, reg 71.

3.46 An example of this is where the paying party deliberately and unreasonably makes additional pension contributions to reduce artificially the amount of gross income that is taken into account on an assessment, or where dividend income has been diverted by the non-resident parent to a third party (for an example of this, see *AS v Secretary of State for Work and Pensions*[17]).

Reviews

3.47 Child maintenance decisions are automatically reviewed once a year (ie 12 months from the initial 'effective date') using updated information obtained from HMRC.

It is possible to request an 'in year' review, but there must have been a change in the payee's financial circumstances of 25% or more – SI 2012/2677, reg 23.

Applications for revision

3.48 Separate to the right to apply for a variation outlined above, if a parent considers there has been error in the way in which child maintenance has been calculated they can apply for a revision.

The grounds on which revision can be sought depend on the timeframe in which a revision is applied for.

3.49 The CMS may revise a decision on any ground (except a change of circumstances that has arisen after the date of the decision) if an application (which includes an application for a variation) has been made within 30 days of the date of notification of the decision (or within 30 days of the date of notification of a 'correction' made of the CMS's own motion) – SI 2012/2677, reg 14(1).

3.50 After the 30 day limit has passed, an application for revision can only be made on the following grounds (see SI 2012/2677, regs 14(1)(b)–(g) and 14(3):

- if the decision was wrong because of a misrepresentation (whether innocent or fraudulent) or a breach of duty to disclose a **material fact** and that decision was more advantageous to the person who misrepresented or failed to disclose that fact than it would have been 'but for the wrongness of the decision';
- if an appeal has been made under CSA 1991, s 20 to the First-tier Tribunal within prescribed time limits but has yet to be determined;
- if the decision arose from an official error;
- if the information held by HMRC in relation to a tax year in respect of which the CMS has determined historic income or unearned income has since been amended;

17 [2018] UKUT 315, [2019] 1 FCR 273.

- if the ground for revision is that a person with respect to whom a maintenance calculation was made was not, at the time the calculation was made, a **parent** of a child to whom the calculation relates.
- where it is an interim or default maintenance decision made pursuant to CSA 1991, s 12.

Applications for supersession

3.51 Supersession is the process through which the CMS is notified of, inter alia, a change in circumstances. Such an application can be made at any time.

A decision may be superseded, on an application or on the Secretary of State's own initiative, where:

- there has been a relevant change of circumstances since the decision had effect or it is expected that a relevant change of circumstances will occur (SI 2012/2677, reg 17(1)(a)); or
- the decision was made in ignorance of, or was based on a mistake as to, some material fact; or
- the decision was wrong in law (unless it was a decision made on appeal).

3.52 Where a non-resident parent makes an application for supersession because their current income has changed or is expected to change, no supersession will be made unless there has been a change of 25% or more. This restriction does not apply, however, where the CMS is making a supersession decision as part of any annual review/periodic check of current income, or where there was an error of law, or where the earlier decision was based on an estimate of current income – SI 2012/2677, reg 23.

APPEALS

3.53 Both non-resident parents and parents with care can appeal most CMS decisions to the First-tier Tribunal and appeals may be brought on the basis of both errors of law and fact as set out at CSA 1991, s 20.

3.54 For decisions made after 28 October 2013 it is necessary to request a review of the decision (sometimes referred to as 'mandatory reconsideration') *before* appealing – SI 2012/2677, reg 14A. The decision (called the Mandatory Reconsideration Notice or MRN) must be sent to the Tribunal together with the Notice of Appeal using form SSCS2.

In the absence of a mandatory reconsideration, the appeal will be treated as a request for such reconsideration instead.

3.55 The time limit for an appeal is one calendar month from the date of the MRN and the time limit can be extended by a maximum of 12 months (Tribunal Procedure (First-tier Tribunal) (Social Entitlement Chamber) Rules 2008, SI 2008/2685, r 22(8)).

3.56 If there has been an error of law by the First-tier Tribunal a party may apply for permission to appeal to the Upper Tribunal.

3.57 The appeals process can be summarised as follows:

Mandatory Reconsideration

- Party unhappy with CMS decision must first apply for a review of the decision.
- If unhappy with the reviewed decision they may then apply to the First Tier Tribunal within 1 calendar month of the date of the Mandatory Reconsideration Notice (MRN). The time limit may be extended by a max of 12 months.
- Use Notice of Appeal on Form SSCS2 which can be downloaded from the GOV.UK website.

Appeal to the First Tier Tribunal

- CMS must provide a response to the Notice of Appeal within 42 days of receipt.
- FTT has wide powers including the ability to summon witnesses. See Tribunal Procedure (First-tier Tribunal) (Social Entitlement Chamber) Rules 2008 for the procedure.
- The hearing will be in public unless the FTT determines otherwise.
- If the appeal is allowed the FTT may make its own decision or remit the case back to the CMS with appropriate directions.
- The FTT's jurisdiction has been described as 'inquisitorial and enabling' (*SC v Child Maintenance and Enforcement Commission and JM* [2011] UKUT 458) and the FTT can raise its own issues if in the public interest to do so.

Appeal to the Upper Tribunal

- If the FTT has made an error of law only. Mistakes or accidental slips may be corrected by the FTT instead and the FTT also has the power to set aside its own decision if, for example, there was a procedural irregularity or a party was not present at a hearing.
- An application for permission to appeal to the UT must be made within 1 month of receipt of the reasons from the FTT.
- There is no right of appeal against a refusal of the UT to grant permission to appeal.
- If satisfied that there has been a **material** error of law, the UT may set aside the decision of the FTT and either remake the decision itself or remit to the FTT for a fresh decision to be made.
- It is more common for appeals to be dealt with without an oral hearing but the parties' views on this will be sought.

COLLECTING PAYMENTS

3.58 The scheme is designed to incentivise parents to arrange payment/collection of maintenance directly between themselves. This is referred to by the CMS as 'Direct Pay'. It is cheaper to use Direct Pay than to use the Collect and Pay Service (where the CMS collects and passes on payments).

With Direct Pay, the CMS calculates the amount owed but does not monitor compliance. If arrears accrue the CMS cannot enforce them.

3.59 The alternative is Collect and Pay, but this method can only be used if either the non-resident parent agrees, or the CMS considers that child maintenance is 'unlikely to be paid' without the service. Once in force, the Child Support Collection (Domestic Abuse) Act 2023 will enable Collect and Pay to be used where the CMS is satisfied, on the basis of evidence of relevant domestic abuse, that it is appropriate to do so.

3.60 Users of Collect and Pay have to pay a fee (which is an uncapped percentage of the amount of child maintenance) each time they make or receive a child maintenance payment using Collect and Pay. The fee is currently:

- 20% (which is added to the payment) for paying parents;
- 4% (which is taken off the payment) for receiving parents.

ENFORCEMENT

3.61 A person with care has no free-standing right to seek enforcement of CMS maintenance by way of a separate civil remedy and they must instead use the CMS's own procedures as set out in the CSA 1991: *R (Kehoe) v Secretary of State for Work and Pensions*[18].

3.62 The range of enforcement remedies includes:

- deducting sums from a non-resident parent's earnings;
- deducting sums from a non-resident parent's bank account;
- making a 'liability order' which then enables the CMS to obtain an order for seizure and sale of the defaulter's property in order to satisfy the debt owed under the liability order or to obtain a charging order or third party debt order. This method can be useful where the defaulter is self-employed and where a deduction of earnings order would not therefore be applicable;
- if a liability order has been obtained, and a charging order/third party debt order or order for distress (seizure and sale of goods) has been made but the debt remains outstanding, an application for committal to prison or for disqualification from driving may be made.

18 [2005] UKHL 48, [2006] 1 AC 42, [2005] 3 WLR 252, [2005] 2 FCR 683, [2005] 2 FLR 1249.

CHAPTER 4

Jurisdiction

Content at a glance:

INTRODUCTION

4.1 This chapter addresses the jurisdiction of the courts, in an international sense, to deal with financial remedies claims for children. Aside from international issues of jurisdiction, before issuing proceedings practitioners also need to consider whether the proposed claim is one over which the Child Maintenance Service has exclusive jurisdiction; this issue is addressed in **Chapter 3**. For the remainder of this chapter references to 'jurisdiction' refer to the concept at an international level, save where indicated otherwise.

4.2 The issue of jurisdiction is governed by statute. It is necessary to consider different statutes depending upon the procedural route that is to be adopted. The different statutes in question feature different gateways for jurisdiction. Two concepts with which practitioners need to be familiar feature in all of them:

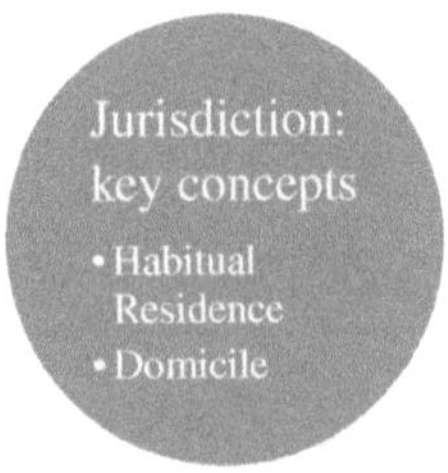

HABITUAL RESIDENCE

4.3 The recent domestic case law on the concept of habitual residence derives from cases decided by the Court of Justice for the European Union, notwithstanding that as result of the departure of the United Kingdom from the EU, with limited exceptions, EU law ceased to have effect at 11pm on 31 December 2020.

4.4 There are two strands of cases in relation to habitual residence: those which relate to children and those which relate to adults.

4.5 The children cases have been decided in relation to the question of jurisdiction to deal with welfare proceedings and have their origins in European cases about the meaning of habitual residence in Council Regulation (EC) No 2201/2003, Art 8.

4.6 The adult cases have been primarily concerned with the meaning of habitual residence for the purposes of determining divorce jurisdiction. These mainly relate to the meaning of the concept for the purposes of Council Regulation (EC) No 2201/2003, Art 3. The principles have evolved from other European cases decided in a non-family sphere.

THE HABITUAL RESIDENCE OF CHILDREN

4.7 The concept of 'habitual residence' is not defined in any of the Acts or treaties in which it is mentioned; nor is it defined in any domestic statute. Its meaning in relation to children has been considered in six cases before the Supreme Court:

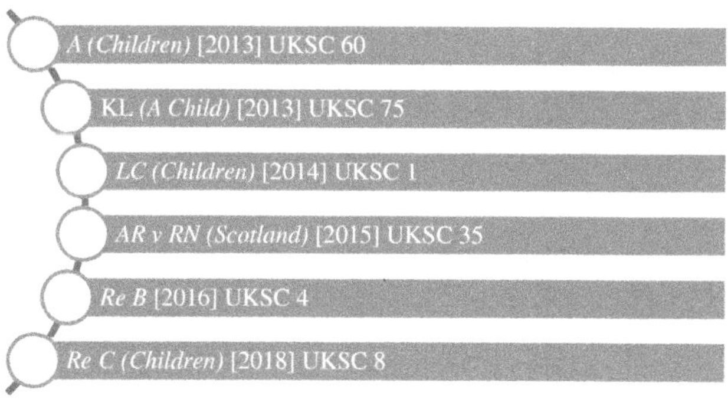

4.8 In *A (Children)*[1], the Supreme Court decided that previous domestic tests to determine the habitual residence of children were no longer applicable.

1 *A v A (Children: Habitual Residence) (Reunite International Child Abduction Centre intervening)* [2013] UKSC 60, [2014] AC 1, [2013] 3 WLR 76, [2013] 3 FCR 559, [2014] 1 FLR 111.

Instead, it adopted the approach of the European courts, in particular in *Mercredi v Chaffe*[2] and *Proceedings brought by A*[3].

Case summary: *Mercredi v Chaffe* CJEU Case C-497/10[4]

Facts:

A child was born in the UK to unmarried parents: M (French) from Réunion (a French *department*) and F (British). A few weeks after the birth, M took the child to Réunion. F did not have parental responsibility. A day after removal, a duty judge made a location order. F then applied for welfare orders and a judge (ex parte) ordered M to return the child to England. In order to determine whether M's retention of the child was wrongful for the purposes of the 1980 Hague Convention, it was necessary to establish whether the child remained habitually resident in England on the date the courts were seised. When the case came before the Court of Appeal, it requested a preliminary ruling from the CJEU to clarify the test for determining the habitual residence of a child.

Held by the CJEU:

- habitual residence is a matter of fact to be resolved in each case;
- to be 'habitual' residence must have 'a certain permanence[5] or regularity';
- a uniform EU wide interpretation of habitual residence was required;
- jurisdictional issues were to be shaped in the light of the best interests of the child and in particular on the criterion of proximity;
- habitual residence corresponds to the place which reflects some degree of integration by the child in a social and family environment;
- reference must be made to the conditions and reasons for the child's stay, as well as to his nationality;
- in addition to physical presence other factors must make it clear that the child's presence is not in any way temporary or intermittent; the intention of the person with parental responsibility to settle permanently with the child in another Member State may constitute an indicator of the transfer of habitual residence;

2 CJEU, Case C-497/10, [2012] Fam 22, [2011] 1 FLR 1293.
3 CJEU, Case C-523/07, [2010] Fam 42, [2009] 2 FLR 1.
4 [2012] Fam 22, [2011] 1 FLR 1293.
5 See *DL v EL* [2013] 2 FLR 163 and *AR v RN (Scotland)* [2015] UKSC 35, [2016] AC 76, [2015] 2 FCR 570, [2015] 2 FLR 503 in which it was held that 'permanence' in this context means 'stability'.

- to distinguish habitual residence from temporary presence, there must be a duration which reflects an adequate degree of permanence[6], although there is no minimum duration; the duration of a stay can only be an indicator in the assessment of the permanence of the residence;
- a child's social and family environment is fundamental in determining their habitual residence, age is also likely to be of particular importance. An infant necessarily shares the social and family environment of the people on whom they are dependent;
- where an infant has been removed to a new Member State and has been there only a matter of days, the factors to be taken into consideration when determining the child's habitual residence include: (i) the duration, regularity, conditions and reasons for the stay in the territory of that Member State and for the parent's move; and (ii) the child's age, the parent's geographic and family origins, and the family and social connections which the parent and child had with the new Member State.

4.9 In *A (Children)*[7], the Supreme Court applied the European cases and held that:

- A child is HR in 'the place which reflects some degree of integration ... in a social and family environment'
- HR is a question of fact, not a legal concept
- There must be consistency between the Hague Conventions, European law and domestic jurisprudence
- The purposes and intentions of parents is merely one of the relevant factors

4.10

Case summary: *A (Children)*[8]

Facts:

The proceedings related to four children, the oldest three of whom were born in the UK. After the birth of the third child, the parents separated. M took the three children to Pakistan for a holiday. Under pressure M agreed to reconcile with F on the basis that the family would return to England although in fact they were forced to remain in Pakistan.

6 See *DL v EL* [2013] FLR 163 and *AR v RN (Scotland)* [2015] UKSC 35, [2016] AC 76, [2015] 2 FCR 570, [2015] 2 FLR 503.
7 [2013] UKSC 60, [2014] AC 1, [2013] 3 FCR 559, [2014] 1 FLR 111.
8 *A v A (Children: Habitual Residence) (Reunite International Child Abduction Centre intervening)* [2013] UKSC 60, [2014] AC 1, [2013] 3 WLR 76, [2013] 3 FCR 559, [2014] 1 FLR 111.

Following the birth of the fourth child, M managed to return to England and issued wardship proceedings. The courts were required to determine whether they had jurisdiction. A critical question concerned the habitual residence of the children on the date of commencement of the proceedings.

Held by the UKSC:

The Supreme Court provided detailed guidance on ascertaining a child's habitual residence, rejecting previous domestic authorities and adopting a simple test: a child is habitually resident in the place which reflects some degree of integration by the child in a social and family environment.

The test to determine habitual residence

4.11 In a summary, at para 54 of *A (Children)*[9] Baroness Hale held:

- habitual residence is a question of fact and not a legal concept such as domicile;
- there is no legal rule akin to that whereby a child automatically takes the domicile of his parents;
- the relevant test is that adopted by the European Court, namely '**the place which reflects some degree of integration by the child in a social and family environment**' in the country concerned. This depends upon numerous factors, including the reasons for the family's stay in the country in question;
- the social and family environment of an infant or young child is shared with those (whether parents or others) upon whom they are dependent. Hence it is necessary to assess the integration of that person or persons in the social and family environment of the country concerned;
- the essentially factual and individual nature of the inquiry should not be glossed with legal concepts;
- it is possible that a child may have no country of habitual residence at a particular point in time.

Parental intention

4.12 Parental intention is a relevant consideration to the determination of a child's habitual residence, but not determinative. In *AR v RN (Scotland)*[10], the Supreme Court upheld the earlier decision of the Court of Appeal in *Re H (Children) (Reunite International Child Abduction Centre intervening)*[11]

9 *A v A and another (Children: Habitual Residence) (Reunite International Child Abduction Centre intervening)* [2013] UKSC 60, [2014] AC 1, [2013] 3 WLR 76, [2013] 3 FCR 559, [2014] 1 FLR 111.

10 [2015] UKSC 35, [2016] AC 76, [2015] 2 FCR 570, [2015] 2 FLR 503.

11 [2014] EWCA Civ 1101; [2015] 1 WLR 863, [2014] 3 FCR 405, [2015] 1 FLR 1132.

that there is no *rule* to prevent one parent changing or bringing about the change of the habitual residence of a child on a unilateral basis.

Simultaneous gaining and losing of habitual residence

4.13 In *Re B (A Child) (Habitual Residence: Inherent Jurisdiction)*[12] it was determined that in general, a child will lose a pre-existing habitual residence at the same time as gaining a new one. It is only in exceptional cases that a child will be 'in limbo' and be found to have no habitual residence at a given time. The position was explained by Lord Wilson at para 45:

Key citation: Re B *(A Child) (Habitual Residence: Inherent Jurisdiction)*[13]

Lord Wilson:

> 'I conclude that the modern concept of a child's habitual residence operates in such a way as to make it highly unlikely, albeit conceivable, that a child will be in the limbo in which the courts below have placed B. The concept operates in the expectation that, when a child gains a new habitual residence, he loses his old one. Simple analogies are best: consider a see-saw. As, probably quite quickly, he puts down those first roots which represent the requisite degree of integration in the environment of the new state, up will probably come the child's roots in that of the old state to the point at which he achieves the requisite de-integration (or, better, disengagement) from it.'

4.14 The seamless transfer of a child's habitual residence from one state to another is illustrated by the following graphic:

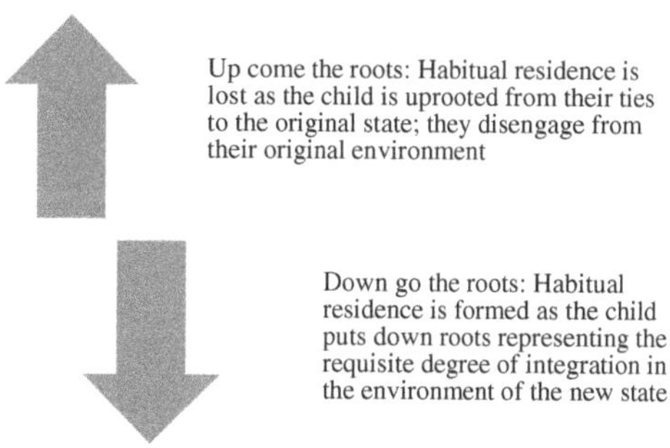

12 [2016] UKSC 4, [2016] AC 606, [2016] 2 FCR 307, [2016] 1 FLR 561.
13 [2016] UKSC 4, [2016] AC 606, [2016] 2 FCR 307, [2016] 1 FLR 561.

4.15 In *Re B*[14] Lord Wilson offered three examples of the matters a court will take into account when determining the point at which habitual residence has been lost and gained:

The deeper the child's integration in old state, probably the less fast the child's achievement of requisite degree of integration in new state

The greater the pre-planning of the move, probably the faster the child's achievement of that requisite degree

Where all central members of the child's life have moved with the child, probably the faster the achievement of a new HR and, conversely, if any of them have remained behind, probably the less fast the child's achievement of it

These expectations were highlighted by Moylan LJ in *Re A (A Child) (Habitual Residence: 1996 Hague Child Protection Convention)*[15].

4.16 In *Re M (Children) (Habitual Residence: 1980 Hague Child Abduction Convention)*[16], however, the Court of Appeal held that:

Key citation: Re *M* (Children) (Habitual Residence: 1980 Hague Child Abduction Convention)[17]

Moylan LJ:

> 'while Lord Wilson's see-saw analogy can assist the court when deciding the question of habitual residence, it does not replace the core guidance given in *A v A* and other cases to the approach which should be taken to the determination of the habitual residence. This requires an analysis of the child's situation in and connections with the state or states in which he or she is said to be habitually resident for the purpose of determining in which state he or she has the requisite degree of integration to mean that their residence there is habitual.
>
> Further, the analogy needs to be used with caution because if it is applied as though it is the test for habitual residence it can, as in

14 *Re B (A Child) (Habitual Residence: Inherent Jurisdiction)* [2016] UKSC 4, [2016] AC 606, [2016] 2 FCR 307, [2016] 1 FLR 561.
15 [2023] EWCA Civ 659.
16 [2020] EWCA Civ 1105 at paras 61–62.
17 [2020] EWCA Civ 1105.

> my view is demonstrated by the present case, result in the court's focus being disproportionately on the extent of a child's continuing roots or connections with and/or on an historical analysis of their previous roots or connections rather than focusing, as is required, on the child's *current* situation (at the relevant date). This is not to say continuing or historical connections are not relevant but they are part of, not the primary focus of, the court's analysis when deciding the critical question which is *where* is the child habitually resident and not, simply, *when* was a previous habitual residence lost.' (emphasis in the original)

Global analysis required to determine habitual residence

4.17 Where there are two states in which a child is potentially habitually resident, the child may have 'some degree of integration' in each of them and an application of this test may not be sufficient to determine in which state the child is habitually resident. Accordingly, the court must undertake a 'global analysis' of the factors which connect the child to each of the two states in question focussing on current, as opposed to historic, connections[18].

General guidance for determining the habitual residence of a child

4.18 The following checklist adopted by Hayden J in *Re B (A Child)*[19] and amended by the Court of Appeal in *Re M (Children) (Habitual Residence: 1980 Hague Child Abduction Convention)*[20] sets out the factors which a court may consider, and upon which practitioners should focus, when dealing with the factual determination of a child's habitual residence:

18 *Re J (A Child) (Finland) (Habitual Residence)* [2017] 2 FCR 542; *Re G-E (Children) (Hague Convention 1980: Repudiatory Retention and Habitual Residence)* [2019] 2 FLR 17; *Re M (Children) (Habitual Residence: 1980 Hague Child Abduction Convention)* [2020] EWCA Civ 1105; *Re B (A Child) (Abduction: Habitual Residence)* [2020] EWCA Civ 1187; *Re A (A Child) (Habitual Residence:1996 Hague Child Protection Convention)* [2023] EWCA 659.

19 *Re B (A Child) (Custody Rights: Habitual Residence)* [2016] EWHC 2174 (Fam), [2016] 4 WLR 156 at para 17.

20 [2020] EWCA Civ 1105.

- Child's HR requires some degree of integration in social and family environment
- Factual enquiry centred on circumstances of child's life likely to illuminate the child's HR
- Meaning of HR shaped in light of best interests, in particular 'practical connection' between child and country concerned
- Parent may unilaterally change HR by removing the child without the consent of the other parent
- Child usually has same HR as the caring parent(s) but it is the child's HR and intergration under consideration, not parent's
- Parental intention is relevant, but not determinative
- Highly unusual for child to have no HR. Usually a child loses pre-existing HR at the same time as gaining a new one
- ***Stability*** of residence as opposed to *permanence* is relevant
- Question is ***some degree*** *of* integration in social/family environment; not whether *fully* integrated before becoming HR
- Requisite integration can develop quickly; possibly in a day
- HR is question of fact focused on child; purposes/intentions of parents merely relevant factors. No requirement of intention by parents to reside permanently or indefinitely

THE HABITUAL RESIDENCE OF AN ADULT

4.19 For a number of years, the Courts of England and Wales applied a test for 'habitual residence' based upon the concept of 'ordinary residence' as it was explained by the House of Lords in *R v Barnet London Borough Council, ex p Shah*[21].

4.20 In *Marinos v Marinos*[22], Munby J considered the meaning of the term for the purposes of Council Regulation (EC) No 2201/2003, Art 3, in order to determine whether the English court had jurisdiction under that Regulation to entertain divorce proceedings. He held that previous domestic authorities including *Shah*[23] were of no application to the interpretation of a European regulation. On the basis of the European case law, he went on to hold that:

21 [1983] 2 AC 309, [1983] 2 WLR 16.
22 [2007] EWHC 2047 (Fam), [2008] 2 FCR 47, [2007] 2 FLR 1018.
23 *R v Barnet London Borough Council, ex p Shah* [2007] EWHC 2047 (Fam), [2008] 2 FCR 47, [2007] 2 FLR 1018.

Test for habitual residence

For the purposes of Regulation 2201/2003, Art 3, the Member State in which a person is habitually resident is the place where the person has established, on a fixed basis, their permanent or habitual centre of interests.

4.21 The so-called 'centre of interests' test for habitual residence has been affirmed in subsequent cases, including by the Court of Appeal in *Tan v Choy*[24].

4.22 As explained by Munby J in *Marinos*[25], by contrast with previous domestic law authorities[26], under the 'centre of interests' test a person can only be habitually resident in one jurisdiction at any given time[27]. He further held that:

- length of residence is not an intrinsic element of habitual residence: following a planned move a new habitual residence can be acquired immediately upon arrival in the new jurisdiction[28];
- in determining where a person has their 'centre of interests' for *divorce* purposes, the court should consider their position as a spouse: accordingly the place where the family home is located – where the person's family lives – is an important factor[29].

4.23 One aspect of the decision in *Marinos*[30] has proved to be controversial[31] and more recently has been held to be wrong: Munby J held that for the purposes of Regulation 2201/2003, Art 3 references to 'residence' should be interpreted as meaning *mere* residence, a concept easier to establish than *habitual* residence. This issue was examined in detail by Moor J in *Pierburg v Pierburg*[32]. He concluded that on this issue, *Marinos* was wrongly decided and when Art 3 refers to 'residence' this is simply short-hand for 'habitual residence'.

24 [2014] EWCA Civ 251, [2015] 1 FLR 492.
25 [2007] EWHC 2047 (Fam), [2008] 2 FCR 47, [2007] 2 FLR 1018.
26 See for example, *Ikimi v Ikimi (Divorce: Habitual Residence)* [2001] EWCA Civ 873, [2002] Fam 72, [2001] 3 WLR 672, [2001] 2 FCR 385, [2001] 2 FLR 1288.
27 The CJEU subsequently reached the same conclusion in *IB v FA (Case C-289/20)* [2022] 2 FLR 294 (see below at **4.26–4.27**).
28 See also *LK v K (No 2)* [2006] EWHC 3280 (Fam); *Swaddling v Chief Adjudication Officer* (Case C-90/97) [1999] ECR 1-01075, [1999] 2 FLR 184.
29 In so deciding, Munby J distinguished certain European authorities in which, in the context of a dispute about a person's entitlement to social security payments, the courts had treated the person's place of employment as significant to the establishment of his centre of interests.
30 [2007] EWHC 2047 (Fam), [2008] 2 FCR 47, [2007] 2 FLR 1018.
31 See *Munro v Munro* [2007] EWHC 3315 (Fam), [2008] 1 FLR 1613.
32 [2019] EWFC 24, [2019] 1 WLR 4335, [2019] 2 FCR 1006, [2019] 2 FLR 527.

4.24

Case summary: *Pierburg v Pierburg*[33]

Facts:

Both parties were born in Germany but moved to Switzerland in 1999. In 2017 they separated, following which W moved to England. The date of the move was disputed: W contended that she had moved on 12 July 2017; H asserted 15 August 2017.

On 12 January 2018, W issued a divorce petition in England on the basis that she was domiciled and habitually resident in England, having resided there for at least six months prior to the petition.

Held by Moor J:

W's petition dismissed. The English court did not have jurisdiction.

For the purposes of Regulation (EC) 2001/2003, Art 3, references to 'residence' meant 'habitual residence'. It was therefore necessary for W to demonstrate that as at the date of her petition she was: (a) domiciled in England and Wales; (b) habitually resident in England and Wales, having been habitually resident here for at least six months.

On the facts, W became habitually resident in England and Wales on 15 August 2017 and therefore had not been habitually resident for the requisite six months as at 12 January 2018. Additionally, at the date of the petition W remained domiciled in Germany, not England.

4.25 In *Nicolaisen v Nicolaisen*[34] Moor J followed his previous decision in *Pierburg*[35] as to the meaning of 'residence' under Regulation 2201/2003, Art 3. In doing so, he relied upon the decision of the CJEU in *IB v FA (Case C-289-20)*, decided in the meantime.

4.26 In *IB v FA (Case C-289/20)*[36] the CJEU held that for the purposes of Regulation 2201/2003, Art 3, a person can only be habitually resident in one

33 [2019] EWFC 24, [2019] 1 WLR 4335, [2019] 2 FCR 1006, [2019] 2 FLR 527.
34 [2022] EWFC 70, [2023] 1 FLR 1163.
35 [2019] EWFC 24, [2019] 1 WLR 4335, [2019] 2 FCR 1006, [2019] 2 FLR 527.
36 [2022] 2 FLR 294.

jurisdiction at a given time (the same conclusion previously reached by Munby J in *Marinos*). It also gave guidance as to the interpretation of habitual residence, drawing attention to features of the habitual residence of an adult which differ from those of a child.

4.27

Case summary: *IB v FA* (Case C-289/20)[37]

Facts:

H was a French national and W was an Irish national. The parties' family home was in Ireland where W continued to live. H contended that from 2010 he had been working in France, doing so on a permanent and stable basis since May 2017. He had, despite this, continued to travel to and stay at the family home in Ireland until the end of 2018. He maintained significant family ties in Ireland.

In December 2018, H filed a divorce application in France and W challenged jurisdiction, asserting that H remained habitually resident in France. The French Court of Appeal referred the matter to the CJEU for a ruling as to whether it was possible to have more than one habitual residence for the purposes of Regulation 2201/2003, Art 3.

Held by the CJEU:

For the purposes of Regulation 2201/2003, Art 3, a person can only have one habitual residence at a given time.

The particular circumstances characterising the place of habitual residence of a child are not identical in every respect to those which make it possible to determine the habitual residence of a spouse.

A spouse may, as a result of a marital crisis, decide to leave the couple's former habitual residence in order to settle in another Member State and apply there for the dissolution of matrimonial ties, while remaining entirely free to retain some social and family ties in the Member State of the couple's former habitual residence.

Unlike a child, particularly an infant, whose environment is, as a general rule, a family environment, the environment of an adult is necessarily more varied,

37 [2022] 2 FLR 294.

> composed of a significantly wider range of activities and diverse interests, concerning, inter alia, professional, sociocultural and financial matters in addition to private and familial matters.

HABITUAL RESIDENCE POST-BREXIT

4.28 The fact that the modern principles of habitual residence in English law all derive from European case law raises a question as to whether those principles continue to apply following the departure of the United Kingdom from the European Union. At the time of writing, there is no case which provides a definitive answer to this question.

4.29 So far as the habitual residence of children is concerned, an essential part of the Supreme Court's decision in *Re A (Children)*[38] was that it was the purpose of the Family Law Act 1986 to adopt a concept (habitual residence) as a basis for jurisdiction which was the same as that adopted in the Hague and European Conventions. Hence, the concept should be interpreted consistently across the board, with the test formulated by the European Court being preferable to that previously adopted by the English courts. This reasoning continues to hold good, notwithstanding the UK ceasing to be a member of the EU. The domestic cases since 1 January 2021 have all continued to adopt the same approach to habitual residence.

4.30 So far as the habitual residence of adults is concerned, the domestic case law is based upon the interpretation of Council Regulation (EC) No 2201/2003, Art 3. This ceased to apply at 11pm on 31 December 2020, but as a consequence the Domicile and Matrimonial Proceedings Act 1973, s 5(2) was amended to incorporate into domestic law the grounds for jurisdiction previously contained in Article 3 (the amended statute virtually replicates Article 3). It was clearly the intention of Parliament in amending the statute in this way to ensure a seamless continuation of the jurisdictional position which existed before Brexit, a proposition which supports the continued application of European law concepts to the meaning of habitual residence.

DOMICILE

4.31 The principles of domicile were set out by Arden LJ in *Barlow Clowes International Ltd (in liquidation) v Henwood*[39] at para 8:

38 *A v A (Children: Habitual Residence) (Reunite International Child Abduction Centre intervening)* [2013] UKSC 60, [2014] AC 1, [2013] 3 WLR 76, [2013] 3 FCR 559, [2014] 1 FLR 111.

39 [2008] EWCA Civ 577.

Key citation: *Barlow Clowes International Ltd (in liquidation) v Henwood*[40]

Arden LJ:

'8. The following principles of law, which are derived from Dicey, Morris and Collins on *The Conflict of Laws* (2006) are not in issue:

(i) A person is, in general, domiciled in the country in which he is considered by English law to have his permanent home. A person may sometimes be domiciled in a country although he does not have his permanent home in it (Dicey, pages 122 to 126).

(ii) No person can be without a domicile (Dicey, page 126).

(iii) No person can at the same time for the same purpose have more than one domicile (Dicey, pages 126 to 128).

(iv) An existing domicile is presumed to continue until it is proved that a new domicile has been acquired (Dicey, pages 128 to 129).

(v) Every person receives at birth a domicile of origin (Dicey, pages 130 to 133).

(vi) Every independent person can acquire a domicile of choice by the combination of residence and an intention of permanent or indefinite residence, but not otherwise (Dicey, pages 133 to 138).

(vii) Any circumstance that is evidence of a person's residence, or of his intention to reside permanently or indefinitely in a country, must be considered in determining whether he has acquired a domicile of choice (Dicey, pages 138 to 143).

(viii) In determining whether a person intends to reside permanently or indefinitely, the court may have regard to the motive for which residence was taken up, the fact that residence was not freely chosen, and the fact that residence was precarious (Dicey, pages 144 to 151).

(ix) A person abandons a domicile of choice in a country by ceasing to reside there and by ceasing to intend to reside there permanently, or indefinitely, and not otherwise (Dicey, pages 151 to 153).

(x) When a domicile of choice is abandoned, a new domicile of choice may be acquired, but, if it is not acquired, the domicile of origin revives (Dicey, pages 151 to 153).'

40 [2008] EWCA Civ 577.

4.32 The position can be summarised by the following graphics:

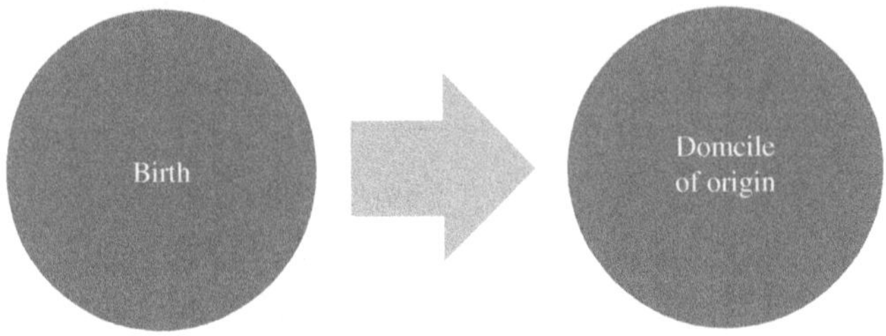

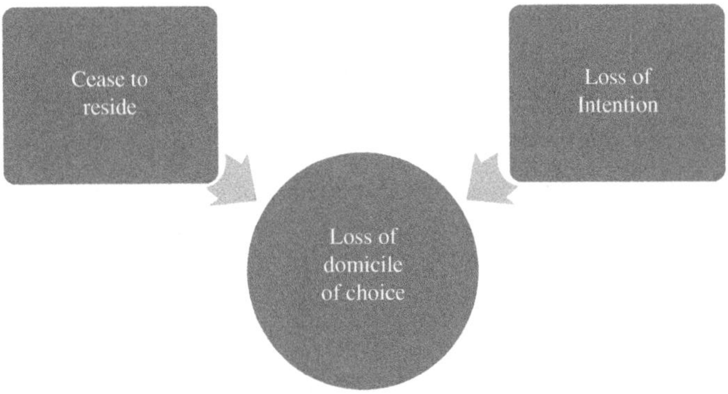

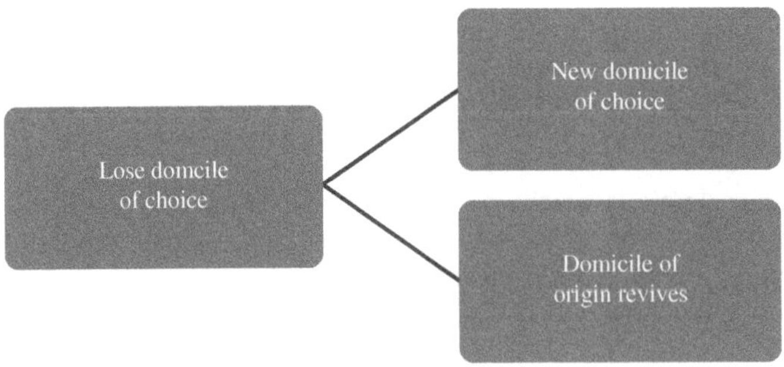

4.33 In *Barlow Clowes*[41] it was further held that:

- the intention of residence must be fixed and must be for the indefinite future. It is not enough, for instance, that at any given point in time its length has not been determined;
- given that a person can only have one domicile at any one time for the same purpose, they must have a singular and distinctive relationship with the country of supposed domicile of choice. That means it must be their ultimate home or the place where they would wish to spend their last days;
- the fact that residence is precarious or illegal is a circumstance that is relevant to the question of intention (but the fact that presence is illegal does not prevent residence)[42];
- a person can acquire a domicile of choice without naturalisation. On the other hand, citizenship is not decisive[43];
- an intention to be buried in a particular place has in some circumstances been treated as an important factor, but in other cases discounted (Dicey, page 140);
- if a person leaves a country to evade their creditors, they may lose their domicile there, unless they plan to return as soon as they have got rid of their debts;
- frequently the subject of a dispute as to domicile will make statements or declarations as to what they intend. But the court should not rely on these statements unless corroborated by action consistent with the declaration.

4.34 In *Agulian v Cyganik*[44] a Greek-Cypriot man who had lived in England for over 30 years was found not to have acquired a domicile of choice in this jurisdiction. In the Court of Appeal, the following was said about the nature of the task of determining domicile:

Key citations: *Agulian v Cyganik*[45]

Mummery LJ at para 16:

> 'Positioned at the date of death in February 2003 the court must look back at the whole of the deceased's life, at what he had done with his life, at what life had done to him and at what were his inferred intentions

41 [2008] EWCA Civ 577.
42 See also *Mark v Mark* [2005] UKHL 42, [2006] 1 AC 98, [2005] 3 WLR 111, [2005] 2 FCR 467, [2005] 2 FLR 1193.
43 *Wahl v Wahl* [1932] 147 LT 382.
44 [2006] EWCA Civ 129, [2006] 1 FCR 406.
45 [2006] EWCA Civ 129, [2006] 1 FCR 406.

> in order to decide whether he had acquired a domicile of choice in England by the date of his death. Soren Kierkegaard's aphorism that "Life must be lived forwards, but can only be understood backwards" resonates in the biographical data of domicile disputes.'
>
> **Longmore LJ at para 53:**
>
> 'All the cases state that a domicile of origin can only be replaced by clear cogent and compelling evidence that the relevant person intended to settle permanently and indefinitely in the alleged domicile of choice.'

4.35 The principles summarised in *Barlow Clowes*[46] were applied by the Court of Appeal in *Kelly v Pyres*[47]. The Court of Appeal held that the judge at first instance had been wrong to find that a domicile of choice had been acquired in England over the course of a 16-year period when the wife had not lived in England for the majority of that period; there had been no co-incidence of residence and intention.

JURISDICTION OF THE COURTS TO DEAL WITH FINANCIAL REMEDIES APPLICATIONS UNDER DIFFERENT STATUTES

Children Act 1989, Sch 1

4.36 The jurisdictional position is governed by CA 1989, Sch 1, para 14.

4.37 In relation to applications made pursuant to CA 1989, Sch 1, para 1 by a parent, a guardian, a special guardian or the holder of a lives with order, the courts of England and Wales have jurisdiction if any of the following are habitually resident or domiciled in England and Wales on the date of the application[48]:

(a) a parent of the child;

(b) a guardian or special guardian of the child;

(c) the holder of a 'lives with' order[49];

(d) the child.

For these purposes a parent includes a party to a marriage or civil partnership in relation to whom the child is 'a child of the family'[50].

46 [2008] EWCA Civ 577.
47 [2018] EWCA Civ 1368, [2018] 3 FCR 374, [2018] 1 FLR 62.
48 CA 1989, Sch 1, para 14(1).
49 Ie person who is named in a child arrangements order as a person with whom the child is to live.
50 CA 1989, Sch 1, para 16(2).

4.38 In relation to applications made pursuant to CA 1989, Sch 1, para 2 by an adult child over the age of 18, the courts of England and Wales have jurisdiction if any of the following are habitually resident or domiciled in England and Wales on the date of the application[51]:

(a) a parent of the child against whom the order is sought or made;

(b) the child.

For these purposes a parent does NOT include a party to a marriage or civil partnership in respect to whom the child is 'a child of the family'; only a legal parent.

Matrimonial Causes Act 1973

4.39 Where an application for financial remedies is made ancillary to proceedings for divorce, nullity or judicial separation, the court will have jurisdiction as long as it has jurisdiction in respect of the proceedings to which the financial remedies application is ancillary.

4.40 Jurisdiction for divorce, nullity and judicial separation is governed by the Domicile and Matrimonial Proceedings Act 1973, s 5(2), which was amended following the departure of the United Kingdom from the European Union. The grounds for jurisdiction are:

> '(a) both parties to the marriage are habitually resident in England and Wales;
>
> (b) both parties to the marriage were last habitually resident in England and Wales and one of them continues to reside there;
>
> (c) the respondent is habitually resident in England and Wales;
>
> (ca) in a joint application only, either of the parties to the marriage is habitually resident in England and Wales;
>
> (d) the applicant is habitually resident in England and Wales and has resided there for at least one year immediately before the application was made;
>
> (e) the applicant is domiciled and habitually resident in England and Wales and has resided there for at least six months immediately before the application was made;
>
> (f) both parties to the marriage are domiciled in England and Wales; or
>
> (g) either of the parties to the marriage is domiciled in England and Wales.'

51 CA 1989, Sch 1, para 14(1).

4.41 In relation to a failure to maintain application under MCA 1973, s 27, the grounds for jurisdiction are as follows[52]:

> '(a) the applicant or the respondent is domiciled in England and Wales on the date of the application;
>
> (b) the applicant has been habitually resident there throughout the period of one year ending with that date; or
>
> (c) the respondent is resident there on that date.'

Practitioners should note that jurisdiction can be founded on the basis of a respondent's mere residence at the date of the application as opposed to their *habitual* residence for a specified period[53].

4.42 Section 27(2A) of MCA 1973 makes clear that in relation to cases governed by the 2007 Hague Convention[54], Art 18 the court may not entertain the application save as permitted by that Article[55].

Civil Partnership Act 2004, Sch 5

4.43 Where an application for financial remedies is made ancillary to proceedings for dissolution of the civil partnership, nullity or legal separation, the court will have jurisdiction as long as it has jurisdiction in respect of the proceedings to which the financial remedies application is ancillary.

4.44 Jurisdiction for dissolution of the civil partnership, nullity and legal separation is governed by the Civil Partnership Act 2004 ('CPA 2004'), ss 219–221 and the Civil Partnership (Jurisdiction and Recognition of Judgments) Regulations 2005 ('CP(JRJ)R 2005'), r 4 which was amended following the departure of the United Kingdom from the European Union. The grounds for jurisdiction under the regulation are the same as those in respect of proceedings for divorce, nullity and judicial separation (see para **4.40** above) save that the domicile of just one of the parties, as opposed to both parties, is not one of the grounds in the regulation.

4.45 If no court has or is recognised as having jurisdiction under CP(JRJ)R 2005, then by virtue of CPA 2004, s 221 the court has jurisdiction in respect of dissolution and separation proceedings if:

- either civil partner is domiciled in England and Wales on the date proceedings are begun; or

52 MCA 1973, s 27(2).

53 For the distinction between 'residence' and 'habitual residence' see *Marinos v Marinos* [2007] EWHC 2047 (Fam), [2008] 2 FCR 47, [2007] 2 FLR 1018.

54 The Hague Convention on the International Recovery of Child Support and Other Forms of Family Maintenance concluded on 23 November 2007.

55 See **4.63** below.

- the parties are registered as civil partners in England and Wales and it appears to the court to be in the interests of justice to assume jurisdiction.

4.46 If no court has or is recognised as having jurisdiction under CP(JRJ)R 2005, then by virtue of CPA 2004, s 221 the court has jurisdiction in respect of nullity proceedings if:

- either civil partner is domiciled in England and Wales on the date proceedings are begun; or
- either civil partner died before proceedings were begin and either was at death domiciled in England and Wales or had been habitually resident in England and Wales throughout the period of one year ending with the date of death; or
- the parties registered as civil partners in England and Wales and it appears to the court to be in the interests of justice to assume jurisdiction.

4.47 In relation to a failure to maintain application under CPA 2004, Sch 5, para 39 the grounds for jurisdiction are as follows[56]:

(a) the applicant or the respondent is domiciled in England and Wales on the date of the application;

(b) the applicant has been habitually resident there throughout the period of one year ending with that date; or

(c) the respondent is resident there on that date.

Practitioners should note that jurisdiction can be founded on the basis of a respondent's mere residence at the date of the application as opposed to their *habitual* residence for a specified period[57].

4.48 Paragraph 39(2) of CPA 2004, Sch 5 makes clear that in relation to cases governed by the 2007 Hague Convention[58], Art 18 the court may not entertain the application save as permitted by that Article[59].

Part III of the Matrimonial and Family Proceedings Act 1984

4.49 Where a person wishes to make an application for financial remedies following an overseas decision for the dissolution or annulment of their marriage or for judicial separation they may be able to pursue a remedy under Part III of the Matrimonial and Family Proceedings Act 1984 ('MFPA 1984'). Section 13

56 CPA 2004, Sch 5, para 39(2).

57 For the distinction between 'residence' and 'habitual residence' see *Marinos v Marinos* [2007] EWHC 2047 (Fam), [2008] 2 FCR 47, [2007] 2 FLR 1018.

58 The Hague Convention on the International Recovery of Child Support and Other Forms of Family Maintenance concluded on 23 November 2007.

59 See **4.63** below.

of MFPA 1984 requires that the leave of the court must be obtained in order to make an application.

4.50 Jurisdiction is governed by MFPA 1984, s 15. The court can only entertain an application for financial remedies under the Act if one of the following jurisdictional criteria is met:

> '(a) either of the parties to the marriage was domiciled in England and Wales on the date of the application for leave under section 13 above or was so domiciled on the date on which the divorce, annulment or legal separation obtained in the overseas country took effect in that country; or
>
> (b) either of the parties to the marriage was habitually resident in England and Wales throughout the period of one year ending with the date of the application for leave or was so resident throughout the period of one year ending with the date on which the divorce, annulment or legal separation obtained in the overseas country took effect in that country; or
>
> (c) either or both of the parties to the marriage had at the date of the application for leave a beneficial interest in possession in a dwelling-house situated in England or Wales which was at some time during the marriage a matrimonial home of the parties to the marriage[60].'

Jurisdiction is, however, subject to the express limitation in Art 18 of the 2007 Hague Convention[61] if the application relates to a matter in relation to which Art 18 applies.

Civil Partnership Act 2004, Sch 7

4.51 Schedule 7 of CPA 2004 provides remedies equivalent to those available under Part III of MFPA 1984 where a civil partnership has been dissolved or annulled, or the civil partners have been legally separated, overseas. In those circumstances, either civil partner can pursue an application for financial remedies, provided that they first obtain the leave of the court[62] (and subject to the applicant not having formed a subsequent civil partnership or marriage[63]).

4.52 The jurisdictional requirements are contained in CPA 2004, Sch 7, para 7 and essentially replicate the equivalent requirements in MFPA 1984, s 15.

60 NB where jurisdiction is based upon the 'dwelling-house ground', the orders which the court can make are restricted to those permitted by MFPA 1984, s 20. These include the following orders to or for the benefit of a child: a lump sum order; a transfer of property order; a settlement of property order; and a variation of settlement order. They do not include periodical payments or secured periodical payments.

61 The Hague Convention on the International Recovery of Child Support and Other Forms of Family Maintenance concluded on 23 November 2007.

62 CPA 2004, Sch 7, para 4.

63 CPA 2004, Sch 7, para 3.

The court shall only have jurisdiction to entertain the application if one or more of the following requirements is satisfied:

- either of the civil partners:
  (a) was domiciled in England and Wales on the date when the leave was applied for; or
  (b) was domiciled in England and Wales on the date when the dissolution, annulment or legal separation took effect in the overseas country in which it was obtained;
- either of the civil partners:
  (a) was habitually resident in England and Wales throughout the period of one year ending with the date when the leave was applied for; or
  (b) was habitually resident in England and Wales throughout the period of one year ending with the date on which the dissolution, annulment or legal separation took effect in the overseas country in which it was obtained;
- either or both of the civil partners had, at the date when the leave was applied for, a beneficial interest in possession in a dwelling-house situated in England or Wales which was at some time during the civil partnership a civil partnership home of the civil partners[64].

Jurisdiction is, however, subject to the express limitation in Art 18 of the 2007 Hague Convention[65] if the application relates to a matter in relation to which Art 18 applies[66].

THE 2007 HAGUE MAINTENANCE CONVENTION

4.53 The 2007 Hague Convention[67] has the force of law in the United Kingdom by virtue of the Private International Law (Implementation of Agreements) Act 2020. This amended the Civil Jurisdiction and Judgments Act 1982 by the insertion of a new s 3E, which gives force to the Convention. A full consideration of the 2007 Hague Convention is beyond the scope of this book. The following paragraphs are intended to provide a high-level overview of its key provisions.

4.54 The Convention creates a means by which applications relating to decisions made in a Contracting State can be transmitted to another Contracting

64 NB where jurisdiction is based upon the 'dwelling-house ground', the orders which the court can make are restricted to those permitted by CPA 2004, Sch 7, para 11. These include the following orders to or for the benefit of a child: a lump sum order; a transfer of property order; a settlement of property order; and a variation of settlement order. They do not include periodical payments or secured periodical payments.

65 The Hague Convention on the International Recovery of Child Support and Other Forms of Family Maintenance concluded on 23 November 2007.

66 CPA 2004, Sch 7, para 7(7).

67 The Hague Convention on the International Recovery of Child Support and Other Forms of Family Maintenance concluded on 23 November 2007.

State via Central Authorities in each of the States in question[68]. The scope of the Convention is governed by Art 2. It applies:

> 'a) to maintenance obligations arising from a parent-child relationship towards a person under the age of 21 years;
>
> b) to recognition and enforcement or enforcement of a decision for spousal support when the application is made with a claim within the scope of sub-paragraph a); and
>
> c) with the exception of Chapters II[69] and III[70], to spousal support.'

4.55 Article 10(1) of the 2007 Hague Convention permits the following applications to be made by a creditor seeking to recover maintenance using the procedure in Chapter III whereby the application can be transmitted via Central Authorities:

> 'a) recognition or recognition and enforcement of a decision;
>
> b) enforcement of a decision made or recognised in the requested State;
>
> c) establishment of a decision in the requested State where there is no existing decision, including where necessary the establishment of parentage;
>
> d) establishment of a decision in the requested State where recognition and enforcement of a decision is not possible, or is refused, because of the lack of a basis for recognition and enforcement under Article 20, or on the grounds specified in Article 22 b) or e);
>
> e) modification of a decision made in the requested State;
>
> f) modification of a decision made in a State other than the requested State.'

4.56 Article 10(2) permits the following applications to be made by a debtor using the Chapter III procedure:

> 'a) recognition of a decision, or an equivalent procedure leading to the suspension, or limiting the enforcement, of a previous decision in the requested State;
>
> b) modification of a decision made in the requested State;
>
> c) modification of a decision made in a State other than the requested State.'

68 See Chapter III of the 2007 Hague Convention.

69 Chapter II is headed 'Administrative Co-operation'. Article 4 specifies the requirement of each Contracting State to designate a Central Authority to discharge certain duties. The functions of the Central Authorities are set out in Arts 5–8.

70 Chapter III creates a scheme through which applications for recognition, enforcement and modification can be transmitted via Central Authorities.

4.57 Practitioners should note that the remedies available under the Convention are essentially procedural rather than substantive in nature. Article 10(3) provides that, save as otherwise provided under the Convention, the available applications in Art 10(1) and (2) shall be determined under the law of the Requested State.

4.58 Article 20 requires decisions made in one Contracting State to be recognised and enforced in others, provided that one of the following conditions is met:

> 'a) the respondent was habitually resident in the State of origin at the time proceedings were instituted;
>
> b) the respondent has submitted to the jurisdiction either expressly or by defending on the merits of the case without objecting to the jurisdiction at the first available opportunity;
>
> c) the creditor was habitually resident in the State of origin at the time proceedings were instituted;
>
> d) the child for whom maintenance was ordered was habitually resident in the State of origin at the time proceedings were instituted, provided that the respondent has lived with the child in that State or has resided in that State and provided support for the child there;
>
> e) except in disputes relating to maintenance obligations in respect of children, there has been agreement to the jurisdiction in writing by the parties; or
>
> f) the decision was made by an authority exercising jurisdiction on a matter of personal status or parental responsibility, unless that jurisdiction was based solely on the nationality of one of the parties.'

4.59 The requirement to recognise and enforce decisions under Art 20, is subject to the exceptions under Art 22. This provides that recognition and enforcement of a decision may be refused in the following circumstances:

> 'a) recognition and enforcement of the decision is manifestly incompatible with the public policy ("*ordre public*") of the State addressed;
>
> b) the decision was obtained by fraud in connection with a matter of procedure;
>
> c) proceedings between the same parties and having the same purpose are pending before an authority of the State addressed and those proceedings were the first to be instituted;
>
> d) the decision is incompatible with a decision rendered between the same parties and having the same purpose, either in the State addressed or in another State, provided that this latter decision fulfils the conditions necessary for its recognition and enforcement in the State addressed;

e) in a case where the respondent has neither appeared nor was represented in proceedings in the State of origin –

i) when the law of the State of origin provides for notice of proceedings, the respondent did not have proper notice of the proceedings and an opportunity to be heard; or

ii) when the law of the State of origin does not provide for notice of the proceedings, the respondent did not have proper notice of the decision and an opportunity to challenge or appeal it on fact and law; or

f) the decision was made in violation of Article 18.'

4.60 Chapter VI of the 2007 Convention is concerned with enforcement. It provides that, subject to the provisions of the Chapter, enforcement shall take place in accordance with the law of the state addressed[71]. Article 33 requires states to provide 'at least' the same range of enforcement methods for cases under the Convention as are available for domestic cases.

4.61 The 2007 Hague Convention (unlike, for example, the 1996 Child Welfare Hague Convention[72]) does not contain a comprehensive jurisdictional framework governing the ability of Contracting States to deal with applications. Article 20, however, requires certain jurisdictional requirements to have been met in order for a decision made by a Contracting State to be capable of recognition and enforcement.

4.62 Article 10(3) provides that, save as otherwise provided under the Convention, the available applications under Art 10(1)(c) to (f) and (2)(b) to (c) shall be subject to the jurisdictional rules applicable in the requested state. The applications in question are for the establishment of decisions (ie the making or an original decision) or the modification of decisions. The jurisdiction of the courts to modify (ie vary) decisions made in other Contracting States is subject to the restriction in Art 18.

4.63 Article 18 of the 2007 Hague Convention contains an express limitation on the jurisdiction of the courts to modify decisions made in Contracting States. Article 18(1) provides as follows:

> 'Where a decision is made in a Contracting State where the creditor is habitually resident, proceedings to modify the decision or to make a new decision cannot be brought by the debtor in any other Contracting State as long as the creditor remains habitually resident in the State where the decision was made.'

71 For enforcement, see **Chapter 15**.

72 The Hague Convention of 19 October 1996 on Jurisdiction, Applicable Law, Recognition, Enforcement and Co-operation in Respect of Parental Responsibility and Measures for the Protection of Children.

This rule, however, does not apply in the circumstances specified in Art 18(2):

'a) where, except in disputes relating to maintenance obligations in respect of children, there is agreement in writing between the parties to the jurisdiction of that other Contracting State;

b) where the creditor submits to the jurisdiction of that other Contracting State either expressly or by defending on the merits of the case without objecting to the jurisdiction at the first available opportunity;

c) where the competent authority in the State of origin cannot, or refuses to, exercise jurisdiction to modify the decision or make a new decision; or

d) where the decision made in the State of origin cannot be recognised or declared enforceable in the Contracting State where proceedings to modify the decision or make a new decision are contemplated.'

CHAPTER 5

Bringing a Claim

Content at a glance:

INTRODUCTION

5.1 This chapter considers the persons who are able to make an application for financial provision in respect of a child and the persons against whom applications may be brought. These may differ, depending upon the statutory regime under which the application is brought and whether the application is made for the benefit of the child or by a child who has attained the age of 18. **Chapter 2** provides an overview of the different statutory regimes which may be available.

WHO MAY BRING A FINANCIAL CLAIM FOR A CHILD?

5.2 Subject to the courts of England and Wales having jurisdiction (considered in further detail in **Chapters 3, 4 and 12**), the following persons may apply to court for a financial remedy in respect of a child:

Who may apply?	For whose benefit?	What orders?
A parent[1]	The child of the applicant	Any of the orders at Children Act 1989 ('CA 1989'), Sch 1, para 1(2), ie: – Periodical payments to applicant for benefit of child[2]; – Periodical payments direct to child[3];

1 CA 1989, Sch 1, para 1(1).
2 CA 1989, Sch 1, para 1(2)(a)(i).
3 CA 1989, Sch 1, para 1(2)(a)(ii).

		– Secured periodical payments to applicant for benefit of child[4]; – Secured periodical payments direct to child[5]; – Lump sum to applicant for benefit of child[6]; – Lump sum to child[7]; – Settlement of property to which either parent is entitled, in favour of a child[8]; – Transfer of property to applicant for benefit of child[9]; – Transfer of property to child[10].
A guardian or special guardian[11]	The child subject to guardianship or special guardianship	Any of the orders at CA 1989, Sch 1, para 1(2), ie: – *per list above.*
A person with the benefit of a child arrangements 'lives with' order[12]	The child subject to the child arrangements order	Any of the orders at CA 1989, Sch 1, para 1(2) ie: – *per list above.*
A spouse on divorce, nullity or judicial separation[13], or at any time thereafter[14]	A 'child of the family'[15]	Any of the orders at Matrimonial Causes Act 1973 ('MCA 1973'), s 23(1)(d), (e) and (f) and s 24, ie: – Periodical payments to applicant[16] (or third party)[17] for benefit of child; – Secured periodical payments to applicant[18] (or third party)[19] for benefit of child; – Periodical payments direct to child[20]; – Secured periodical payments direct to child[21];

4 CA 1989, Sch 1, para 1(2)(b)(i).
5 CA 1989, Sch 1, para 1(2)(b)(ii).
6 CA 1989, Sch 1, para 1(2)(c)(i).
7 CA 1989, Sch 1, para 1(2)(c)(ii).
8 CA 1989, Sch 1, para 1(2)(d).
9 CA 1989, Sch 1, para 1(2)(e)(i).
10 CA 1989, Sch 1, para 1(2)(e)(ii).
11 CA 1989, Sch 1, para 1(1).
12 CA 1989, Sch 1, para 1(1).
13 MCA 1973, s 23(1).
14 MCA 1973, s 24(4).
15 Per MCA 1973, s 29(1) and (3), the court may not make orders for financial provision where the child has reached the age of 18, unless the child is (or would otherwise be) in education or training, or there are special circumstances.
16 MCA 1973, s 23(1)(a).
17 MCA 1973, s 23(1)(d).
18 MCA 1973, s 23(1)(b).
19 MCA 1973, s 23(1)(e).
20 MCA 1973, s 23(1)(d).
21 MCA 1973, s 23(1)(e).

		– Lump sum to applicant[22] (or third party)[23] for benefit of child; – Lump sum to child[24]; – Transfer of property to applicant (or third party) for benefit of child[25]; – Transfer of property to child[26]; – Settlement of property to which either spouse is entitled, in favour of a child[27]; – Variation of an ante-nuptial or post-nuptial settlement (including one made by will or codicil) made to the parties of the marriage other than in the form of a pension arrangement, for the benefit of the parties to the marriage and of the children of the family[28].
A party to a subsisting marriage, on satisfying the grounds of a failure to maintain pursuant to MCA 1973, s 27[29]	A 'child of the family'[30]	Any of the orders at MCA 1973, s 27(6), ie: – Periodical payments to a named person for benefit of child[31]; – Secured periodical payments to a named person for benefit of child[32]; – Lump sum to a named person for benefit of child[33]; – Periodical payments direct to child[34]; – Secured periodical payments direct to child[35]; – Lump sum to child[36].
A civil partner on dissolution, nullity or separation order[37], or at any time thereafter[38]	A 'child of the family'[39]	Any of the orders at Civil Partnership Act 2004 ('CPA 2004'), Sch 5, paras 2(1) and 7(1), ie: – Periodical payments to a named person for benefit of child[40];

22 MCA 1973, s 23(1)(c).
23 MCA 1973, s 23(1)(f).
24 MCA 1973, s 23 (1)(f).
25 MCA 1973, s 24(1)(a).
26 MCA 1973, s 24(1)(a).
27 MCA 1973, s 24(1)(b).
28 MCA 1973, s 24(1)(c).
29 MCA 1973, s 27(1), subject to the jurisdictional requirements at s 27(2) and (2A).
30 Per MCA 1973, s 29(1) and (3), the court may not make orders for financial provision where the child has reached the age of 18, unless the child is (or would otherwise be) in education or training, or there are special circumstances.
31 MCA 1973, s 27(6)(d).
32 MCA 1973, s 27(6)(e).
33 MCA 1973, s 27(6)(f).
34 MCA 1973, s 27(6)(d).
35 MCA 1973, s 27(6)(e).
36 MCA 1973, s 27(6)(f).
37 CPA 2004, Sch 5, para 1(1).
38 CPA 2004, Sch 5, paras 1(1)(b) and (3).
39 Per CPA 2004, Sch 5, paras 49(1) and (5), the court may not make orders for periodical payments, secured periodical payments, lump sums, transfer of property, settlement property, or to remedy a failure to maintain, where the child has reached the age of 18, unless the child is (or would otherwise be) in education or training, or there are special circumstances. See also CPA 2004, Sch 5, paras 5 and 9.
40 CPA 2004, Sch 5, para 2(1)(d)(i).

		– Secured periodical payments to a named person for benefit of child[41]; – Lump sum to a named person for benefit of child[42]; – Periodical payments direct to child[43]; – Secured periodical payments direct to child[44]; – Lump sum to child[45]; – Transfer of property to applicant[46] (or other third party)[47] for benefit of child; – Transfer of property to child[48]; – Settlement of property to which either civil partner is entitled, in favour of a child[49]; – Variation of a 'relevant settlement' (a settlement made during the subsistence of the civil partnership or in anticipation of its formation, including one made by will or codicil, but not including one in the form of a pension arrangement) for the benefit of the children of the family[50].
A party to a subsisting civil partnership, on satisfying the grounds of a failure to maintain pursuant to CPA 2004, Sch 5, para 39[51]	A 'child of the family'[52]	Any of the orders at CPA 2004, Sch 5, para 41(1), ie: – Periodical payments to any named person for benefit of child[53]; – Secured periodical payments to any named person for benefit of child[54]; – Lump sum to any named person for benefit of child[55]; – Periodical payments direct to child[56]; – Secured periodical payments direct to child[57]; – Lump sum to child[58].

41 CPA 2004, Sch 5, para 2(1)(e)(i).
42 CPA 2004, Sch 5, para 2(1)(f)(i).
43 CPA 2004, Sch 5, para 2 (1)(d)(ii).
44 CPA 2004, Sch 5, para 2(1)(e)(ii).
45 CPA 2004, Sch 5, para 2(1)(f)(ii).
46 CPA 2004, Sch 5, paras 6 and 7(1)(a)(i).
47 CPA 2004, Sch 5, paras 6 and 7(1)(a)(iii).
48 CPA 2004, Sch 5, paras 6 and 7(1)(a)(ii).
49 CPA 2004, Sch 5, paras 6 and 7(1)(b).
50 CPA 2004, Sch 5, paras 6 and 7(1)(c). The definition of 'relevant settlement' is found at para 7(3).
51 CPA 2004, Sch 5, para 39(1), subject to the jurisdictional requirements at para 39(2) and (2A).
52 Per CPA 2004, Sch 5, paras 49(1) and (5), the court may not make orders for periodical payments, secured periodical payments, lump sums, transfer of property, settlement property, or to remedy a failure to maintain, where the child has reached the age of 18, unless the child is (or would otherwise be) in education or training, or there are special circumstances. See also CPA 2004, Sch 5, paras 5 and 9.
53 CPA 2004, Sch 5, para 41(1)(d)(i).
54 CPA 2004, Sch 5, para 41(1)(e)(i).
55 CPA 2004, Sch 5, para 41(1)(f)(i).
56 CPA 2004, Sch 5, para 41(1)(d)(ii).
57 CPA 2004, Sch 5, para 41(1)(e)(ii).
58 CPA 2004, Sch 5, para 41(1)(f)(ii).

A child who is over the age of 18 provided: – he or she is receiving instruction at an educational establishment or undergoing training for a trade, profession or vocation[59]; or – there are special circumstances which justify the making of an order[60]. Albeit an order may not be made if: – a periodical payments order was in force with respect to this child immediately prior to his or her turning 16[61]; or – the parents of the child are living together in the same household when the application is made[62].	The applicant child	Any of the orders at CA 1989, Sch 1, para 2(2), ie: – Periodical payments to the child[63]; – Lump sum to the child[64].

59 CA 1989, Sch 1, para 2(1)(a).
60 CA 1989, Sch 1, para 2(1)(b).
61 CA 1989, Sch 1, para 2(3).
62 CA 1989, Sch 1, para 2(4).
63 CA 1989, Sch 1, para 2(2)(a).
64 CA 1989, Sch 1, para 2(2)(b).

An ex-spouse who has been given permission to proceed with an application for financial remedies in England and Wales after an overseas divorce under Matrimonial and Family Proceedings Act 1984 ('MFPA 1984'), Part III	A 'child of the family'[65]	Any of the orders at MCA 1973, ss 23(1)(d), (e) or (f) or s 24[66]: – *per list above.*
An ex-civil partner who has been given permission to proceed with an application for financial remedies in England and Wales after an overseas dissolution under CPA 2004, Sch 7	A 'child of the family'	Any of the orders available in respect of a child of the family under CPA 2004, Sch 5 – *per list above.*

5.3 In addition, if a child is a ward of court, or if a court is making, varying or discharging a child arrangements order, the court may exercise *any* of its powers under CA 1989, Sch 1 of its own motion, even if no application has been made[67].

5.4 The court retains jurisdiction to determine a claim brought 'for the benefit' of a child under CA 1989, Sch 1, para 1 after the child in question has reached the age of 18 provided they were under the age of 18 at the date of the application[68].

65 Per MFPA 1984, s 17, which imports to the court all the powers under MCA 1973, Part II.
66 Per MFPA 1984, s 17, which imports to the court all the powers under MCA 1973, Part II. Note, however, the jurisdictional obstacles to bringing a MFPA 1984, Part III claim, and in particular that (per MFPA 1984, s 20) if the jurisdiction to hear the claim is derived only by existence of a former matrimonial home in England and Wales, not all of these powers will be available to the court.
67 CA 1989, Sch 1, paras 1(6) and (7).
68 *UD v DN (Schedule 1, Children Act 1989: Capital Provision)* [2021] EWCA Civ 1947, [2022] Fam 289, [2022] 2 WLR 1047, [2022] 2 FLR 308.

Bringing a fresh claim under a new statutory heading after a dismissal/disposal in another claim

5.5 In practice most applicants will have more than one basis for bringing a claim. A spouse or civil partner with a valid MCA 1973 or CPA 2004 claim in respect of a child will often also be a parent entitled to bring an application against the same respondent under CA 1989, Sch 1. Remedies under these different statutes may be available simultaneously or successively.

5.6 It was suggested by Mostyn J in *Collardeau-Fuchs v Fuchs*[69] that when a claim is brought in respect of a child in a matrimonial context where a corresponding full spousal claim is not before the court (for example, because the length of the marriage or the existence of a prenuptial agreement limits the spousal claim in some way) the CA 1989, Sch 1 case law may be applicable even in a MCA 1973 context.

5.7 Courts should rarely allow principles such as *res judicata* or *estoppel* to constrain a child's right to bring a financial claim against a parent (albeit a pre-existing award may be relevant to the substantive merits of any claim)[70]. A matrimonial clean break between spouses or civil partners does not act as a dismissal of a claim brought on behalf of a child under MCA 1973, CPA 2004 or CA 1989, Sch 1. Moreover, 'the doctrine of estoppel ought … to be sparingly applied in cases concerning children'[71].

Case summary: *MB v KB*[72]

Facts:

F applied to strike out M's claim for a settlement of property and lump sum brought under CA 1989, Sch 1 some four years after a consent order had been made in ancillary relief proceedings pursuant to which M's housing claim had been settled on the basis of a grant of an assured shorthold tenancy M shared with her sister (who was herself the mother of the father's brother's child, with her own financial claim against him).

Held by Baron J:

Application dismissed.

69 *Collardeau-Fuchs v Fuchs* [2022] EWFC 135, [2023] 2 FLR 345.

70 *MB v KB* [2007] EWHC 789 (Fam), [2007] 2 FLR 586, Baron J at paras 25–26, and *MG v FG (Schedule 1: Application to strike out; Estoppel; Legal costs funding)* [2016] EWHC 1964 (Fam) [2016] 3 FCR 480, per Cobb J at para 25.

71 Per Cobb J at para 25 in *MG v FG (Schedule 1: Application to strike out; Estoppel; Legal costs funding)* [2016] EWHC 1964 (Fam) [2016] 3 FCR 480.

72 *MB v KB* [2007] EWHC 789 (Fam), [2007] 2 FLR 586, Baron J.

M's agreement in respect of her own housing claim qua spouse had not compromised her right to make financial claims on behalf of the child.

A settlement between the adults (to which the child was not a party) could not oust the jurisdiction of the court in relation to the child.

5.8 Since *MB v KB*[73] concerned a strike out application, the case primarily addressed jurisdiction rather than the substantive merits of the case. As to the latter, it was relevant (on the facts of *MB v KB*[74] at least) that in the matrimonial proceedings long-term housing had not been addressed definitively.

5.9 Despite the existence of the jurisdiction, in *PK v BC*[75] Moor J held that it would be 'exceptional' for a court to award fresh capital provision under CA 1989, Sch 1 after the same claim had been addressed on the basis of a clean break under the MCA 1973.

Case summary: *PK v BC*[76]

Facts:

M and F were married for eight years and had one child together. When they divorced M received an award worth £950,000 on a clean break basis (which covered both income and housing needs) plus F was ordered to pay £15,000 pa by way of child maintenance and additional sums for school fees.

F subsequently lost his job and when he recommenced work his income had fallen beneath the CSA maximum threshold. He applied to the CSA for an assessment of his maintenance obligations, which were found to be £8,468 pa. He reduced the child maintenance payments to this level, but continued to pay the school fees and extras under the original order.

M applied under CA 1989, Sch 1 for further financial provision, effectively to recoup the shortfall between the payments required under the original financial order and the current payments being made, and to provide for housing and a new car.

By the time of the hearing before Moor J, M had accepted the court had no jurisdiction to make an enhanced order for child maintenance. The CSA would govern that part of her claim. However she pursued her application for further capital provision for housing and a car.

73 *MB v KB* [2007] EWHC 789 (Fam), [2007] 2 FLR 586, Baron J.
74 *MB v KB* [2007] EWHC 789 (Fam), [2007] 2 FLR 586, Baron J.
75 *PK v BC (Financial Remedies: Schedule 1)* [2012] EWHC 1382 (Fam), [2012] 2 FLR 1426, Moor J.
76 *PK v BC (Financial Remedies: Schedule 1)* [2012] EWHC 1382 (Fam), [2012] 2 FLR 1426, Moor J.

Her application was made just 3.5 years after the original order. At that time she owned a property worth £572,500 mortgage free.

Held by Moor J:

M's application dismissed as 'entirely misconceived' (para 15). She was ordered to pay 50% of F's costs.

The court had jurisdiction to hear an application for further capital provision under CA 1989, Sch 1 after a dismissal of MCA 1973 claims, but an applicant would have a 'very high hurdle' to overcome to obtain any substantive award. Especially where, as here, the MCA 1973 order had specifically addressed housing claims on a permanent basis (para 13).

In this case, the lump sum M had received of £950,000 had been intended to meet in full her needs and those of the child for housing and a car, and there was no reason to conclude that sum had not been sufficient: 'that is effectively … capital provision which this mother has already had.' (para 12).

5.10 A fresh financial claim may occasionally be struck out summarily. In *GN v MA*[77] a mother's claim for an increase in child periodical payments was struck out by Bodey J, rather than be allowed to proceed to a full hearing. This is a rare example based upon extreme facts.

Case summary: *GN v MA (Child Maintenance: Children Act Sch 1)*[78]

Facts:

The parties had a 7-year old child. They had never lived together and although they had gone through an Islamic marriage ceremony it was found to have had no legal effect so the financial claims were limited to CA 1989, Sch 1. F was a member of a Middle Eastern royal family. He had never met the child and had no wish to play a part in his life. M was born into an affluent Middle Eastern family, but averred latterly to 'serious financial troubles'.

In earlier proceedings, M had obtained an order requiring the father to pay £204,000 pa (index linked) plus provision for housing, schooling, and other capital expenses including to discharge her debts.

77 *GN v MA (Child Maintenance: Children Act Sch 1)* [2015] EWHC 3939 (Fam), [2017] 1 FLR 285 at [23]–[25].

78 *GN v MA (Child Maintenance: Children Act Sch 1)* [2015] EWHC 3939 (Fam), [2017] 1 FLR 285, Bodey J.

Immediately after this order was made, M sought to appeal the order, based on her claim that the quantum of payments did not sufficiently reflect F's royal status. The Court of Appeal rejected the appeal, describing the High Court Judge's analysis as 'faultless'. The Supreme Court refused M permission to appeal further.

Seven months after M's attempts to appeal had been exhausted, she issued a fresh application to the High Court, this time seeking an increase in the payments to £780,000 pa.

Held by Bodey J:

M's claim was a repetition of her first application and a reflection of her dissatisfaction with the award (and at the refusal of her attempted appeal) rather than motivated by a change in circumstances.

Applying *Vince v Wyatt*[79], it was appropriate to strike out M's claim to vary the periodical payments since her maintenance claim had already been finally determined and therefore her renewed application was 'an abuse' (para 32).

As a secondary position, the Court could undertake a summary assessment of M's claim since the discretionary factors at CA 1989, Sch 1, para 4 included 'all the circumstances', one of which was the fact that the court had only recently investigated (in depth) the question of financial provision for the child (para 34).

5.11 In *MG v FG*[80], Cobb J refused to be drawn on whether the appropriate test for renewed applications after substantive provision was 'exceptionality', but commented that in practice they would be 'few and far between'. The facts of *MG v FG*[81] demonstrate how rarely the power to strike out a Sch 1 claim should be exercised.

Case summary: *MG v FG (Schedule 1: Application to strike out; Estoppel; Legal costs funding)*[82]

Facts:

This was a short marriage (16 months) with one child. After divorce, M remained in Australia. F returned to England, remarried and had two further children.

79 *Vince v Wyatt* [2015] UKSC 14, [2015] 1 WLR 1228, [2015] 1 FLR 972, SC.

80 *MG v FG (Schedule 1: Application to strike out; Estoppel; Legal costs funding)* [2016] EWHC 1964 (Fam) [2016] 3 FCR 480, Cobb J.

81 *MG v FG (Schedule 1: Application to strike out; Estoppel; Legal costs funding)* [2016] EWHC 1964 (Fam) [2016] 3 FCR 480, Cobb J.

82 *MG v FG (Schedule 1: Application to strike out; Estoppel; Legal costs funding)* [2016] EWHC 1964 (Fam) [2016] 3 FCR 480, Cobb J.

Financial remedy proceedings in Australia concluded with a series of 'binding agreements' covering (inter alia): spousal maintenance; child maintenance; and capital provision. These were effective in Australia (akin to court orders).

Two years later M applied in England for financial provision under CA 1989, Sch 1 in the following circumstances.

M had agreed to dismiss her application without determination of the merits. Less than six months later, she had issued an application in Australia for variation of the binding agreements. This was dismissed later the same year. M then made a further application in Australia to set aside the agreements on the basis of duress and/or fraud, non-disclosure, a material change of circumstances and negligent legal advice. Her applications were all dismissed.

Six months later, M applied in England for leave to pursue financial proceedings for herself under MFPA 1984, Pt III. She was refused leave and was ordered to pay F's costs. Permission to appeal was refused by the Court of Appeal.

Six days later, M made an application under CA 1989, Sch 1 for a full range of financial orders for the child's benefit.

F asserted her claim amounted to an 'abuse of process' particularly in light of the refusal of leave to proceed under Part III.

Held by Cobb J:

Strike out application refused.

The following principles can be discerned from the judgment:

- the court has a power to strike out an application which 'discloses no reasonable grounds for bringing or defending the application' per FPR 2010, r 4.4(1)(a) or 'is an abuse of process' per r 4.4(1)(b);
- there is no power to strike out the majority of applications concerning children. However an application under Sch 1 for a financial remedy is governed by FPR 2010, Pt 9 and not Pt 12, and therefore the power to strike out a claim under r 4.4 does exist;
- however, following *Vince v Wyatt*[83], an application to strike out a claim must be decided without reference to 'real prospects of success'. The claim should be heard if it is 'legally recognisable';
- neither the Australian court nor the English court had determined the financial claim for the child on *merits*, nor tested whether the original provision under the binding agreements met her needs more recently;

83 *Wyatt v Vince* [2015] UKSC 14, [2015] 1 WLR 1228, [2015] 1 FLR 972.

– the doctrine of estoppel, if available, ought 'to be sparingly applied in cases concerning children':

> 'Cases concerning children are not static; the court should be slow to knock out a claim without consideration of the merits (particularly where the previous determination is some time ago) where the result may affect or even interfere with thc continuing needs of a child.'[84]

Cobb J did not define the test for renewed applications, specifically refusing to import a test of 'exceptionality', though he noted in practice such applications would rarely succeed.

5.12 In *TK v LK*[85] DHCJ Nicholas Allen KC made substantive CA 1989, Sch 1 orders in favour of a father against a mother who had received an inheritance while serving a custodial sentence, despite there previously having been a clean break in respect of matrimonial claims.

Case summary: *TK v LK*[86]

Facts:

The parties were married for just over two years and had a pre-marital agreement. Consequently, their spousal financial claims were limited, and by consent were resolved on the basis of no substantive provision and a clean break.

After the separation the parties became embroiled in 'prolonged and bitterly contested' private law proceedings, and later in public law proceedings when M made false allegations of sexual abuse against F. A Circuit Judge called her behaviour 'the most sustained conduct of parental influence and manipulation I have seen for some time.'

In 2020 M was convicted of a criminal offence against the parties' child and sentenced to 19 years' imprisonment. A lifetime restraining order was put in place between her and the child.

After a period in foster care, the child was placed in F's care and a 'lives with' order was later made in his favour.

F brought a CA 1989, Sch 1 claim against M, seeking lump sum orders for various needs including housing. M resisted his claim, relying in part on the clean break within the divorce.

84 *MG v FG (Schedule 1: Application to strike out; Estoppel; Legal costs funding)* [2016] EWHC 1964 (Fam) [2016] 3 FCR 480, per Cobb J at para 25.
85 *TK v LK* [2024] EWFC 71.
86 *TK v LK* [2024] EWFC 71.

Held by DHCJ Nicholas Allen KC:

It was not necessary to consider whether the making of a further order under CA 1989, Sch 1 after an MCA 1973 dismissal required the case to be 'exceptional', as this case plainly was.

The court allowed a full range of capital orders to meet the child's housing and other needs, including therapeutic support.

M's expected inheritance was £341,715, from which she was ordered to make lump sums to F for the child's benefit totalling £309,750. She was additionally required to pay the balance (£31,965) to F towards his legal costs.

AGAINST WHOM MAY A CLAIM BE BROUGHT?

Overview

5.13 Just as the nature of the *applicant* is defined by the statutory provision pursuant to which the claim is made, so too is the identity of potential *respondents*.

Basis of claim	Against whom can orders be made?	How defined?
An order under CA 1989, Sch 1, para 1	A 'parent' of the subject child	– A legal parent (see below) – A step-parent, i.e. any party to a marriage or civil partnership (whether or not subsisting) in relation to whom the child was a child of the family[87]
An order under CA 1989, Sch 2, para 2	A 'parent' of the subject child	– A legal parent (see below)
An order under MCA 1973	A 'party to the marriage'	– A party to the marriage
An order under CPA 2004	A 'civil partner'	– A civil partner

Respondents to CA 1989, Sch 1 claims

5.14 For the purposes of CA 1989, Sch 1, the category of potential respondents is narrower than that of potential applicants. There are people (eg the holders of a 'lives with' order) who have status to *bring* a claim for financial provision, but against whom such an application *cannot be made* unless they are also a 'parent' within the meaning of the statute.

87 CA 1989, Sch 1, para 16(2).

'Parent' is defined more broadly for claims under CA 1989, Sch 1, para 1 than under para 2. The class of respondents is wider for claims brought under CA 1989, Sch 1, para 1 (claims brought on behalf of a minor child) rather than under para 2 (claims brought by a child over the age of 18).

5.15 CA 1989, Sch 1, para 16 extends the definition of 'parent' to include:

- any party to a marriage (whether or not subsisting) in relation to whom the child concerned is a child of the family[88]; and
- any civil partner in a civil partnership (whether or not subsisting) in relation to whom the child concerned is a child of the family;

This extension (expressly – per CA 1989, Sch 1, para 16(2)) does not apply to claims brought under CA 1989, Sch 1, para 2.

Definition of 'parent' for all CA 1989, Sch 1 claims

5.16 The definition of 'parent' for the purpose of identifying a *respondent* to a Sch 1 application is narrow. The concepts of 'social' or 'psychological' parent, which have developed in private law children cases concerning aspects to do with the upbringing of a child[89], do not apply analogously to CA 1989, Sch 1 applications. Nor does the definition cover all persons with parental responsibility. Following *T v B*[90], the term 'parent' is restricted for the purposes of a financial application under CA 1989, Sch 1 to legal parents and those falling within the ambit of CA 1989, Sch 1, para 16(2).

Case summary: *T v B*[91]

Facts:

A lesbian couple underwent assisted reproduction via donor insemination leading one of them to become pregnant. The couple was not married nor in a civil partnership but had lived together for 13 years and their application to the clinic was made jointly. Their relationship ended when the child was seven years old.

The non-biological parent ('the respondent') acquired parental responsibility by virtue of a shared residence order.

88 For the meaning of 'child of the family' see **Chapter 12** at **12.13**.

89 See, for instance, paras 33–37 of the judgment of Baroness Hale in *Re G (Children) (Residence: Same-sex partner)* [2006] UKHL 43, [2006] 1 WLR 2305, [2006] 2 FLR 629), adapting the concept of 'parent' to give recognition of parental roles that may be genetic, gestational or social/psychological.

90 *T v B* [2010] EWHC 1444 (Fam), [2010] Fam 193, [2010] 2 FLR 1966.

91 *T v B* [2010] EWHC 1444 (Fam), [2010] Fam 193, [2010] 2 FLR 1966.

The birth mother ('the applicant') subsequently sought financial provision from the respondent under CA 1989, Sch 1. The respondent resisted that application, on the basis that she was not defined as a 'parent' for the purposes of Sch 1.

Held by Moylan J:

Application dismissed.

> For the purposes of CA 1989, Sch 1, para 1, the term 'parent' did not apply to all persons who hold parental responsibility. If Parliament had intended otherwise, the definition of 'parent' in para 16 of Sch 1 would not have needed expressly to include for para 1 purposes (and not for para 2) the mother's spouse (and, by later amendment, her civil partner), as such person would already hold parental responsibility, without the additional qualification required by para 16 of Sch 1 that to be a 'parent' for the purpose of para 1 that spouse must also have treated the child as a child of the family: '… in my view Schedule 1 is not using the word "parent" in a broad welfare-informed sense but **is confined to legal parent**'[92].

Thus no financial order could be made against the respondent.

5.17 The Privy Council applied the same test, albeit with a different outcome on the facts, in the Jersey appeal of *C v C*[93]. In *C v C* the respondent was not the biological father of the child but he had obtained a declaration of parentage in the Latvian courts which (by operation of law) conveyed on him the status of 'parent' in Latvia. That status was entitled to recognition in Jersey, as it would have satisfied the requirement for obtaining a declaration of parentage under English law (there being no Jersey equivalent to the Family Law Act 1986 ('FLA 1986'), s 55A). The respondent *was* therefore to be recognised as a 'parent' by operation of law.

5.18 Had the facts of *T v B*[94] occurred more recently, application of the same principles would have led to the opposite outcome. A person in the position of the respondent in *T v B*[95] *would* be recognised as the second female parent of the child under the Human Fertilisation and Embryology Act 2008 ('HFEA 2008'), s 43. A claim under CA 1989, Sch1 *could* therefore now be brought against such a person.

92 *T v B* [2010] EWHC 1444 (Fam), [2010] Fam 193, [2010] 2 FLR 1966, per Moylan J at para 60.
93 *C v C* [2019] UKPC 40, [2020] 1 WLR 1711, [2020] 1 FLR 641, PC.
94 *T v B* [2010] EWHC 1444 (Fam), [2010] Fam 193, [2010] 2 FLR 1966.
95 *T v B* [2010] EWHC 1444 (Fam), [2010] Fam 193, [2010] 2 FLR 1966.

Who *is* a legal parent for CA 1989, Sch 1 purposes?

- A woman who gives birth to a child[96].
- A man who is the genetic father (subject to the rebuttable common law presumption that a husband of the child's mother is the genetic father if the child is born during the subsistence of the marriage, unless a decree of judicial separation has been pronounced).
- A man who is married to a woman who has received placement of an embryo or insemination of sperm that is not his or her genetic material unless it can be shown that he did not consent to the placement or insemination[97].
- A woman who is married to or in a civil partnership with a woman who has received placement of an embryo or insemination of sperm unless it can be shown that she (the spouse or civil partner) did not consent to the placement or insemination[98].
- A person in whose favour an adoption order is made[99].
- A person in whose favour a parental order is made[100].
- A person who holds a declaration of parentage[101] pursuant to FLA 1986, s 55A.
- A man who has complied with agreed 'fatherhood conditions' when a woman has received fertility treatment pursuant to HFEA 2008, s 36[102].
- A woman who has complied with agreed 'female parenthood conditions' when a woman has received fertility treatment pursuant to HFEA 2008, s 43. Provided there is no man who is treated as father of the child pursuant to HFEA, s 35 and no woman as a parent pursuant to HFEA, s 42[103].
- A man whose sperm was inseminated (or an embryo conceived with his sperm was implanted) posthumously to conceive a child, provided the conditions of HFEA 2008, s 39 are followed[104].

96 HFEA 2008, ss 33(1) and 48. Prior to the HFEA 2008, this was recognised at common law. The birth mother's status as a parent can only be extinguished by an adoption order being made in favour of a third party.
97 HFEA 2008, s 35.
98 HFEA 2008, s 42.
99 Adoption and Children Act 2002, ss 50 and 51.
100 HFEA 2008, s 54.
101 See also *C v C* [2019] UKPC 40, [2020] 1 WLR 1711, [2020] 1 FLR 641, PC where the Latvian equivalent of the FLA 1986, s 55A declaration was recognised by the Privy Council in a Jersey case.
102 See also HFEA 2008, s 43.
103 HFEA 2008, s 43.
104 HFEA 2008, s 39.

- A deceased woman who gave consent in writing (not withdrawn by the time of her death) for the implantation of her embryo in her civil partner, provided the partner elects in writing she also consents for the deceased woman to be treated as a parent[105].

Who is *not* a legal parent (for Sch 1 purposes)?

- A guardian or special guardian.
- A holder of parental responsibility who does not otherwise hold the status of 'parent' (as above).
- A social or psychological parent.
- A spouse or civil partner of the parent (*unless* they have treated the child as a child of the family – in which case CA 1989, Sch 1, para 16(2) defines them as a parent for the purposes of orders under CA 1989, Sch 1, para 1 (but not para 2).

Orders against non-legal parents under CA 1989, Sch 1

5.19 In deciding whether to exercise its powers under CA 1989, Sch 1, para 1 against a person who is not the mother or father of the child (orders cannot be made under para 2 against a non-parent but they can under para 1 as set out above) the statute requires the court to consider the following factors[106]:

Matters to which the court will have regard when considering whether to make an order against a respondent who is not the child's mother or father

- Whether the respondent had assumed responsibility for the maintenance of the child, and if so, the extent, basis and length of the period in which they did so.
- Whether the respondent assumed responsibility for the maintenance of the child knowing that the child was not their child.
- The liability of any other person to maintain the child.

105 HFEA 2008, s 64.
106 CA 1989, Sch 1, para 4(2); see also para 4(5).

The same checklist applies in relation to claims under MCA 1973 and CPA 2004 in respect of a 'child of the family' who is not the child of the respondent (see **Chapter 12** at **12.21** and the cases cited at **12.13**; see also the statutory definitions of 'child of the family' at **5.23** below).

5.20 If the court makes an order against a respondent who is not the father of a child (or, in a case where the child has a parent by virtue of HFEA 2008, ss 42 and 43, the respondent is not the second female parent), it shall record that fact on the order[107].

Class of respondent to MCA 1973 or CPA 2004 applications

5.21 The class of respondents to an MCA 1973 or CPA 2004, Sch 5 application is more straightforward to define, since such claims are included within the wider menu of orders for financial relief which may be sought by a party to a marriage or civil partnership.

5.22 If the court has jurisdiction to determine a claim against a party to the marriage or civil partnership, such a person may also be the respondent to claims brought on behalf of a relevant child. The issue of whether the child is within the class of persons in respect of whom a claim can be brought is considered below.

FOR WHOSE BENEFIT MAY A CLAIM BE BROUGHT?

Definitions

5.23 All three statutes include express definition sections as to what constitutes 'a child' or 'child of the family':

107 CA 1989, Sch 1, para 4(3) and (5).

CA 1989, Sch 1

- 'Child' within the Children Act generally = 'subject to [CA 1989, Sch 1, para 16], a person under the age of eighteen' **[CA 1989, s 105(1)]**

- 'Child' within Schedule 1 specificially = 'In [CA 1989, Sch 1] "child" includes, in any case where an application is made under [CA 1989, Sch 1, paras 2 or 6] in relation to a person who has reached the age of eighteen, that person' **[CA 1989, Sch 1, para 16]**

- 'Child of the family' = 'in relation to parties to a marriage, or to two people who are civil partners of each other' means either 'a child of both of them' or 'any other child, other than a child placed with them as foster parents by a local authority or voluntary organisation, who has been treated by both of them as a child of their family.' **[CA 1989, s 105(1)]**

CPA 2004, Sch 5

- 'Child of the family' = 'a child of both' civil partners and 'any other child, other than a child placed with them as foster parents by a local authority or voluntary organisation, who has been treated by both the civil partners as a child of their family' **[CPA 2004, Sch 5, para 80(2)]**

MCA 1973

- 'Child' of one or both parties defined to include 'an illegitimate ... child of that party or, as the case may be, of both parties.' **[MCA 1973, s 52(1)]**

- 'Child of the family' = 'a child of both' of the parties to a marriage and 'any other child, not being a child who is placed with those parties as foster parents by a local authority or voluntary organisation, who has been treated by both of those parties as a child of their family' **[MCA 1973, s 52(1)]**

Claims brought by adult children

5.24 A claim for financial provision may be brought by a 'child' who is over the age of 18 pursuant to CA 1989, Sch 1, para 2, albeit such claim will be limited to orders for periodical payments and lump sums (only)[108]. Such claims may only be brought if the applicant is in education or training[109], or there be special circumstances justifying the making of an order[110].

5.25 A child may bring a claim under CA 1989, Sch 1, para 2 against a parent, but not a step-parent[111].

5.26 An order cannot be made under CA 1989, Sch 1, para 2 if the child's parents share a household[112] or if immediately prior to the child's 16th birthday a periodical payments order was in force with respect to the child[113].

5.27 The exercise of the court's powers in relation to claims brought by or on behalf of children who are over the age of 18 relating to needs arising from education, disability or health is considered in **Chapter 13**.

108 CA 1989, Sch 1, para 2(2)(a) and (b).
109 CA 1989, Sch 1, para 2(1)(a); see also **Chapter 13**.
110 CA 1989, Sch 1, para 2(1)(b); see also **Chapter 13**.
111 CA 1989, Sch 1, para 16(2).
112 CA 1989, Sch 1, para 2(4).
113 CA 1989, Sch 1, para 2(3).

CHAPTER 6

Related Claims against Property

Content at a glance:

Introduction

Concurrent proceedings

Case management – principles

Case management – overview

Orders for sale

INTRODUCTION

6.1 Where parties have been married or in a civil partnership, under the Matrimonial Causes Act 1973 ('MCA 1973') or the Civil Partnership Act 2004 ('CPA 2004'), Sch 5 the court may make orders to or for the benefit of respectively a spouse or civil partner (as well as any children). These powers include outright property transfers pursuant to MCA 1973, s 24 or CPA 2004, Sch 5, paras 6–7 and orders for sale of property pursuant to MCA 1973, s 24A or CPA 2004, Sch 5, para 10. Notably, given the court is exercising its broad discretionary powers under MCA 1973 and CPA 2004, there is usually no need to consider what the ownership of property as between the spouses or civil partners may be (eg whether both parties are beneficially entitled to the family home and, if so, in what shares)[1].

6.2 In contrast, where parties are not married or civil partners and have children, under the Children Act 1989 ('CA 1989'), Sch 1, the court may only make orders in favour of or for the benefit of a child. Whilst these powers include provision of a lump sum for housing, property settlement orders for the benefit of a child and property transfer orders to or for the benefit of a child, the provision will be made in such a way that, in the absence of special circumstances, any property reverts to the payer once the relevant child attains the age of 18 or ceases

1 *Fielding v Fielding* [1977] 1 WLR 1146; *De Lasala v De Lasala* [1980] AC 546, [1979] 3 WLR 390; *Mortimer v de Mortimer-Griffin* [1986] 2 FLR 315; *Tee v Tee and Hillman* [1999] 3 FCR 409, [1999] 2 FLR 613; *Prazic v Prazic* [2006] EWCA Civ 497, [2006] 3 WLR 470, [2007] 1 FCR 503, [2006] 2 FLR 1128; *Bromfield v Bromfield (Jamaica)* [2015] UKPC 19, [2016] 1 FLR 482.

full-time education[2]. Thus, there will often be a need to consider the nature and extent of any ownership of property as between parties as it will be relevant to the court's discretionary powers and the need for further housing provision. It should further be noted that there is no power to order the sale of property under CA 1989, Sch 1.

6.3 Accordingly, where parties are not married or civil partners and have children, the court's powers under the Trusts of Land and Appointment of Trustees Act 1996 ('TLATA 1996') may[3] also need to be used by a party in conjunction with CA 1989, Sch 1 to deal with real property. Equally, the court's powers under CA 1989, Sch 1 are often deployed in response to a claim under TLATA 1996.

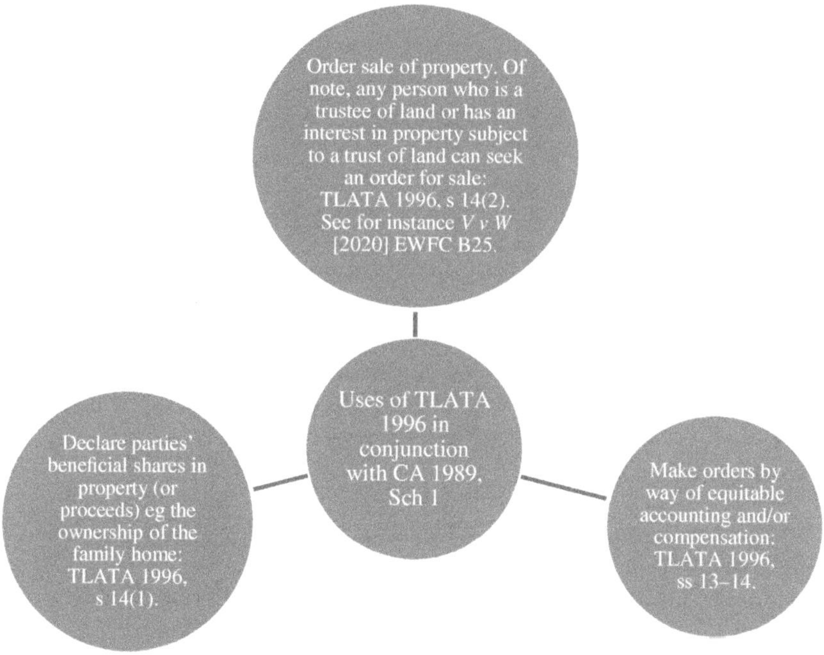

2 *A v A (A Minor) (Financial Provision)* [1995] 1 FCR 309, [1994] 1 FLR 657; *N (A Child) (Financial Provision: Dependency)* [2009] EWHC 11 (Fam), [2009] 1 WLR 1621, [2009] 1 FCR 606, [2009] 1 FLR 1442; *PG v TW (No 2) (Child: Financial Provision)* [2012] EWHC B36 (Fam); *UD v DN (Sch 1, Children Act 1989: Capital Provision)* [2021] EWCA Civ 1947, [2022] Fam 289, [2022] 2 WLR 1047, [2022] 2 FLR 308.

3 It is notable that the Family Court is quite capable of joining a third party to financial remedy proceedings to resolve issues of beneficial ownership without separate TLATA 1996 proceedings being issued (and no issue can seriously be taken that the Family Court *could not* declare the property rights and interests as between a husband and wife notwithstanding this will usually be unnecessary): see *Tebbutt v Haynes* [1981] 2 All ER 238. Thus, it is arguable that TLATA does not always need to be used to determine what is (or what is not) within the court's dispositive powers under Sch 1.

6.4 It is to emphasised, however, that the task of the judge determining a TLATA 1996 dispute is completely different in nature from the discretionary exercise under CA 1989, Sch 1. A judge will apply the law of property, equity and trusts in exactly the same way as they would if the case arose in free-standing civil proceedings[4]. Moreover, the hearing of a TLATA 1996 dispute is adversarial and not, as in financial remedy proceedings, 'quasi-inquisitorial': see *Parra v Parra*[5].

CONCURRENT PROCEEDINGS

6.5 TLATA claims are 'chancery business'[6] which can only be issued in the High Court and the county court[7]. The Civil Procedure Rules 1998 ('CPR 1998') apply.

6.6 In contrast, CA 1989, Sch 1 applications are 'family business'[8] assigned to the High Court Family Division and to the family court. The Family Procedure Rules 2010 ('FPR 2010') apply.

6.7 The Family Court currently has no power to deal with TLATA 1996 claims[9] (and the county court has no power to deal with CA 1989, Sch 1 applications). Accordingly, specialist courts such as the Central Family Court will not issue and cannot deal with TLATA 1996 claims[10].

6.8 Where a prospective claimant/applicant wishes to bring proceedings under both TLATA 1996 and CA 1989, Sch 1, the applications should be issued either at the High Court or at a court where judges exercise both family court and county court jurisdiction.

6.9 The different nature of TLATA 1996 and CA 1989, Sch 1 proceedings means that they cannot be *consolidated*. However, in *White v White*[11], Arden LJ made observations about the desirability of the proceedings being *conjoined*:

4 See *Pettitt v Pettitt* [1970] AC 777, [1969] 2 WLR 966.
5 [2002] EWCA Civ 1886, [2003] 1 FCR 97, [2003] 1 FLR 942.
6 County Courts Act 1984, s 23(b).
7 TLATA 1996, s 23(3).
8 Matrimonial and Family Proceedings Act 1984, s 32.
9 President's Guidance, Jurisdiction of the Family Court: allocation of cases within the Family Court to High Court judge level and transfer of cases from the Family Court to the High Court (28 February 2018), para 13.
10 An exception arises where a case is listed before a judge who sits as a judge of the High Court or a judge of the Principal Registry of the Family Division.
11 [2003] EWCA Civ 924, [2004] 2 FLR 321.

Key Citation: *White v White*[12]

Arden LJ at para 27 [emphasis added]:

> 'Finally, I would like to add an observation about the overlap of jurisdiction between [TLATA] and the Children Act 1989. Where there are children and where both parties have an interest in property, prima facie both Acts will apply. There are some differences between the two Acts. For example, under Schedule 1 to the Children Act 1989 orders can be made for the benefit of the children. Likewise, section 13 of the 1996 Act confers an express power to restrict the entitlement of a party to occupation with power to order compensation or to adjust the benefits to which a party is entitled under the trust. The powers under each Act are not therefore co-extensive. **Unless for some special reason it is not desired that the court should consider exercising powers under both Acts, it seems to me that the application should be under both Acts and the exercise of the powers under each Act should be considered by the same court and at the same time.**'

6.10 Directions to ensure that the two sets of proceedings can be heard together can be made under both CPR 1998, r 3.1(2)(h) and FPR 2010, r 4.1(3)(i).

CASE MANAGEMENT – PRINCIPLES

6.11 The question of case management directions gives rise to the issue of which set of proceedings should be given priority. In *White v White*[13], Thorpe LJ observed that the CA 1989, Sch 1 proceedings might be given '*leading status*' because of the court's discretionary as opposed to declaratory powers:

Key Citation: *White v White*[14]

Thorpe LJ at para 5:

> 'As a matter of sensible management in the county court, if one co-owner invokes one statutory power and the other invokes a

12 [2003] EWCA Civ 924, [2004] 2 FLR 321.
13 [2003] EWCA Civ 924, [2004] 2 FLR 321.
14 [2003] EWCA Civ 924, [2004] 2 FLR 321.

> different statutory power, sensible management demands that the competing applications be conjoined. If one had to be given leading status, I would have myself assumed that it would be the application under Schedule 1, since that statute confers upon the court a much more extensive power, namely the power to make adjustive orders between the co-owners. Of course, I recognise that the applicant under Schedule 1 for any form of capital provision has no personal claim but only a claim on behalf of and perhaps therefore through the children. But, even so, the fact remains that there is within the court the power to make adjustive and not merely declaratory orders …'

6.12 It should be noted that *White v White*[15] did not involve any dispute as to the beneficial ownership of the family home; the issue between the parties was whether an order for sale should be made or deferred. Where beneficial ownership is in dispute, a different approach may be more appropriate. It is suggested that courts are likely to deal with the matter as follows:

- CA 1989, Sch 1 claims should ordinarily be given '*leading status*' in respect of case management and directions as this is reflective of the court's more extensive powers when compared to TLATA 1996; but
- where parties disagree as to their beneficial ownership of a property, that issue logically falls to be determined first before considering what further powers the court should exercise under CA 1989, Sch 1. After all, CA 1989, Sch 1, para 4(1)(a) requires the court to have regard to the property and other financial resources of each party. Such an approach was adopted in *Moutreuil v Andreewitch*[16].

CASE MANAGEMENT – OVERVIEW

6.13 **Chapter 7** provides a detailed overview of the procedure relevant to claims for financial provision for children under CA 1989, Sch 1 and other statutes. The following diagram sets out a high-level procedural overview for cases involving the determination of TLATA 1996 and CA 1989, Sch 1 proceedings together. The CPR 1998 apply to the former and FPR 2010 to the latter.

15 [2003] EWCA Civ 924, [2004] 2 FLR 321.
16 [2020] EWHC 2068 (Fam), [2021] 1 FCR 654, [2021] 2 FLR 165.

Pre-action

- Pre-application protocol (annexed to FPR 2010, PD9A) applies to CA 1989, Sch 1. Parties expected to exchange financial and other relevant information to identify and narrow or resolve the issues. Breach of the pre-application protocol relevant to costs.
- Applicants required to attend a MIAM before application (unless excemption applies).
- Parties expected to follow general Practice Direction on Pre-Action Conduct before issuing a TLATA 1996 claim. Breach relevant to costs. PD requires parties to (1) exchange sufficent infromation to comply with objectives in the PD (2) consider ADR (3) disclose any key documents.
- It is suggested that these two separate pre-action procedures can be combined in the interests of proportionality and saving costs.

Alternative Dispute Resolution

- In respect of both proceedings, court will expect parties to have considered ADR. Litigation should be a last resort.
- TLATA 1996 claim: court can order parties to attend ADR (provided power is not exercised so as to impair Art 6 rights): *Churchill v Merthyr Tydfil CBC* [2023] EWCA Civ 1416.
- Under FPR 2010, if the court considers ADR appropriate, it can adjourn a hearing or the proceedings to facilitate FDR. A recent example is *NA v LA* [2024] EWFC 113.
- ADR to cover both issues may well be appropriate, cheaper and more proportionate.

Applications

- CA 1989, Sch 1 application made in Form A or, where periodical payments only (or the variation but not capitalisation thereof) are sought, Form A1.
- TLATA 1996 claim made under either Part 7 (Form N1) or Part 8 (Form N208). Part 8 used where case unlikely to involve a substantial dispute of fact. It is suggested that Part 8 suitable if no serious issue as to beneficial ownership but the issues relate to order/timing of sale, the interpretation of a trust deed or equitable accounting.
- There are key differences between Part 7 and Part 8. Eg, Part 7 requires detailed statements of case. Part 8 does not: merely that the claim be supported by written evidence.

First Hearing(s)

- First Appointment ordinarily be listed on receipt of CA 1989, Sch 1 application.
- Directions hearing will be listed on receipt of Part 8 claim. For Part 7 claim, parties required to file directions questionnaires; ordinarily TLATA 1996 claim allocated to the multi-track such that a costs budgeting and case management conference will be listed (costs budget by Precedent H must be completed by each party). No automatic costs management for Part 8.
- Generally, parties should agree and seek that these hearings are listed at the same time before the same judge.

Directions

- Conjoined directions hearing. Consideration of: further statements of case; disclosure; further evidence; expert/valuation evidence; listing further hearing (including FDR). Court should be mindful of duplication between the two proceedings. Vigorous case management should be expected.
- If Part 7 applies, the parties may wish to seek that costs budgeting and management is dispensed with. Otherwise, the court will amend or approve the parties' costs budgets in Precedent H.

Disclosure

- CA 1989, Sch 1: financial statement (usually Form E1; in more complex cases, Form E); replies to questionnaires (if court-sanctioned); updating of further disclosure (as necessary).
- TLATA 1996 (CPR 1998, Part 7 claim): scope and timetable for disclosure usually decided after statements of case.
- Court will ordinarily decide, having regard to the overriding objective and the need to limit disclosure to that which is necessary to deal with the case justly, whether to (a) dispense with disclosure (b) order specific disclosure (c) direct issue-by-issue or limited disclosure (eg by questionnaire) (d) order standard disclosure (generally by list using Form N265 and inspection).

Evidence

- CPR 1998, Part 8 claim: claimant's evidence 'must' be filed with application. Court primarily concerned with timetabling defendant's response. By contrast, in a Part 7 claim, evidence ordinarily follows statements of case and disclosure.
- As with CA 1989, Sch 1, it is a case management question as to whether to order evidence under Part 7 before the FDR.
- TLATA 1996: expert evidence rules in CPR 1998, Part 35; expert may be directed if reasonably required to resolve the proceedings. Such evidence may be required for: property value; occupation rent; increase in value through improvements.
- CA 1989, Sch 1: expert evidence rules in FPR 2010, Part 25; evidence must be 'necessary' to assist the court in resolving the proceedings justly.

FDR and beyond

- CA 1989, Sch 1 appications on the standard procedure: FDR must be listed unless the First Appointment used as FDR or it is otherwise inappropriate.
- FDRs are widely used in TLATA 1996 claims (a 'Chancery FDR' having been an accepted form of ADR since 2016 when incorporated into the Chancery Guide).
- Conjoined FDR should ordinarily be listed.
- In default of settlement, court should make further directions as necessary including listing a (conjoined) final hearing.

ORDERS FOR SALE

6.14 Any person who is a trustee of land or has an interest in property subject to a trust of land, ie the legal and beneficial owners, may seek orders relating to the exercise of any of the trustees' functions: TLATA 1996, s 14(2)(a). This gives the court the broad-ranging powers of an absolute owner. Accordingly, the court has the power to order a property to be sold or even mortgaged.

6.15 Under TLATA 1996, s 15(1), the court is to have regard to certain matters in determining an application for such an order of sale:

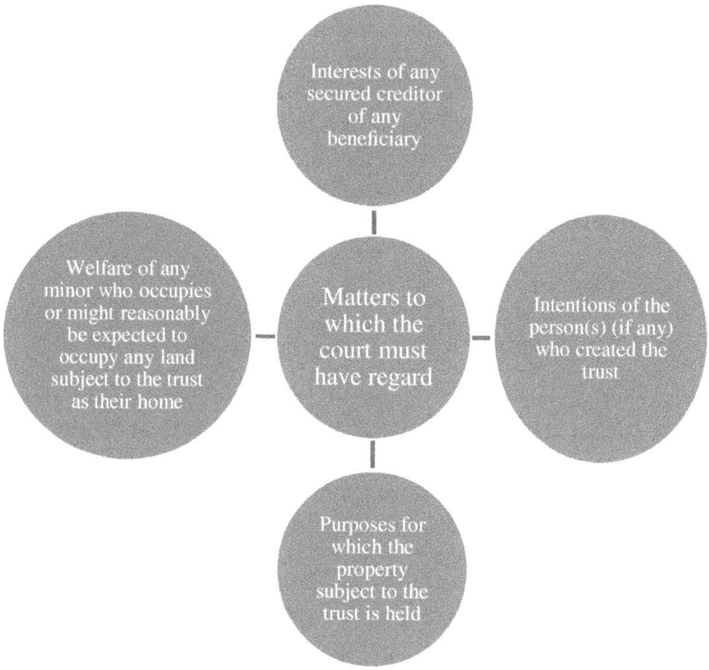

6.16 The factors in the diagram above are non-exhaustive and the court has a wide discretion. There will be other relevant factors which the court will consider depending on the facts of the case in question[17]. No one factor has overriding significance. The court has a far greater discretion than it did under the section it replaced: the Law of Property Act 1925 ('LPA 1925'), s 30[18]. Additional factors will often include the circumstances and wishes of any beneficiaries (where they are of full age and entitled to an interest in possession): TLATA 1996, s 15(3).

6.17 An order for sale can be immediate, or deferred, as was sought (unsuccessfully) in *V v W*[19].

17 *Gandesha v Gandesha* [2020] EWHC 1743 (QB), [2020] 4 WLR 120.
18 *Mortgage Corporation v Shaire* [2000] EWHC (Ch) 452, [2001] Ch. 743, [2001] 3 WLR 639, [2000] 2 FCR 222, [2000] 1 FLR 973. LPA 1925, s 30 provided a statutory presumption that there be an order for sale.
19 [2020] EWFC B25.

Case Summary: *V v W*[20]

Facts:

V applied under TLATA 1996 for a declaration as to the parties' beneficial interests and an order for sale. W applied under CA 1989, Sch 1 for V's share of the family home to be held on trust for the benefit of the parties' youngest child (aged 14) until he ceased full-time (university) education. W initially alleged that the beneficial interest in the family home was held 85:15 in his favour. However, one working day before the hearing, W conceded that the property was held by the parties equally.

Held by HHJ Vincent:

In terms of approach, HHJ Vincent observed at para 67:

> 'In respect of each of the applications the parties have the same position; the Applicant seeks a sale as soon as possible, the Respondent seeks the sale to be deferred for a further seven or eight years. While the ToLATA and Schedule 1 applications place emphasis on different factors, both require the Court to consider all the circumstances. I therefore consider the applications together.'

Having done so, HHJ Vincent concluded that there should be an immediate order for sale. Amongst other things, there was a significant risk that the family home would be repossessed if there was a deferred order for sale as W could not afford to keep up the mortgage payments and it was not foreseeable that he would be able to do so in the future. Both parties were in debt and W did not provide any indication of how he would service the debts without a sale. The youngest child did not need to live in the family home but rather to be financially supported and have his daily needs provided for. A eferred order for sale would leave V in an unfair and difficult position which would have restricted her ability to separate herself financially from the relationship and rehouse (enabling her to spend time with the parties' two children).

6.18 The court's powers under TLATA 1996, s 14, whilst including the power to order sale, do not include the transfer or adjustment of legal and/or beneficial interests between beneficiaries. By extension, the court does not have the power to direct that one beneficiary sell or transfer their beneficial interest to another beneficiary[21].

20 [2020] EWFC B25.

21 *Rahnema v Rahbari* [2008] 2 P & CR DG5; *Bagum v Hafiz* [2015] EWCA Civ 801, [2016] Ch 241, [2015] 3 WLR 1495, [2016] 2 FLR 337. The court is however entitled to direct that the property

6.19 The court has powers of enforcement where it makes an order for sale including[22]:

- ordering a party in occupation to vacate/delivery-up possession;
- ordering who is to have conduct of sale;
- signing the contract for sale where a party refuses to do so.

may be sold by the trustees upon terms that one beneficiary has a right to a pre-emptive bid at a price determined by the court reflecting market value (in default of which, the property would be sold on the open market). This is effectively a work around of the court's powers and remains an 'unusual order'. See also *Chaston v Chaston* [2018] EWHC 1672 (Ch), [2019] 1 FLR 624.

22 CPR 1998, r 40.16, CPR 1998, r 40.17 and CPR 1998, PD30D, para 2.

CHAPTER 7

Procedure

Content at a glance:

Introduction

Commencing an application

Financial Remedies Court

Fast-track and standard-track procedure

Hearings

Disclosure

INTRODUCTION

7.1 This chapter will consider the procedural requirements for bringing an application for financial provision for children, under the Matrimonial Causes Act 1973 ('MCA 1973'), the Children Act 1989 ('CA 1989'), Sch 1 and the Civil Partnership Act 2004 ('CPA 2004'), Sch 5[1]. It is also possible, with the leave of the court, to seek financial provision for children after an overseas divorce pursuant to Part III of the Matrimonial and Family Proceedings Act 1984 ('MFPA 1984') or the overseas dissolution of a civil partnership (CPA 2004, Sch 7). In practice, it is unlikely that leave would be granted to make a freestanding application for financial provision for a child under MFPA 1984 or CPA 2004, Sch 7 if the jurisdictional requirements in CA 1989, Sch 1 were not met[2].

7.2 Applications to the Child Maintenance Service do not engage the court – at least to begin with – and are considered in **Chapter 3**.

7.3 Although they can be aimed at achieving the same ultimate financial provision, there are a number of differences between the procedural routes for applications made under MCA 1973 and those made under CA 1989, Sch 1.

1 This corresponds to the financial relief available after divorce under the MCA 1973 and so includes provision for children; references to financial provision for children pursuant to the MCA 1973 therefore encapsulates provision for children under the CPA 2004.

2 See CA 1989, Sch 1, para 14 and **Chapter 4**.

COMMENCING AN APPLICATION

Pre-action protocol

7.4 Practice Direction 9A of the Family Procedure Rules 2010 ('FPR 2010') annexes to it a pre-action protocol. Whilst this is not applied as stringently as the equivalent pre-action protocol in civil proceedings, FPR 2010, PD9A, para 2.2 states that compliance with it may be relevant to costs. The protocol is intended to apply to all applications for a financial remedy.

7.5 The relevant features of the protocol are summarised in the diagram below.

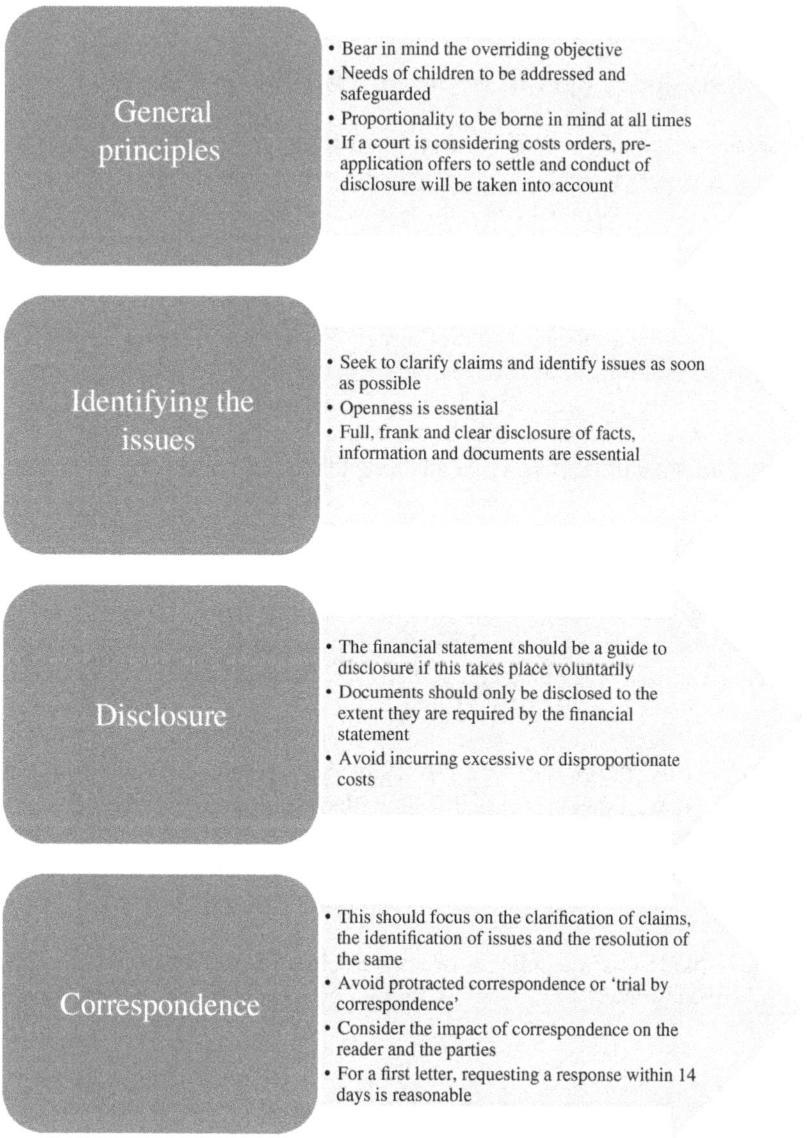

7.6 Prior to commencing an application, a Mediation Information and Assessment Meeting ('MIAM') must be attended, pursuant to FPR 2010, rr 3.5–3.10.

Applications within proceedings for divorce or dissolution of a civil partnership

7.7 An application for a financial order upon divorce or dissolution of a civil partnership can include financial provision for children. Such an application is made by Form A: FPR 2010, PD5A. The application for a financial order can also be included within the substantive claim for divorce or dissolution, as per FPR 2010, r 9.4(a), although in practice a Form A will still be required.

Applications under Part III of the MFPA 1984 or CPA 2004, Sch 7

7.8 Where financial provision for children is sought, following an overseas divorce or dissolution of a civil partnership, under the MFPA 1984 or the CPA 2004, Sch 7, commencing an application is a two-stage process as permission is first required for the claim to be brought. The application should be made in Form D50E (for permission) and Form D50F (for the substantive application), as per FPR 2010, PD5A. The application needs to be supported by a statement from the applicant and draft order. At the time of writing, FPR 2010, r 8.25 provides that the application should be made initially without notice to the respondent; however, in practice, following the decision of the Supreme Court in *Potanin v Potanina*[3] it is more likely that applications will be directed to be heard on notice. The same principles will apply to applications under CPA 2004, Sch 7.

Applications under CA 1989, Sch 1

7.9 An order for financial provision under CA 1989, Sch 1 does not fall within the definition of a 'financial order' for the purposes of FPR 2010, but is part of the wider definition of a 'financial remedy'[4]. Such an application is made in Form A1, as set out in FPR 2010, PD5A.

7.10 Ordinarily, the parties to a CA 1989, Sch 1 claim are the two parents of the child. It is, however, possible that the child(ren) could be joined as respondents. Under FPR 2010, r 9.11(2), the court *may* direct that the child is separately represented. If it does so, the court may appoint the Official Solicitor or some other consenting person to be the children's guardian[5].

7.11 It is likely that exceptional or special circumstances would be required for a child to be joined as a party to an application for financial provision for

3 [2024] UKSC 3, [2024] AC 1063, [2024] 2 WLR 540, [2024] 2 FCR 154, [2024] 1 FLR 1040.
4 FPR r 2.3: the definition of financial remedies includes financial orders but not vice versa.
5 FPR r 9.11(3).

that child's benefit. Whilst this step was not taken in the case, *Re S (Unmarried Parents: Financial Provisions)*[6] provides a flavour of when it may be appropriate.

Case summary: *Re S (Unmarried Parents: Financial Provisions)*[7]

Facts:

The parties were two unmarried parents of a nine year old girl. M applied for financial relief for the child and sought housing in Kensington, where the child currently attended school, at a cost of £1.6–2m. F proposed housing in Parsons Green or Fulham, at a cost of £500,000–550,000. The first instance judge, as well as judges in private law proceedings, had considered M to be egocentric and manipulative, and held that her wish to remain in Kensington was part of her own selfish need. F had persistently given false evidence as to his financial circumstances, and at final hearing the judge found that, as a best estimate, his worth was around £4m. It was ordered that F should provide a sum of £800,000, to revert to him when the child was 18, for housing. M appealed.

Held by Court of Appeal:

The judge had been wrong to consider the case of *Re P (Child: Financial Provision)*[8] as a benchmark and scale down accordingly to reflect this father's lower level of wealth. The judge had failed to focus on the child's needs as separate and distinct from the needs of the mother.

It was not the practice for children to be represented in such cases, but this case demonstrated when it may be advantageous. Thorpe LJ stated that the battle was '*intense and bitter*' between two adults, 'the mother striving to harm the father by extracting the maximum investment fund, the father striving to worst the mother by concealing the extent of his fortune. It is easy to see how, in such circumstances, the real crux of the case can be lost to view unless there is some advocate there to urge constantly the needs and interests of the child. For that, in the end, is what the award is largely designed to satisfy.'

FINANCIAL REMEDIES COURT

7.12 All applications for a financial remedy or a financial order, within the definitions set out in FPR 2010 r 2.3 and for enforcement of the same will now be

6 [2006] EWCA Civ 479, [2006] 2 FLR 950.
7 [2006] EWCA Civ 479, [2006] 2 FLR 950.
8 [2003] EWCA Civ 837, [2003] 2 FCR 481, [2003] 2 FLR 865.

dealt with by the Financial Remedies Court ('FRC'). This has been established as a subsidiary structure within the family court.

7.13 There are a number of FRC zones. Where a case is to be dealt with in a specific FRC zone, only an FRC judge will be able to deal with a case involving financial remedies.

7.14 For practitioners' purposes, this is significant for the FRC-specific procedural principles, guidance and rules that the creation of the FRC has spawned. Whilst the rules set out in the FPR 2010 remain in full force and effect, there are specific additional requirements which have been introduced by the lead judges of the FRC.

FAST-TRACK AND STANDARD-TRACK PROCEDURE

7.15 Where an application is made for either *only* periodical payments or a variation of periodical payments[9], ordinarily the application will immediately be dealt with under the fast-track procedure, pursuant to FPR 2010, r 9.9B(3).

Fast-track procedure

- Applications for only a periodical payments order
- Applications for variation of a periodical payments order
- Applications made under the Domestic Proceedings and Magistrates' Courts Act 1978, Schedule 6 of the Civil Partnership Act 2004, Article 56 of the Maintenance Regulation or Article 10 of the 2007 Hague Convention

Standard procedure

- An application for a financial remedy, save for the above
- Any application where the court orders the standard procedure to be used

7.16 It can be seen that applications for financial provision for children can be allocated to either track: where just a periodical payments order (or variation thereof) is sought, as may be the case when seeking provision for children, this will be allocated to the fast-track. Where wider-ranging financial provision is sought, for example housing or other capital, the standard procedure will be appropriate.

9 Unless the applicant seeks the dismissal of the periodical payments order and its substitution with a lump sum order, property adjustment order, pension sharing order and/or pension compensation sharing order.

7.17 It is open to either party to request that the standard procedure be applied where, ordinarily, the fast-track procedure would apply: FPR 2010, r 9.18A. Should either party do this, the court will determine the request without notice to the parties and, crucially, prior to the first hearing, make any consequent directions that may be necessary.

Standard procedure

7.18 The first stages of the standard procedure are as follows:

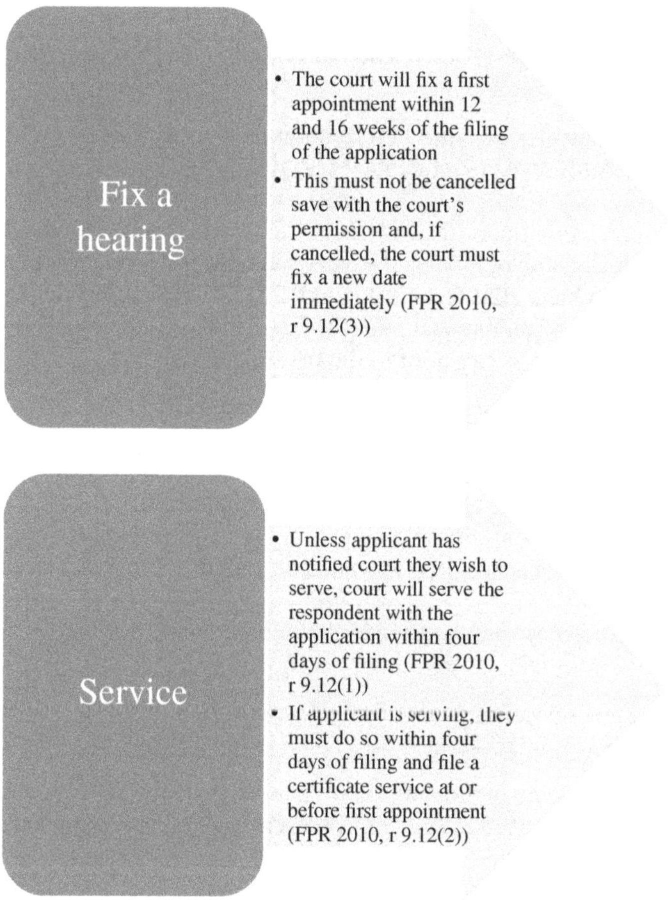

7.19 In accordance with FPR 2010, r 9.14(1), no less than 35 days before the first appointment, the parties must exchange a financial statement as set out in FPR 2010, PD5A. The type of form to be used depends on what application is being pursued:

– for a financial order or an order under the MFPA 1984 or CPA 2004, Sch 7, Form E is required;

- for an application to vary a financial order, it is Form E2;
- for all other financial remedy applications (including, therefore, CA 1989, Sch 1 applications), Form E1 should be completed.

Disclosure is dealt with further at **7.56** below.

7.20 Various other documents are required no less than 14 days prior to the first appointment pursuant to FPR 2010, r 9.14(5), namely:

- a concise statement of issues;
- a chronology;
- a questionnaire setting out further information and documents requested from the other party; and
- a notice stating whether the first appointment can be used as a Financial Dispute Resolution Appointment ('FDR')[10].

7.21 The procedure under the FPR 2010 has been amended by the Statement on the Efficient Conduct of Financial Remedy Hearings ('Efficiency Statement'), issued by Mostyn J and HHJ Hess in January 2022. This requires that in addition to the documents required pursuant to FPR 2010, r 9.14(5) the following must be filed by the applicant one day prior to the first appointment:

- a composite case summary in Template ES1; and
- composite schedule of assets and income in Template ES2.

Although the information to be provided in Template ES1 overlaps with that contained in the statement of issues and chronology, the FPR 2010 obligation to file those documents has not been amended or varied.

7.22 The Efficiency Statement additionally requires the parties to do the following:

- jointly to obtain a market appraisal of any property used as a family home (unless it proves impossible to do so on a joint basis);
- to file estate agent particulars of properties suitable to meet the parties' housing needs (limited to three for themselves and three for the other party); and
- to file jointly obtained brief indicative material on their respective borrowing capacities.

These provisions do not apply only in cases where the parties seek to use the first appointment as an FDR, but for any hearing. Their purpose is to assist the court in managing the case moving forward.

10 For FDRs see **7.31** below.

Fast-track procedure

7.23 The fast-track procedure is set out in FPR 2010, Part 9, Ch 4, rr 9.18–9.21. The key features of the fast-track procedure, and in particular those which differ from the standard procedure are summarised in the diagram below.

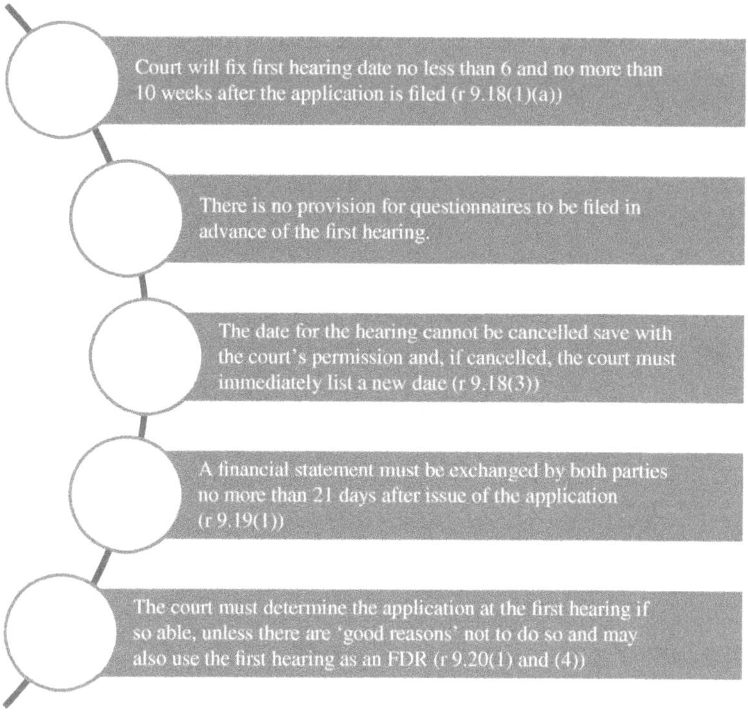

7.24 It can be seen that the fast-track procedure is designed to avoid drawn out proceedings and enable resolution at the earliest opportunity.

HEARINGS

7.25 The progression chart below is based upon a typical case which follows the standard procedure; a fast-track case will likely proceed directly to a FDR appointment (or, indeed, the court could seek to determine the application at the first hearing).

7.26 It may be that other interim applications are needed, such as for interim provision. Such application would likely require additional hearings to those set out above.

7.27 The purpose of the First Appointment is set out in FPR 2010, r 9.15. The matters to be dealt with at the hearing are:

The extent to which the information and documentation requested should be provided and directions for such further documents as may be necessary

- Per the questionnaires filed in advance

Necessary directions for the valuation of assets; the obtaining and exchanging of expert evidence; evidence to be adduced by the parties; further chronologies or schedules

- This could be for valuation of property or chattels, the instruction of accountants or other professional expert evidence or medical evidence.

Referral to an FDR appointment

- This is a mandatory step in proceedings, unless: (a) the first appointment, or part thereof, has been treated as a FDR; or (b) there are exceptional reasons making such a referral inappropriate.
- If an FDR appointment is not appropriate, the court must fix either a further directions appointment, an appointment for the making of an interim order, or a final hearing.
- This can also include a private FDR, on which see **7.34** below.

Accelerated first appointment procedure

7.28 It is possible to use the accelerated first appointment procedure[11]. In such cases, attendance at the hearing is not required and the order will be considered on the papers. This is not the same as simply agreeing a directions order by consent shortly before the hearing, but rather has its own independent procedural requirements.

7.29 Under the accelerated procedure, the parties must file the following documents at least 14 days prior to the date of the first appointment:

- a draft agreed directions order signed by both parties in the standard template form;
- the body of each party's financial statement, excluding attachments;
- each party's first appointment documentation (namely a statement of issues, chronology and questionnaire);
- any other documentation vital to the court's ability to approve the draft order.

11 This is set out in a schedule to the Primary Principles document applicable to the Financial Remedies Court.

7.30 The accelerated procedure is not an available option for the parties if they seek for a FDR appointment to be dispensed with. The court's express decision-making at a hearing is required in such circumstances.

Financial Dispute Resolution appointment

7.31 The FDR is a key part of the financial remedies process and both parties must therefore attend the appointment personally unless the court directs otherwise. Its purpose is to facilitate, encourage and promote discussion and negotiation, such that agreement can be reached.

7.32 The FPR 2010, both in Part 9 and PD 9A, makes clear the importance of the FDR appointment, emphasising the following:

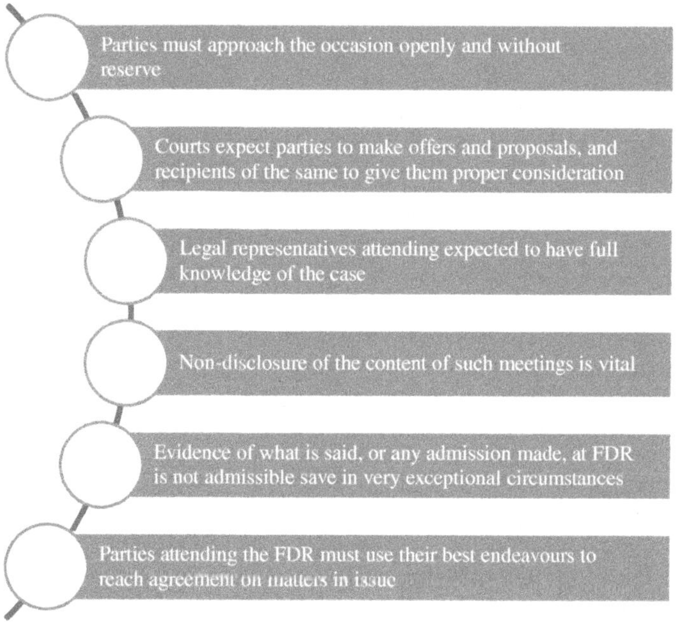

7.33 The importance of the FDR process was recently emphasised in *GH v GH*[12], where the court overturned a case management decision to dispense with a FDR. Peel J highlighted that FPR 2010, r 9.15(4)(b) provides that 'exceptional reasons' must be present to make referral to a FDR inappropriate. In that case, the factual dispute about the wife's earning capacity and the fact her position had not crystallised were not considered to be such exceptional reasons.

12 [2024] EWHC 2547 (Fam), [2024] 4 WLR 90.

Key citation: *GH v GH*[13]

Peel J:

> 'The FDR (which for these purposes includes the increasingly popular Private FDR) is an integral part of the court process. Its value has been proved time and again. Its without prejudice status allows the judge to look behind the litigation posturing which is so familiar in these cases and give clear, robust views. Anecdotally, it facilitates settlement in a significant number of cases. It is not only relatively straightforward cases which are susceptible to settlement at FDR. So, too, are complex cases. In my personal experience, even the most intractable case can yield to settlement at the FDR. The purpose of it is to enable the parties to hear (probably for the first time) an independent evaluation of the likely outcome, and the risks (in terms of costs, uncertainty, delay and emotional toll) of continued litigation. The FDR judge is there to tell the parties if their proposals are sound or devoid of merit, or if particular points or arguments are or are not likely to find favour at trial. It is often those hard cases where one or other party appears utterly intransigent that the FDR judge's indication and observations can be of greatest utility. The FDR judge is well able to deal with factual issues (such as, in this case, W's earning capacity), not by determining them but by expressing a view as to how they appear on the available evidence and how relevant they are. The FDR judge is also well able to give a clear overview even if (as the judge assumed to be the case here) one or other party's position is not fully crystallised).
>
> It is very hard to envisage a situation where the FDR should be dispensed with. Perhaps if one party has not engaged at all, including not attending court hearings, and has stated that they will not attend the FDR. No doubt there are other situations which might justify proceeding from First Appointment to final hearing without the FDR. But these will be very few and far between.'

Private-FDRs

7.34 It is permissible for the in-court FDR process to be dispensed with in favour of a private FDR, namely where a barrister, solicitor or other appropriate expert acts as the tribunal to provide a non-binding indication for the parties. Provision for a private FDR will often be contained in the directions order made at the first appointment.

13 [2024] EWHC 2547 (Fam), [2024] 4 WLR 90.

7.35 Following a private FDR a mention hearing will be listed to avoid delay in the progress of the case. However, it is important to note that stepping outside the court process for the purpose of a private FDR does not enable either party to seek to subvert the requirement for engagement with the FDR. The directions order will contain a standard provision which requires the parties to attend the private FDR. A further court order will be needed if either or both parties seek to adjourn it.

Case summary: *AS v CS*[14]

Facts:

The parties agreed to arbitrate their first appointment, which the court approved by the making of an order setting this out. The same order directed that a private FDR would take place some 3.5 months later. The parties later agreed to adjourn that FDR. The adjournment was approved by a consent order which provided that the private FDR would take place in a further six months. After receipt of a SJE report, W's solicitors wrote a letter stating that it was neither cost-effective nor proportionate to hold the private FDR and suggested that the private FDR judge be released to allow time for the husband and SJE to answer further questions. It was proposed that after the questions had been answered the FDR could be relisted. H then sought for the post-FDR directions hearing to be converted into an FDR.

Held by Mostyn J:

> 'Where an agreement is reached that a private FDR will be held then an order should be made which (a) disapplies the in-court FDR process, (b) requires the parties to attend a private FDR on a specified date, and (c) provides that the date may only be altered by an order of the court (which may, of course, be made by consent).'

If a party considers that either a court-based or private FDR cannot be effective, it is incumbent upon them to apply for an adjournment or seek agreement on the same.

Settlement proposals

7.36 If settlement is not possible at the FDR, it is a requirement that open offers are exchanged 21 days afterwards unless the court disapplies this requirement[15]. Offers are also required to be exchanged in advance of a final hearing, so that the court can be provided with a schedule of those open offers which have been

14 [2021] EWFC 34, [2021] 4 WLR 68, [2021] 2 FCR 559.
15 FPR 2010, r 9.27A(1).

made. The applicant must set out the orders they invite the court to make no less than 14 days prior to the final hearing, and the respondent must do the same no more than seven days later[16].

Final hearing

7.37 The structure and approach taken at a final hearing will depend on the issues to be decided. It is likely that both parties will be required to file and serve witness statements, with this to stand as their evidence-in-chief. The Efficiency Statement provides that such witness statements should not exceed 15 pages, albeit this is a statement of best practice and does not override the 25 page limit set out in FPR 2010, PD 27A, para 5.2A.1. Further evidence will only be allowed only if the court permits it.

7.38 Position statements (or skeleton arguments) should be filed prior to the final hearing; the best practice as set out in the Efficiency Statement provides for these to be limited to 15 pages although PD27A permits 20 pages. A template or timetable is required for such final hearings and should incorporate sufficient time for both judicial reading and judgment writing. Generally, the court will not allow more than 30 minutes for opening (albeit, in practice, this does not often happen); nor will evidence-in-chief usually be permitted.

7.39 There may be experts instructed in proceedings where financial provision for children is sought. The general rule in FPR 2010, r 25.9 is that the expert's evidence shall be given in writing, namely through the provision of a written report. It may be necessary for the expert to be cross-examined, although it will be expected that written questions have first been posed in accordance with r 25.10, if such request is made. Where there is more than one expert, the court may direct a discussion between them; the Efficiency Statement provides that the parties must agree for this to happen no later than 28 days before the final hearing.

Vulnerability and domestic abuse

7.40 The court has a duty at all stages of proceedings, under FPR 2010, Part 3A, to identify any party or witness who may be a vulnerable person. If such a person is identified, the court must consider participation directions. A person who is or is at risk of being a victim of domestic abuse from another party is assumed to be a vulnerable person, pursuant to PD3A, para 3A.2A(1).

7.41 This is of particular relevance to a final hearing as it may engage MFPA 1984, Part 4B, as amended by the Domestic Abuse Act 2021. This

16 FPR 2010, r 9.28.

prohibits cross-examination by and of victims and alleged victims of domestic abuse by perpetrators and alleged perpetrators. These provisions apply to financial applications issued after 21 July 2022.

7.42 If the court decides that a prohibition on cross-examination applies, there is no identified alternative to cross-examination. If the prohibited party does not have and does not intend to have a lawyer, the court can appoint a publicly funded 'qualified legal representative' ('QLR') to conduct that cross-examination if it is necessary in the interests of justice to do so, in accordance with MFPA 1984, s 31W. The QLR does not represent the prohibited party; their function is to undertake cross-examination on their behalf. If such a step is taken, the QLR will be invited to attend any pre-trial review or ground rules hearing[17]. A ground rules hearing is required to ensure that possible participation directions are put in place in advance of the hearing. Where a vulnerable witness is to give evidence, such a hearing must take place in accordance with FPR 2010, PD3AA, para 5.2.

7.43 In practice, there is a shortage of available QLRs and it is not always possible for one to be found. The question then arises of what is to be done in such circumstances. This problem was considered in *Re Z (Prohibition on Cross-examination: No QLR)*[18]. It had already been suggested by the President in June 2023 that if no QLR could be found within 28 days of the order directing one, a further directions hearing should be listed with information from HMCTS about the difficulties. At that stage, Sir Andrew McFarlane, P considered the options to be as follows, albeit he considered that this list was non-exhaustive:

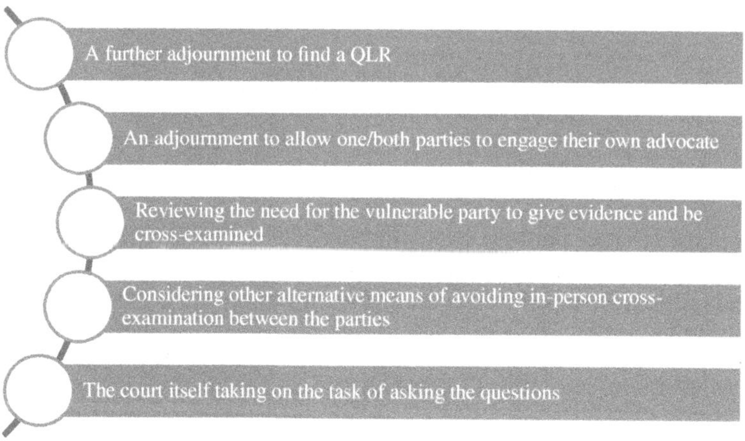

17 This was considered to be beneficial by Sir Andrew McFarlane, P in *Re Z (Prohibition on Cross-examination: No QLR)* [2024] EWFC 22, [2024] 1 WLR 2170, [2024] 2 FCR 96, [2024] 2 FLR 306 although their attendance can be remote where it is otherwise impractical for them to attend in person or may affect their ability to act.

18 [2024] EWFC 22, [2024] 1 WLR 2170, [2024] 2 FCR 96, [2024] 2 FLR 306.

Alternative Dispute Resolution

7.44 As referred to in *AS v CS*[19], there is a growing push towards out-of-court dispute resolution. This can all be facilitated by, and incorporated within, the above procedure.

7.45

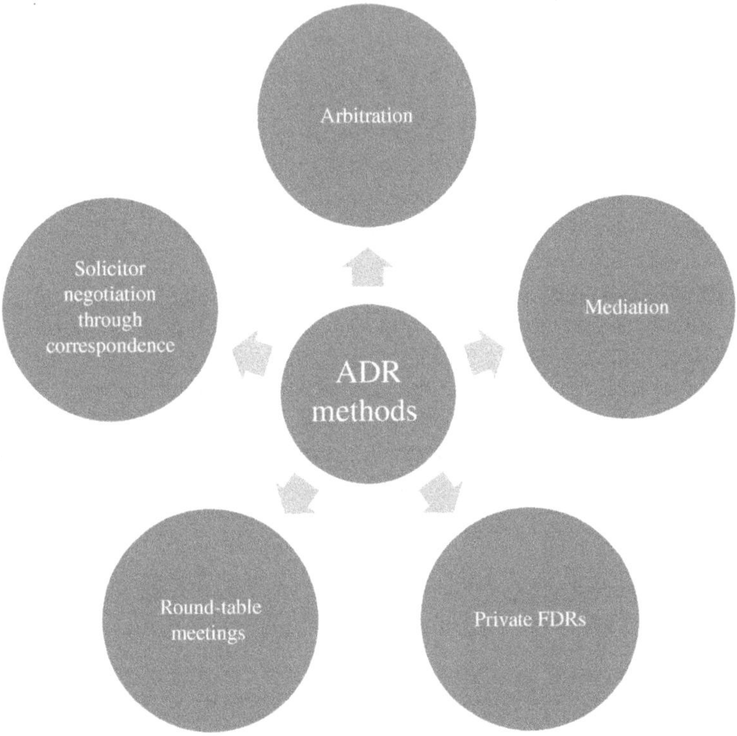

7.46 In accordance with the overriding objective in FPR 2010, r 1, the court always has the power (and, indeed, the obligation) to manage the case in a way that is proportionate, expeditious, fair and designed to save expense.

7.47 Since 29 April 2024, amendments to the FPR 2010 focus on encouraging and facilitating non-court dispute resolution to resolve matters. These go beyond simply *permitting* the court to facilitate out-of-court dispute resolution; they require the court actively to encourage it regardless of the parties' stances.

7.48 First, parties are required to file and serve a form FM5 setting out their views on using non-court dispute resolution as a means to resolve matters in the proceedings. This will be required to be filed at least seven days prior to the First Appointment, pursuant to FPR 2010, r 3.3(1A) and PD3A, paragraph 10C, and at least seven days prior to any subsequent hearing, or within such time as the court may direct. Such a document will be an 'open' one, meaning the court will be

19 [2021] EWFC 34, [2021] 4 WLR 68, [2021] 2 FCR 559.

aware at all stages of the parties' positions in this regard. It will, in this sense, also go beyond the 'yes/no/unsure' answers currently contained within the Form ES1.

7.49 Additionally, FPR 2010, r 3.4(1A) (as amended) enables the court to adjourn proceedings to encourage parties to undertake non-court dispute resolution where the overall timetable for the proceedings will not be prejudiced by taking such a step. Although a provision to similar effect is contained at FPR 2010, r 3.4(1)(b), this only permits the court to so adjourn if the parties agree. The amended FPR 2010, r 3.4(1A) does not require agreement. Although the court cannot then *force* engagement with such dispute resolution methods, the potential costs consequences of not doing so (on which see **Chapter 16** at **16.11–16.13**) means that the parties will have a strong incentive to engage.

Case summary: *NA v LA*[20]

Facts:

W had sought ex parte non-molestation and occupation orders and an interim order for the preservation of two properties, on the basis of very short and informal notice to H. W then filed her divorce petition and Form A on the same day, with applications for MPS and an LSPO the following week. The matter returned to court for the return dates of both of those hearings, which compromised the original applications. The court raised the possibility of adjourning or staying the proceedings for non-court dispute resolution; H was supportive but W considered a first appointment was needed.

Held by Nicholas Allen KC (sitting as a Deputy High Court Judge):

The proceedings were stayed, and no first appointment was to be listed. The parties were to update the court within six weeks for the appropriate way forward to be considered.

There is no need for financial disclosure to be given prior to parties engaging with NCDR and such process can include disclosure as part of the process, even for 'reluctant' disclosers. The urgency of the applications made meant no MIAM had been attended and the exemption had been claimed.

In accordance with the court's duties of active case management and the amended rules, it was a 'paradigm' case for the court to exercise its powers.

7.50 Where an out-of-court dispute resolution method is used, the court can be invited both:

(a) to sanction this step by delaying the usual hearing timetable or staying proceedings; and

(b) to approve any agreed (or arbitrated) outcome by way of a consent order.

20 [2024] EWFC 113, [2024] 3 FCR 391.

Agreements and consent orders

7.51 Rule 9.26 of FPR 2010 contains the procedure for applying to the court for approval of a consent order. In addition to the consent order itself, parties are required to file:

(a) a statement of information in Form D81; and

(b) confirmation that the order is agreed to.

7.52 The consent order procedure can also be used where the court is asked to approve an order following an arbitration process. However, arbitration for financial remedy applications is not subject to the Arbitration Act 1996. Accordingly, where one party considers that the arbitral award should *not* be converted into an order of the court, this challenge proceeds by way of an appeal.

7.53

Case summary: *Haley v Haley*[21]

Facts:

A divorcing couple agreed to submit their financial remedy dispute to arbitration via Form ARB1 FS. H was unhappy with the final award and applied to the High Court for an order that the award not be made into an order of the court under the MCA 1973. The judge refused the application and made the award into an order of the court, holding that the test to be satisfied before refusing to make an order was akin to the test for challenging an arbitral award on the grounds of serious irregularity or by way of an appeal on a point of law (notwithstanding that the Arbitration Act 1996 did not apply to family arbitration). The husband appealed.

Held by Court of Appeal:

The court could decline to make an order under the MCA 1973 where there were good and substantial grounds for concluding an injustice would be done if the order were made, and so the discretion to refuse to make an order following an arbitral award was wider than set out in the Arbitration Act 1996.

Moreover, the logical approach to determining such an issue was by reference to the appeal procedure in FPR 2010, Part 30. Accordingly, the court should first require the challenging party to show cause why the order should *not* be made and, if there was a real prospect of success on those grounds, the matter would be heard at a hearing, which should be a review rather than rehearing.

21 [2020] EWCA Civ 1369, [2021] Fam 317, [2021] 2 WLR 357, [2020] 3 FCR 695, [2021] 1 FLR 1429.

7.54 The same procedure applies where the challenge to the arbitral award comes in CA 1989, Sch 1 proceedings[22]. The decision in *Re A and B (Schedule 1: Arbitral Award: Appeal)*[23] provides a salutary warning of the costs and risks of proceeding with such challenges.

7.55

Case summary: *Re A and B (Schedule 1: Arbitral Award: Appeal)*[24]

Facts:

The case was an appeal against a decision of a Circuit Judge who had declined to convert an arbitral award into a substantive order. The arbitral award had been made in August 2022 within a CA 1989, Sch 1 application. The parents had two children, aged seven and five. M and children lived in an apartment owned by F, and F lived in a separate property which he also owned. The properties were heavily mortgaged. The children spent equal time with both parents and there was a nil CMS assessment in place (as a result of the equal shared care regime). The parties had spent £1 million on legal fees by the time of the arbitration.

Broadly, the appeal revolved around whether there was power for an order to be made, the effect of which required F to borrow money via a mortgage on a joint purchase with M. F also challenged a number of factual findings and asserted that his financial circumstances had deteriorated to such an extent that it would be unfair to make the award into an order. The judge hearing the 'appeal' considered that it was wrong to make an order compelling the father to borrow money *and* that the changed financial circumstances made it unfair to make the award. M appealed against this decision and sought that the arbitral award be converted into an order, notwithstanding the delay since it had been made.

Held by Cobb J:

The court confirmed the principles set out in *Haley* as applicable to the challenge, but found the judge had erred in finding that there was no power to take account of F's ability to borrow when making a settlement of property order. Given the delay, however, it was not appropriate to simply convert the arbitral award into an order of the court.

22 This is also the approach to challenges to arbitral awards made in Children Act 1989 welfare applications: per Peel J in *G v G* [2022] EWFC 151, [2023] 1 WLR 804, [2023] 1 FCR 506, [2023] 2 FLR 491.
23 [2024] EWHC 778 (Fam), [2024] 1 WLR 4157, [2024] 2 FCR 815, [2024] 2 FLR 807.
24 [2024] EWHC 778 (Fam), [2024] 1 WLR 4157, [2024] 2 FCR 815, [2024] 2 FLR 807.

The judge determined that the matter should be remitted for further consideration and made the following concluding observation:

> 'I can only express my despair, which I suspect is shared by all those in this case, that the remittance of the cross-applications for re-hearing will inevitably lead to further cost and delay in the resolution of these already long-drawn-out proceedings. Within the time now available to the parties, and before any further step is taken, they may like once again to consider non-court dispute resolution in a final effort to resolve this painful and destructive dispute.'

DISCLOSURE

7.56 As set out above at **7.19**, the financial statements required from each party differ depending on what application is made and/or what orders are sought. The three financial statements are Form E, Form E1 and Form E2.

7.57 The forms to be used for each application are set out below.

Form E	Form E1	Form E2
• For applications under the MCA 1973/CPA 2004, or financial relief after an overseas divorce	• For a financial remedy other than that which requires form E, eg CA 1989, Sch 1	• For variation of an order for a financial remedy, save where a periodical payments order is sought to be substituted for a lump sum order, property adjustment order or pension sharing order

7.58 In broad outline, Form E requires the most thorough and extensive disclosure while Form E1 involves a less significant inquiry into the party's financial position. Form E2 requires less still – since this is relates to variation of periodical payments orders, the focus is predominantly on income and outgoings. In cases where the default position is that Form E1 or Form E2 should be filed, the court has the power to direct that Form E be filed instead, either in full or in a modified form (eg omitting the narrative sections which may not be relevant to the application under consideration). This may be appropriate where the financial affairs of one of the parties are complex.

7.59 Each financial statement must be accompanied by a Schedule of Documents; what is required varies between the relevant forms and is set out at the conclusion of each of them. The extent of documentary evidence to be provided mirrors the thoroughness of the form itself.

7.60 Some detail about the content of the different financial statements is set out below.

Form E	Form E1	Form E2
Property values, including the outstanding mortgage	Employment status	Any dependents and what is paid for them
All bank accounts and investments	Income from employment, self-employment, any other sources and/or state benefits	Details of variation sought
Monies owed to you, cash sums in excess of £500 and chattels in excess of £500	Capital in property, land or buildings	Employment status
Any liabilities and possible tax liabilities	Bank accounts and investments	Bank account average balances over 6 month period
Business assets	Other assets	Property value if owned
Pension provision	Liabilities	Weekly or monthly income
Any other assets	Income needs for self and children	Weekly or monthly expenses
Income from employment, self-employment, any other sources and/or state benefits		Any money owed on essential bills or other financial commitments
Income and capital needs		

Millionaire's defence

7.61 A number of applications for financial provision for children, particularly those which are reported, will involve a very wealthy parent, usually the proposed payor. In those cases, it may be that the 'millionaire's defence' is run, namely where the party asserts that they can afford to meet any order the court may make such that full disclosure is not necessary or appropriate.

7.62 In MCA 1973 cases, the millionaire's defence is generally considered inconsistent with the principles of sharing and fairness, although it was held in *AH v PH (Scandinavian Marriage Settlement)*[25] that, where the assets were solely non-matrimonial, such that there was no sharing claim and the applicant's entitlement was confined to needs, a broad outline of wealth was likely to be sufficient.

7.63 In CA 1989, Sch 1 applications, however, principles of sharing and compensation do not play a role; it is therefore possible for the paying party to rely

25 [2013] EWHC 3873 (Fam), [2014] 2 FLR 251; see case summary at **7.69** below.

upon the millionaire's defence as an alternative to making full disclosure. This was confirmed by the Court of Appeal in *Re A (A Child: Financial Provision)*[26].

Case summary: *Re A (A Child: Financial Provision)*[27]

Facts:

The case concerned a six year old child. F was a very wealthy member of a Middle Eastern royal family who had asserted the millionaire's defence. Though the parents had been religiously married, this was not recognised and so M had no financial claims in her own right. At trial, M was awarded a £3.5 million house, which would revert to F at the end of the child's tertiary education, in addition to periodical payments of £204,000 per annum, a school fees order, car allowance, ongoing house upkeep costs, a £25,000 redecoration fund and a £770,000 lump sum to clear her debts. Her legal fees, of almost £1 million, were also funded by F.

M appealed. One of her arguments on appeal concerned the absence of disclosure from F.

Held by the Court of Appeal:

The appeal was dismissed.

Although the extent of the non-residential parent's wealth would inform both reasonableness of claims and ability to pay, the focus was on ensuring appropriate financial support for the child – as opposed to benefitting the resident parent – and this was done by reference to the circumstances of the child, as opposed to simply the wealth of the paying parent.

It was in line with the overriding objective to permit the millionaire's defence in circumstances of significant wealth, in CA 1989, Sch 1 cases, and this remained permissible notwithstanding the requirements within the FPR 2010.

7.64 The continued availability of the millionaire's defence is consistent with the overriding objective under FPR 2010 and the need for proportionality. It avoids prolonged disclosure and ensures that only focused information is needed. It can also be flexible, in that the court can direct for as much or as little disclosure as is required.

7.65 The use of the millionaire's defence will impact on the approach to disclosure throughout proceedings. Some disclosure is likely to be required as

26 [2014] EWCA Civ 1577, [2015] Fam 277, [2015] 3 WLR 48, [2015] 2 FLR 625.
27 [2014] EWCA Civ 1577, [2015] Fam 277, [2015] 3 WLR 48, [2015] 2 FLR 625.

the extent of the paying party's resources is relevant to the quantification of the claim. It is unlikely, however, that lengthy questionnaires will be permitted to delve into expenditure. The court will generally confine disclosure to that which is necessary to establish the general scale of wealth that is at hand.

7.66 By way of illustration, in *Re Z (No 2) (Schedule 1: Further Legal Costs Funding Order; Further Interim Financial Provision)*[28], following the father's confirmation that he was running the 'millionaire's defence', the mother nevertheless sought details of the father's spending to 'illuminate' her case and claims for the child. Cobb J considered it to be disproportionate and unnecessary for significant questions to be raised, or answered, on this topic and confined the question to one about the father's income for the preceding three years, so as to set context for the claim[29].

7.67

Case summary: *Y v Z*[30]

Facts:

The case concerned two children aged two and four. M was a former professional equestrian and F a member of a Middle Eastern royal family. The parties married religiously, but not legally. During the relationship, the parties' expenditure was around £2 million per year, but both due to their young ages and the COVID pandemic this was not a lifestyle 'enjoyed' by the children in the same sense.

Held by Peel J:

F accepted early in proceedings that he had both the liquidity and resources to meet any reasonable orders made, which was described as 'a standard version of the so-called "millionaire's defence"' and recorded on the face of an order. He was directed to file a Form E, without providing the documentary evidence in support; this ensured the presentation of the wealth was supported by a Statement of Truth.

M was permitted to raise some questions of F's Form E notwithstanding the defence. F was said not to have adhered to the terms of the defence in respect of security, denying that he had more than equity of £2 million for this purpose: it was noted that this 'flew in the face' of the recital.

28 [2021] EWFC 72, [2022] 3 FCR 419.

29 At [18], the question required to be answered was 'Provide a brief letter from [name], the Respondent Father's accountants, setting out the Respondent Father's gross and net income over the last three tax years.'

30 [2024] EWFC 4, [2024] 1 FCR 894.

The court considered that *some* disclosure would usually be necessary:

- to enable the other party and the court to have an understanding of the scale and structure of the wealth;
- to enable thought to be given to the structure and enforceability of an award; and
- as the extent of wealth can inform the reasonableness of the budgetary claims.

7.68 In MCA 1973 and CPA 2004 applications, the approach taken to disclosure is likely to depend on whether the application concerns *only* provision for the child(ren) or whether all matrimonial claims are being dealt with and, if so, the nature of those claims. It is not the case that the millionaire's defence is *only* available in cases solely concerned with provision for children, although it is likely that it will feature more commonly in such cases.

7.69

Case summary: *AH v PH (Scandinavian Marriage Settlement)*[31]

Facts:

The parties were married in Scandinavia, but lived in the UK during their marriage where two children (aged four and five) were born. H's family were very wealthy, and he was gifted a significant amount of capital before marriage. Both parties signed a marriage settlement after receiving legal advice which gave the wife a £850,000 share of the matrimonial property, but no maintenance for herself or future children. The settlement was declined for registration, and a further draft was never signed. During the marriage, the parties enjoyed a high standard of living and lived in a £6 million property. H honoured the settlement prior to the hearing and provided W with just under £1 million. Asset-wise, W had £760,000 available to her while H owned 99% of the family company worth £76 million and a property with equity of £1 million.

Held by Moor J:

In a case that does not involve sharing of the marital assets but is rather based on the needs of the other party, a broad outline of one's overall wealth followed by the millionaire's defence is appropriate. Such an approach is sensible, proportionate and cost-effective.

31 [2013] EWHC 3873 (Fam), [2014] 2 FLR 251.

> It is, however, important to know whether the court is dealing with 'a case involving millions of pounds, tens of millions, hundreds of millions or even billions of pounds but there is absolutely no need to go further'.

7.70 Where a party seeks to rely on the millionaire's defence, it is prudent to make this clear at the earliest opportunity to ensure it has the maximum effect in terms of proportionality and avoiding unnecessary cost. One of the benefits of such a defence, where it is appropriately deployed, is that it can avoid significant costs being spent on disclosure. Such benefits are undermined, if not lost entirely, where the defence is raised too late in proceedings[32].

32 In *CA v DR* [2021] EWFC 21, [2021] 3 FCR 331 Roberts J noted that the father had confirmed he could 'afford to meet any reasonable order which this court might make' although had 'provided a significant amount of disclosure during the course of these proceedings'. The mother's costs totalled almost £240,000 in this case and she owed £97,000 at the conclusion of proceedings.

CHAPTER 8

Interim Provision

Content at a glance:

INTRODUCTION

8.1 The process of pursuing financial provision through the courts can be lengthy. As can be seen from **Chapter 5**, there are a number of procedural steps to be taken and, even were the courts not so heavily over-burdened, the process would be time-consuming. During that time, the caring parent may not be receiving any financial provision for the child(ren) and may have an urgent need for support.

8.2 In such cases, a party may seek interim financial provision prior to the final long-term decision being made. This can include provision for the funding of legal costs for the proceedings. Legal services funding is considered in **Chapter 9** and is not, therefore, addressed in this Chapter. It is a key aspect of the court's power to award interim provision.

FORMS OF INTERIM PROVISION

8.3 Applications for interim financial provision for children can be in the form of either periodical payments or lump sums. It is important to note that interim provision by way of lump sum is permissible under the Matrimonial Causes Act 1973 ('MCA 1973') and the Civil Partnership Act 2004 ('CPA 2004'), Sch 5 only in relation to children.

8.4 Examples of what interim provision may be directed towards is set out in the graphic below:

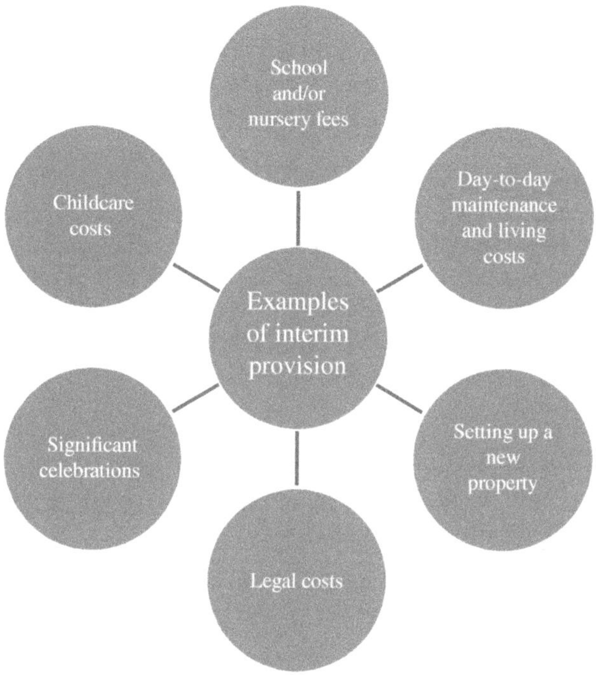

INTERIM PROVISION UNDER THE CHILDREN ACT 1989, SCH 1

8.5 There is limited reference in the Children Act 1989 ('CA 1989'), Sch 1 to interim provision, save in paragraph 9 which sets out the power to make orders for interim periodical payments.

> **Children Act 1989, Sch 1, para 9(1)**
>
> (1) Where an application is made under paragraph 1 or 2 the court may, at any time before it disposes of the application, make an interim order—
>
> (a) requiring either or both parents to make such periodical payments, at such times and for such term as the court thinks fit; and
>
> (b) giving any direction which the court thinks fit.

8.6 It is clear from CA 1989, Sch 1, para 9(2) that payments can be backdated, but the commencement date of an order can be no earlier than the date on which the application was made.

8.7 The power of the court to make orders for interim periodical payments remains subject to the constraints on ordering maintenance payments contained in the Child Support Act 1991 ('CSA 1991'). Accordingly, it is only in cases where a maximum Child Maintenance Service ('CMS') assessment is in place or one of the other exceptions applies that the court will have the power to make such orders. The jurisdiction of the CMS and the exceptions to its otherwise exclusive jurisdiction is addressed in **Chapter 3** at **3.12** to **3.15**.

8.8 Interim provision can also be made by way of lump sum. There is no restriction upon the number of lump sums a court can order for the benefit of a child under CA 1989, Sch 1[1] (nor under MCA 1973[2] or CPA 2004, Sch 5[3]). This contrasts with the position under MCA 1973 and CPA 2004 in relation to lump sums made for the benefit of a spouse or civil partner. Each of the statutes contains provisions making it clear that lump sums can be ordered to meet expenditure incurred before the making of the application. For example, CA 1989, Sch 1, para 5(1)[4] provides that:

> 'Without prejudice to the generality of paragraph 1, an order under that paragraph for the payment of a lump sum may be made for the purpose of enabling any liabilities or expenses—
>
> (a) incurred in connection with the birth of the child or in maintaining the child; and
>
> (b) reasonably incurred before the making of the order,
>
> to be met.'

8.9 It is not possible for an application to be made prior to the birth of the child for interim expenses to be covered; any pre-birth expenditure can only be recouped with an application made after the birth.

PRINCIPLES APPLIED

8.10 Interim orders are usually made at a stage where there is a relative lack of information about the parties' financial positions and where the court does not have the opportunity to consider the claims in detail.

8.11 An important case about interim provision concerns a child referred to as 'Zoe'. On the date when proceedings were commenced she was just one day

1 CA 1989, Sch 1, para 1(5)(a).
2 MCA 1973, s 23(4).
3 CPA 2004, Sch 5, para 1(3).
4 Similar provisions exist under MCA 1973, s 23(3) and CPA 2004, Sch 5, para 3; these provisions do not refer in terms to expenses incurred in connection with the birth of the child, but such expenditure would come within the ambit of 'liabilities or expenses reasonably incurred' for the benefit of the child before the making of the application.

old[5]. There are a number of reported judgments in relation to this child; the first one provides a useful guide and overview as to the approach taken to interim financial provision for a child.

8.12

Case summary: *Re Z (Schedule 1: Legal Costs Funding Order: Interim Provision)*[6]

Facts:

At the time of hearing, the child 'Zoe' was three weeks old. The parents had begun living together in 2020 in the USA, enjoying a lifestyle commensurate with F's significant wealth. They became engaged and M became pregnant in February 2020, but the relationship deteriorated and the parties began living separately. M returned to England and moved in with her family in the North East in July 2020. F issued proceedings in the USA in September 2020 to secure jurisdiction. M issued CA 1989, Sch 1 proceedings the day after the child's birth in October 2020 and the USA proceedings were stayed.

M sought interim provision for the setting up of a new home in London (on a rental basis) and interim maintenance, as well as legal costs funding for both the CA 1989, Sch 1 and welfare proceedings under CA 1989, s 8.

Held by Cobb J:

The judge was satisfied that M required: (a) relocation to London, where she had always previously lived as an adult; and (b) a sum to do so and set up a home for herself and the child, some costs of which would not then need to be claimed again.

As to interim maintenance, the focus was on achieving appropriate temporary accommodation and a reasonable household budget. This required consideration of the matters specifically set out in CA 1989, Sch 1, para 4, as well as the father's 'extraordinary' wealth. The court noted that this was not a final decision, and that the focus should be on the child. Overall, the court's award was said to be enough to achieve a 'good-to-luxurious' lifestyle, which 'does justice to the case'.

M was awarded £70,000 to set up a home and £15,000 as a deposit on a rental property. Interim maintenance was ordered at £9,612 pm, plus £4,750 pm for rent and £5,600 pm for a nanny (with provision for a step-down in the nanny provision).

5 Indeed, the father in fact initiated anticipatory proceedings in the USA prior to her birth.
6 [2020] EWFC 80, [2021] 1 FCR 719, [2021] 2 FLR 727.

8.13 Following the above judgment, at the first appointment the mother applied for further interim provision and legal funding. The application was made primarily to cover the funding for a nanny, without the step-down in support originally planned for, in light of the child's newly discovered health needs and a forthcoming operation, and a proposed increase in domestic help. The former was permitted; the latter was not.

INTERIM PROVISION FOR CHILDREN UNDER THE MATRIMONIAL CAUSES ACT 1973 AND THE CIVIL PARTNERSHIP ACT 2004

8.14 The court can make orders for interim provision for children under the MCA 1973 and CPA 2004, Sch 5. These can be by way of interim periodical payments or, if specifically for the children, interim lump sums[7].

8.15 Under the MCA 1973 and CPA 2004, the court has jurisdiction to make interim orders for periodical payments only from the date of the application for divorce, nullity or judicial separation (MCA 1973) or the application dissolution, nullity or legal separation (CPA 2004): it is from this point that the court's jurisdiction to make such orders is 'activated'.

'Segal' or 'global' orders

8.16 The restrictions on the jurisdiction of the court to make child maintenance payments contained in CSA 1991[8], make necessary to ensure that the statutory child support scheme is not being subverted. Where an application for interim provision is made under the MCA 1973 or CPA 2004, Sch 5, so-called *Segal* orders[9] can be used to enable interim provision to be made for both a spouse/civil partner and a child of the family where a maximum CMS assessment is not (yet) in place. A *Segal* order is an order which provides a global combined sum for the benefit of both the spouse/civil partner and the relevant child, drafted in such a way that it reduces automatically by the amount of any sum assessed to be payable by the CMS.

8.17 *Segal* orders were approved by the Court of Appeal in *Dorney-Kingdom v Dorney-Kingdom*[10].

7 Interim lump sums are *only* permissible under the MCA 1973 for the benefit of a child – spouses cannot be supported in the interim through these means.

8 See **Chapter 3** at **3.12**.

9 See **Chapter 3** at **3.15**.

10 [2000] 3 FCR 20, [2000] 2 FLR 855.

Case summary: *Dorney-Kingdom v Dorney-Kingdom*[11]

Facts:

The parties separated and the three children remained with M at the former matrimonial home. F voluntarily vacated the home (valued at £260,000) but sought a deferred '*Mesher*'[12] charge of 30%. The district judge ordered that M should receive the entirety of the house outright due to her commitments to the children. It was also found that her entitlement to maintenance was nominal, but F should pay £200 pm per child subject to adjustment in the event of a Child Support Agency assessment. On appeal, the circuit judge again found the mother's claim to be nominal but increased the periodical payments for the children to £1000 pm in total, again to be reduced by sums assessed as payable by the Child Support Agency. A *Mesher* order was again refused. F appealed for a second time.

Held by the Court of Appeal:

The appeal was successful in respect of the *Mesher* order, with the father being given a charge of 25%.

As to the periodical payments, it was determined that where the mother did not have a claim in her own right the court could only make an order for child periodical payments if the parties consented (which was not the case here). Whilst a *Segal* order for spousal maintenance incorporating child maintenance, to be reduced by the sums due under a Child Support Agency assessment could be made in some circumstances, any such order needed genuinely to include a substantial element of spousal support to be legitimate.

8.18 Accordingly, *Dorney-Kingdom*[13] determined that the court has jurisdiction to make a Segal order, notwithstanding that the decision was set aside in that particular case. The decision has been applied in subsequent cases. In *AB v CD (Jurisdiction Global Maintenance Orders)*[14] the court was referred to an article written by DJ Segal (the judge after whom the orders are named) where he suggested that such orders may have particular relevance on an application for interim provision, although it was not determined that such orders were only available on interim applications.

11 [2000] 3 FCR 20, [2000] 2 FLR 855.
12 See *Mesher v Mesher* [1980] 1 All ER 126.
13 [2000] 3 FCR 20, [2000] 2 FLR 855.
14 [2017] EWHC 3164 (Fam), [2018] 1 FCR 199, [2018] 2 FLR 150.

8.19

Case summary: *AB v CD (Jurisdiction Global Maintenance Orders)*[15]

Facts:

The parties had been married for 15 years and had three children. Both were lawyers, but M had not worked outside the home since the eldest child was born. They had lived in Dubai for ten years but returned when the eldest child was diagnosed with diabetes. At the conclusion of financial remedy proceedings, it was ordered that the former matrimonial home be sold and the proceeds paid to M, with F additionally paying lump sums totalling £240,000. F was ordered to pay £39,000 pa in global maintenance for M and the children until 2026, with a corresponding reduction in the event of a CMS calculation. F appealed, including upon grounds that there was no jurisdiction to make the global maintenance order.

Held by Roberts J:

Appeal dismissed in full.

The court held that *Segal* orders were not an impermissible device to circumvent the Child Support Act 1991 and the failure to apportion an amount to the mother, in light of the finding that the father's income crossed the threshold for a maximum assessment in all likelihood would do into the future, did not give reason to set it aside.

NB: the court was referred to an article written by District Judge Segal, the 'architect' of the orders, in which he stated that:

> 'early in the ancillary relief proceedings, where there has been no CSA assessment, no first directions hearing and no disclosure, if a parent applies for maintenance pending suit or interim periodical payments, the court may – as a short term measure – make an order in favour of that parent, which includes an element of support for the child, but I stress that this is a short-term order'.

The court declined to hold that global orders could only be made in those circumstances.

15 [2017] EWHC 3164 (Fam), [2018] 1 FCR 199, [2018] 2 FLR 150.

Interim lump sums under MCA 1973 and CPA 2004

8.20 Under the MCA 1973 and CPA 2004, Sch 5, it is possible for lump sums to be made on an interim basis for the benefit of children[16]. In *Re G (A Child) (Maintenance Pending Suit)*[17] the court considered the jurisdiction to make such an order. It made reference to CA 1989, Sch 1, but did not engage directly with the specific provision under the MCA 1973 which confers jurisdiction under that statute.

Case summary: *Re G (A Child) (Maintenance Pending Suit)*[18]

Facts:

H and W appealed against maintenance pending suit orders, in which H was ordered to pay £10,000 pm (backdated to the date of service of the application) for the benefit of W and the four children. He was also ordered to pay £2,000 in respect of her legal fees. H sought a reduction of the quantum and for such payments to start from the date of the hearing, and for the order in respect of legal fees to be discharged. W sought the backdating of the maintenance pending suit to the date of her divorce petition and an order for H to meet the costs of their eldest son's bar mitzvah.

Held by Munby J:

Both parties' appeals were dismissed, save for W's appeal in respect of the bar mitzvah costs. Although H challenged the judge's power to make interim lump sum orders, which he claimed was capital provision, it was accepted that this could be done under CA 1989, Sch 1. On the basis of the disclosure provided, there were capital sums available to meet this need. £45,000 was ordered to be paid for this purpose.

APPROACH OF THE COURT ON AN INTERIM APPLICATION

8.21 When considering interim periodical payments for children, the interim nature of the application means that the court will undertake a broad-brush assessment of both the receiving parent's needs and the paying parent's ability to pay. As Moylan LJ said in *G v G (Child Maintenance: Interim Costs Provision)*[19], the court's jurisdiction at an interim stage is a broad one. Paragraph 9 of CA 1989,

16 MCA 1973, s 23(3) and (4); CPA 2004, Sch 5, paras 1(3) and 3.
17 [2006] EWHC 1834 (Fam), [2007] 1 FLR 1674.
18 [2006] EWHC 1834 (Fam), [2007] 1 FLR 1674.
19 [2009] EWHC 2080 (Fam), [2010] 2 FLR 1264.

Sch 1 makes clear that the determining factor is simply that the order must be one which the court thinks fit.

8.22 The Court of Appeal in *Rattan v Kuwad*[20] considered the approach to be taken to applications for maintenance pending suit. The guidance given can usefully be applied in the context of applications for interim provision for a child:

Key citation: *Rattan v Kuwad*[21]

Moylan LJ:

> '[48] … The court is not required to undertake any greater "critical" analysis of a schedule of income needs than is required of any other aspect of the case. The court is required to undertake such analysis as is sufficient to be satisfied that the ultimate award is "reasonable". In some cases this might require a detailed examination of a budget, in others, such as the present case, it will be immediately apparent whether the listed items represent a fair guide to the applicant's income needs.
>
> [49] I also do not consider that the judge was right to exclude certain items from the wife's budget as not being "immediate expenditure needs". The word "immediate", in this context, does no more than reflect the fact that the court is concerned with an order for maintenance *pending* the final resolution of the financial dispute between the parties. However, the use of this word does not mean that the court should embark on the type of exercise undertaken by the Judge in this case. The fact that some items of expenditure are not incurred every month does not mean they should be excluded for the purposes of determining what maintenance is reasonable.'

8.23 In *Rattan v Kuwad*[22], the Court of Appeal also approved the principles set out by Nicholas Mostyn QC (sitting as a Deputy High Court Judge) in *TL v ML (Ancillary Relief: Claim against Assets of Extended Family)*[23]. These too can be applied by analogy to applications for interim provision for children.

20 [2021] EWCA Civ 1, [2021] 1 WLR 3141, [2021] 1 FCR 618, [2021] 2 FLR 817.
21 [2021] EWCA Civ 1, [2021] 1 WLR 3141, [2021] 1 FCR 618, [2021] 2 FLR 817.
22 [2021] EWCA Civ 1, [2021] 1 WLR 3141, [2021] 1 FCR 618, [2021] 2 FLR 817 at para 23.
23 [2006] 1 FCR 465, [2005] EWHC 2860 (Fam), [2006] 1 FLR 1263.

Key citation: *TL v ML*[24]

Nicholas Mostyn QC (sitting as a Deputy High Court Judge):

'From these cases I derive the following principles:

(i) The sole criterion to be applied in determining the application is "reasonableness" (s 22 Matrimonial Causes Act 1973), which, to my mind, is synonymous with "fairness".

(ii) A very important factor in determining fairness is the marital standard of living (*F v F*). This is not to say that the exercise is merely to replicate that standard (*M v M*).

(iii) In every maintenance pending suit application there should be a specific maintenance pending suit budget which excludes capital or long term expenditure, more aptly to be considered on a final hearing (*F v F*). That budget should be examined critically in every case to exclude forensic exaggeration (*F v F*).

(iv) Where the affidavit or Form E disclosure by the payer is obviously deficient the court should not hesitate to make robust assumptions about his ability to pay. The court is not confined to the mere say-so of the payer as to the extent of his income or resources (*G v G, M v M*). In such a situation, the court should err in favour of the payee.

(v) Where the paying party has historically been supported through the bounty of an outsider, and where the payer is asserting that the bounty had been curtailed but where the position of the outsider is ambiguous or unclear, then the court is justified in assuming that the third party will continue to supply the bounty, at least until final trial (*M v M*).'

8.24 All of the factors which fall to be considered on an application for a final order under CA 1989, Sch 1, MCA 1973 or CPA 2004, Sch 5 may be relevant to the question of interim provision. The factors under CA 1989, Sch 1, para 4 include:

24 [2006] 1 FCR 465, [2005] EWHC 2860 (Fam), [2006] 1 FLR 1263 at para 124.

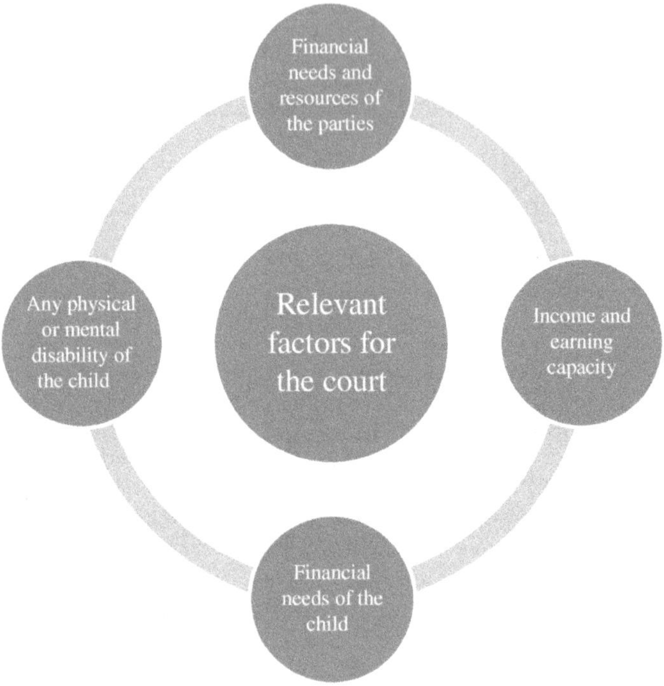

8.25 At the stage of interim provision, the court is not making long-term decisions – it is necessarily focused on meeting short to medium-term needs. An interim order does not tie the court's hands in respect of long-term assessments of needs[25]. The court will acknowledge that the assessments made at the interim stage may need to be adjusted as the case progresses, either with the benefit of further disclosure or after the hearing of full evidence.

PROCEDURE

8.26 The procedure applicable to applications for financial provision for children is set out fully in **Chapter 5**. An application for interim provision can be made within Form A (or Form A1) when an application is initially made. If the need for interim provision arises after this date, a separate application should be made using Form D11 and should be supported by evidence.

8.27 Part 18 of the Family Procedure Rules 2010 ('FPR 2010'), and Practice Direction 18A, is applicable to interim applications.

8.28 Some of the key features of FPR 2010, PD18A, as applicable to applications for interim provision are set out below:

25 See for example *Y v Z* [2024] EWFC 4, [2024] 1 FCR 894, where the final order for child periodical payments was set at a level lower than the interim provision which had been made.

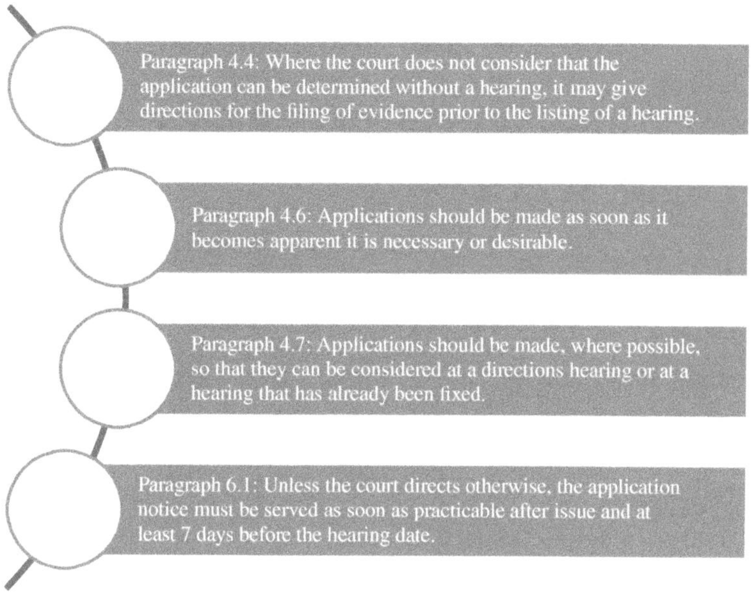

8.29 It is possible for interim applications to be made, and considered, at the outset of proceedings, and thus before there has been full financial disclosure through the exchange of financial statements. In such circumstances, the written evidence in support of the application must set out the party's current financial situation, albeit this may well be more limited than the information which would be contained in a full financial statement. The respondent party must also file and serve a statement of means.

8.30 Care must also be taken with interim applications by both an applicant and respondent, because of the possibility of costs orders. Whilst this may be less of a concern where one party is supported by legal funding, it is important to note that there is no general rule of 'no order' at this interim stage whether the application is made pursuant to the MCA 1973, CPA 2004, Sch 5 or CA 1989, Sch 1. Costs are considered more fully in **Chapter 14**.

CHAPTER 9

Applications for a Costs Allowance for Legal Services

Content at a glance:

Introduction

Jurisdiction

Principles – whether to make an order

Principles – quantum and structure

Procedure

INTRODUCTION

9.1 The statutory power to make legal services payment orders is contained in the Matrimonial Causes Act 1973 ('MCA 1973'), ss 22ZA and 22ZB and the Civil Partnership Act 2004 ('CPA 2004'), Sch 5, paras 38A and 38B. Although there is no equivalent to those statutory provisions in the Children Act 1989 ('CA 1989'), Sch 1, the court does also have the power under Sch 1 to order interim payments for a party's legal services – ie make orders for costs allowances. Orders are frequently made to cover the costs of litigation of substantive CA 1989, Sch 1 proceedings but also other proceedings relating to children, for instance for private law children disputes.

JURISDICTION

9.2 In the absence of a bespoke statutory provision, the court's interim powers under CA 1989, Sch 1 have been broadly interpreted to cover the payment of legal fees (as they had been under the MCA 1973 prior to statutory codification). There are two potential routes which may be used either in tandem (where available) or separately.

By periodical payments order

- The court may either utilise its power under CA 1989, Sch 1, para 1(2)(a) or, where the application is made by an adult child, its power under Sch 1, para 2(2)(a).
- The court may exercise these above powers at any time under CA 1989, Sch 1, paras 1(3) and 2(7) respectively. There is express provision that the court may make interim orders under Sch 1, para 9(1)(a).
- However, the court may only make such a periodical payments order where it has jurisdiction to award child maintenance generally. If the court is prevented from making child periodical payment orders because the Child Maintenance Service has or would otherwise have jurisdiction, the court will have no power to make a cost allowance order via periodical payments: see *R v F (Child Maintenance: Costs of Contact Proceedings)* [2011] 2 FLR 991.

By lump sum order

- This is the only method of using CA 1989, Sch 1 to fund a costs allowance where the court does not or would not have jurisdiction to deal with child maintenance: *CF v KM (Financial Provision for Child: Costs of Legal Proceedings)* [2010] EWHC 1754 (Fam), [2011] 1 FLR 208.
- The court may either utilise its power under CA 1989, Sch 1, para 1(2)(c) or, where the application is made by an adult child, its power under Sch 1, para 2(2)(b).
- As with periodical payments orders, the court may exercise its power to order a lump sum at any time under CA 1989, Sch 1, paras 1(3) and 2(7) respectively. Moreover, the lump sum powers may be exercised by the court more than once under Sch 1, paras 1(5)(a) and 2(8), although it is worth noting that, where the application is made by an adult child, under para 2(8) the court may only do so if it has made an order for periodical payments which remains extant: see Sch 1, para 5(3).
- Payments may be made by instalments under CA 1989, Sch 1, para 5(5).

9.3 Whilst there is no bespoke statutory power to order costs allowances, the CA 1989, Sch 1 jurisdiction exists to enable the court to make orders 'for the benefit of the child': see *M-T v T*[1]; *R v F (Child Maintenance: Costs of Contact Proceedings)*[2]; *BC v DE (Rev 1)*[3].

9.4 This power to make orders has been interpreted so as to include legal services funding for substantive CA 1989, Sch 1 proceedings: see *G v G*[4]. This can potentially include alternative dispute resolution such as mediation or arbitration: *Rubin v Rubin*[5].

9.5 However, the expression 'for the benefit of the child' has been interpreted more broadly than covering only Sch 1 proceedings. Examples of proceedings for which funding can be obtained through an application under CA 1989, Sch 1 are set out in the diagram below:

1 [2006] EWHC 2494 (Fam), [2007] 2 FLR 925.
2 [2011] 2 FLR 991.
3 Also reported as *Re F (A Child) (Financial Provision: Legal Costs Funding)* [2016] EWHC 1806 (Fam), [2016] 1 WLR 4720, [2017] 1 FLR 1521.
4 [2009] EWHC 2080 (Fam), [2010] 2 FLR 1264.
5 [2014] EWHC 611 (Fam), [2014] 1 WLR 3289, [2014] 2 FLR 1018.

Children Act proceedings	Appeal costs	Foreign proceedings
•This is the most obvious extension of the court's power to award cost allowances. •There are thus numerous reported examples, see for instance: *MT v OT, CF v KM, R v F, MG v JF (Child Maintenance: Costs Allowance)* [2015] EWHC 564 (Fam), [2016] 1 FLR 424; *BC v DE (Rev 1), Re Z (No 1) (Schedule 1: Legal Costs Funding Order; Interim Financial Provision)* [2020] EWFC 80, [2021] 2 FLR 727; *MB v CD* [2024] EWHC 751 (Fam).	•Legal fees relating to an appeal can be covered by a cost allowance order: see *Dickson v Rennie* [2014] EWHC 4306 (Fam), [2015] 2 FLR 978; *Al Maktoum v Al Hussein* [2021] EWHC 303 (Fam). •However, as noted in *Xanthopoulos v Rakshina* [2022] EWFC 30, whilst the jurisdiction to make an award may exist, it should be exercised extremely cautiously, particularly so in circumstances where permission to appeal has not been granted.	•It has been stated that there can be no justification for seeking to distinguish between legal proceedings in this jurisdiction and those in another so long as those proceedings remain '*for the benefit of the child*': *G v G*. •Naturally, this most readily applies to the foreign equivalent of Children Act and/or CA 1989, Sch 1 proceedings but has also been held to include divorce and financial remedy proceedings in *M-T v T* and enforcement proceedings in *S (A Child) (Financial Provision)* [2004] EWCA Civ 1685, [2005] Fam 316.

9.6 The fact that jurisdiction itself is in dispute does not prevent the court from making an interim order, but this is a matter which is likely to be relevant to the court's discretion both as to whether to make an order and as to quantum: see *MET v HAT (Interim Maintenance)*[6]; *Rubin v Rubin*[7]; *MG v GM*[8].

PRINCIPLES – WHETHER TO MAKE AN ORDER

9.7 In deciding whether the court shall exercise its powers under CA 1989, Sch 1, paras 1 or 2, and if so in what manner, the court will have regard to all the circumstances including the factors listed at CA 1989, Sch 1, para 4(1)(a)–(f)[9]. These bear some similarity (but are not identical) to the relevant factors under MCA 1973, s 25 and CPA 2004, Sch 5, paras 20–22 (see **Chapter 12** at **12.21–12.22**).

9.8 The statutory codification of costs allowances pursuant to MCA 1973, ss 22ZA and 22ZB, and CPA 2004, Sch 5, paras 38A and 38B reflect the principles which had been developed judicially before those provisions came

6 [2013] EWHC 4247 (Fam), [2015] 1 FCR 296, [2014] 2 FLR 692.
7 [2014] EWHC 611 (Fam), [2014] 1 WLR 3289, [2014] 2 FLR 1018.
8 [2022] EWFC 8, [2023] 1 FCR 197, [2023] 1 FLR 253.
9 Additionally, in deciding whether to exercise its powers against a person who is not the mother or father of the child, and if so in what manner, the court shall also have regard to three further factors listed at CA 1989, Sch 1, para 4(2).

into effect: see *Rubin v Rubin*[10]. Similarly, in CA 1989, Sch 1 proceedings, the court will have particular regard to the decisions of *Currey v Currey (No 2)*[11] and *Rubin v Rubin*[12]. It has been held that the list of 14 principles set out by Mostyn J in *Rubin* at para 13 are relevant, with adaptations, to CA 1989, Sch 1 cost allowances: see for instance *MG v JF (Child Maintenance: Costs Allowance)*[13]; *R v F (Child Maintenance: Costs of Contact Proceedings)*[14]; *BC v DE (Rev 1)*[15]; *LP v AE*[16].

Case Summary: *Rubin v Rubin*[17]

Facts:

Following the conclusion of child abduction proceedings, W made applications under MCA 1973, s 22ZA and CA 1989, Sch 1 for H to make legal services payments to her in respect of:

- costs incurred by her in financial remedy proceedings;
- costs incurred by her in concluded abduction proceedings.

The divorce and financial remedy proceedings were stayed by a District Judge, save that he allowed W to pursue her claim for legal services payments.

H appealed.

Held by Mostyn J:

Appeal allowed. Following the stay of the divorce suit, there was no power to deal with an application for a legal services order under MCA 1973, s 22ZA as such an application was ancillary to the main suit.

W's claim for a legal services payment order ('LSPO') dismissed.

The following key principles in relation to applications for LSPOs were identified at para 13:

(i) The court is required to have regard to all the matters mentioned in s 22ZB(1)–(3).

10 [2014] EWHC 611 (Fam), [2014] 1 WLR 3289, [2014] 2 FLR 1018.
11 [2006] EWCA Civ 1338, [2007] 1 FLR 946.
12 [2014] EWHC 611 (Fam), [2014] 1 WLR 3289, [2014] 2 FLR 1018.
13 [2015] EWHC 564 (Fam), [2016] 1 FLR 424.
14 [2011] 2 FLR 991.
15 Also reported as *Re F (A Child) (Financial Provision: Legal Costs Funding)* [2016] EWHC 1806 (Fam), [2016] 1 WLR 4720, [2017] 1 FLR 1521.
16 [2020] EWHC 1668 (Fam), [2021] 1 FCR 353.
17 [2014] EWHC 611 (Fam), [2014] 1 WLR 3289, [2014] 2 FLR 1018.

(ii) The ability of the respondent to pay should be judged by reference to the principles summarised in *TL v ML (Ancillary Relief: Claim Against Assets of Extended Family)*[18].

(iii) Where the claim for substantive relief appears doubtful, the court should judge the application with caution. The more doubtful it is, the more cautious it should be.

(iv) The court cannot make an order unless it is satisfied that without the payment the applicant would not reasonably be able to obtain appropriate legal services for the proceedings. Therefore, the exercise essentially looks to the future. It is important that the jurisdiction is not used to outflank or supplant the powers and principles governing an award of costs in CPR Part 44. Thus a LSPO should only be awarded to cover historic unpaid costs where the court is satisfied that without such a payment the applicant will not reasonably be able to obtain in the future appropriate legal services for the proceedings.

(v) The court would be unlikely to expect an applicant to sell or charge her home or to deplete a modest fund of savings. This aspect is however highly fact-specific.

(vi) Evidence of refusals by two commercial lenders of repute will normally dispose of any issue whether a litigation loan is available.

(vii) In determining whether a Sears Tooth arrangement[19] can be entered into, a statement of refusal by the applicant's solicitors should normally answer the question.

(viii) If a litigation loan is offered at a very high rate of interest it would be unlikely to be reasonable to expect the applicant to take it unless the respondent offered an undertaking to meet that interest, if the court later considered it just so to order.

(ix) The order should normally contain an undertaking by the applicant that she will repay such part of the amount ordered if the court at the conclusion of the proceedings, considers that she ought to do so.

(x) The court should make clear which of the legal services mentioned in s 22ZA(10) the payment is for.

18 [2005] EWHC 2860 (Fam), [2006] 1 FLR 1263, at para [124](iv) and (v) where Mostyn J held: '(iv) Where the affidavit or Form E disclosure by the payer is obviously deficient the court should not hesitate to make robust assumptions about his ability to pay. The court is not confined to the mere say-so of the payer as to the extent of his income or resources. In such a situation the court should err in favour of the payee. (v) Where the paying party has historically been supported through the bounty of an outsider, and where the payer is asserting that the bounty had been curtailed but where the position of the outsider is ambiguous or unclear, then the court is justified in assuming that the third party will continue to supply the bounty, at least until final trial.'

19 A '*Sears Tooth* arrangement' takes its name from *Sears Tooth (a firm) v Payne Hicks Beach (a firm)* [1998] 1 FCR 231, [1997] 2 FLR 116. It is an agreement whereby solicitors act on a client's behalf extending them credit on the basis of a charge in respect of any settlement which the applicant may recover in the proceedings.

(xi) Generally speaking, the court should not fund the applicant beyond the FDR, but should list a hearing date for further funding to be considered shortly after the FDR.

(xii) When ordering costs funding for a specified period, monthly instalments are to be preferred to a single lump sum payment.

(xiii) If the application for a LSPO seeks an award including the costs of that very application, the court should bear in mind s 22ZA(9), whereby a party's bill of costs in assessment proceedings is treated as reduced by the amount of any LSPO made in his or her favour. Thus, if a LSPO is made in an amount which includes the anticipated costs of that very application for the LSPO, then an order for the costs of that application will not bite save to the extent that the actual costs of the application may exceed such part of the LSPO as is referable thereto.

(xiv) A LSPO is to be made under the Part 18 procedure.

9.9 The following diagram contains a summary of some of the key principles:

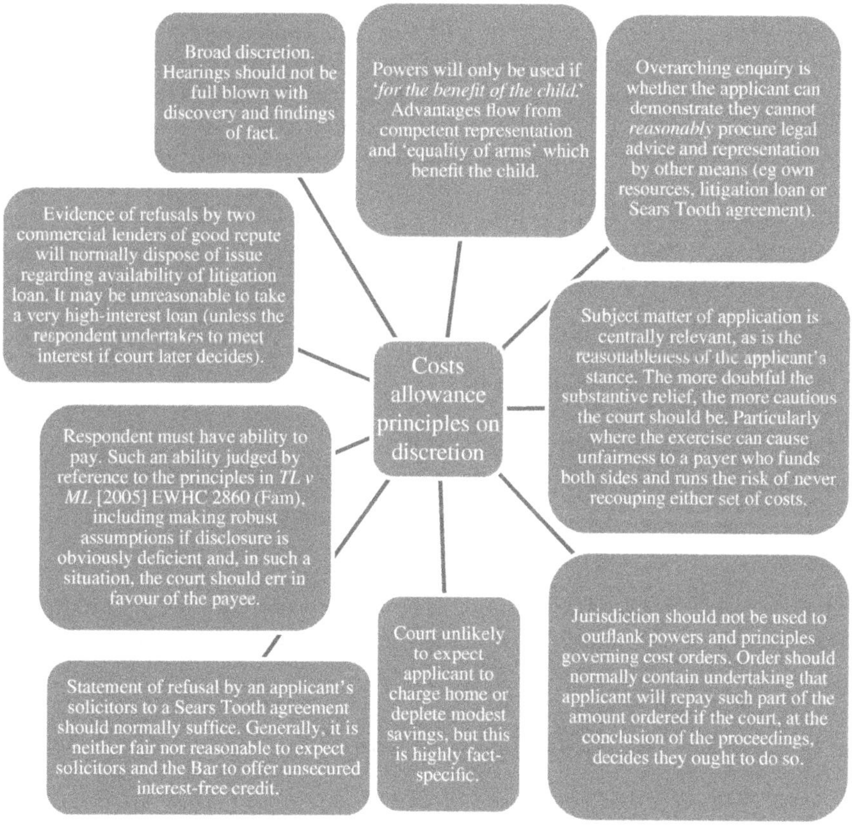

Historic costs

9.10 Whether an application for previously incurred costs will be granted will hinge on how closely such costs are related to the existing proceedings and whether, without such payment, the applicant cannot reasonably procure further legal advice and representation. Accordingly, the court will only make such an award sparingly.

9.11 On the one hand, an application for costs reasonably and legitimately incurred within ongoing proceedings with a party's current solicitors may likely be accepted. Particularly if it can be shown that there is a serious risk that the solicitors will not continue to act without it: *DR v ES*[20]. Specific sworn evidence of an intention by the solicitor in the particular case to refuse to act unless the previously incurred costs are paid, notwithstanding the grant of a costs allowance for future costs, is generally advisable (over and above general reliance on the principle that firms and the Bar should not carry credit in circumstances where they are not charities or credit agents).

9.12 On the other hand, the position is different in relation to former solicitors, as they have already ceased acting, so payment of their outstanding costs is unlikely to have relevance to the question of whether a party can continue to access representation: see *Re Z (No 1) (A Child) (Schedule 1: Legal Costs Funding Order; Interim Financial Provision)*[21]; *Xanthopoulos v Rakshina*[22]. This was so even where there was an undertaking by the current solicitors not to act unless the historical costs from the previous solicitors were paid (which the court described as a 'transparent artifice'): *DH v RH*[23]. It is understood that a historic costs allowance for previous solicitors remains unprecedented.

9.13 Further, a costs allowance application for historic costs relating to concluded, inactive or paused proceedings is highly likely to be rejected: see for instance *Re Z (No 1) (A Child) (Schedule 1: Legal Costs Funding Order; Interim Financial Provision)*[24].

Case Summary: Re Z (No 1) (Schedule 1: Legal Costs Funding Order: Interim Financial Provision)[25]

Facts:

M made interim applications against the non-resident (and extremely wealthy) F in respect of their child Z including for legal costs funding for both her

20 [2022] EWFC 62.
21 [2020] EWFC 80, [2021] 1 FCR 719, [2021] 2 FLR 727.
22 [2022] EWFC 30, [2022] 2 FCR 712, [2023] 1 FLR 388.
23 [2023] EWFC 111.
24 [2020] EWFC 80, [2021] 1 FCR 719, [2021] 2 FLR 727.
25 Also reported as *X v Y* [2020] EWFC 80, [2021] 1 FCR 719, [2021] 2 FLR 727.

previously incurred legal costs and future legal costs. M's applications were made when Z was one-day old and heard when Z was three-weeks old.

M's previously incurred legal costs included the outstanding and unmet costs of her previous solicitors, her legal costs in the US and the costs already incurred with her current solicitors.

M's future legal costs were in relation to both Sch 1 proceedings up to FDR and private law children proceedings up to the Dispute Resolution Appointment.

Held by Cobb J:

M's application partially allowed.

It was not necessary for the costs of M's previous solicitors to be met as this would have no bearing on M's ability to reasonably procure legal services for future proceedings. Further, any award should not have the effect of outflanking or supplanting the court's power to make costs orders. Thus, M received no award in respect of both her previous solicitors in the UK or for her legal costs in the US.

However, the costs in respect of M's currently instructed solicitors were in a different category. The firm should not carry a significant debt in working for M. It was neither fair nor reasonable to expect the firm and counsel to offer unsecured interest-free credit to undertake their work; M and her solicitors should not become bound or beholden to each other by the existing debt. M was awarded her claimed costs less a 30% reduction for a notional standard of assessment.

M's future legal costs were considered to be grossly inflated. It was material in respect of the claimed costs for the Sch 1 proceedings to take into account F's current and projected costs as a benchmark; these were around 40% of M's costs. This was to be paid in six monthly instalments (broadly reflecting the amount of time to FDR).

M's claim for costs in respect of future private law children proceedings was substantially reduced as there was no indication of a significant dispute between the parties; F had offered to engage in mediation and pay the relevant fees (which M had declined). M was accordingly provided with a modest award to cover correspondence and negotiation only. Again, this was to be paid in six monthly instalments.

PRINCIPLES – QUANTUM AND STRUCTURE

9.14 In determining the level and structure of any costs allowance, whether by lump sum or periodical payments, the court's discretion remains a broad one. Of course, by necessity, there is a large overlap between the principles involved in determining whether the court would make an order and how it should make that order.

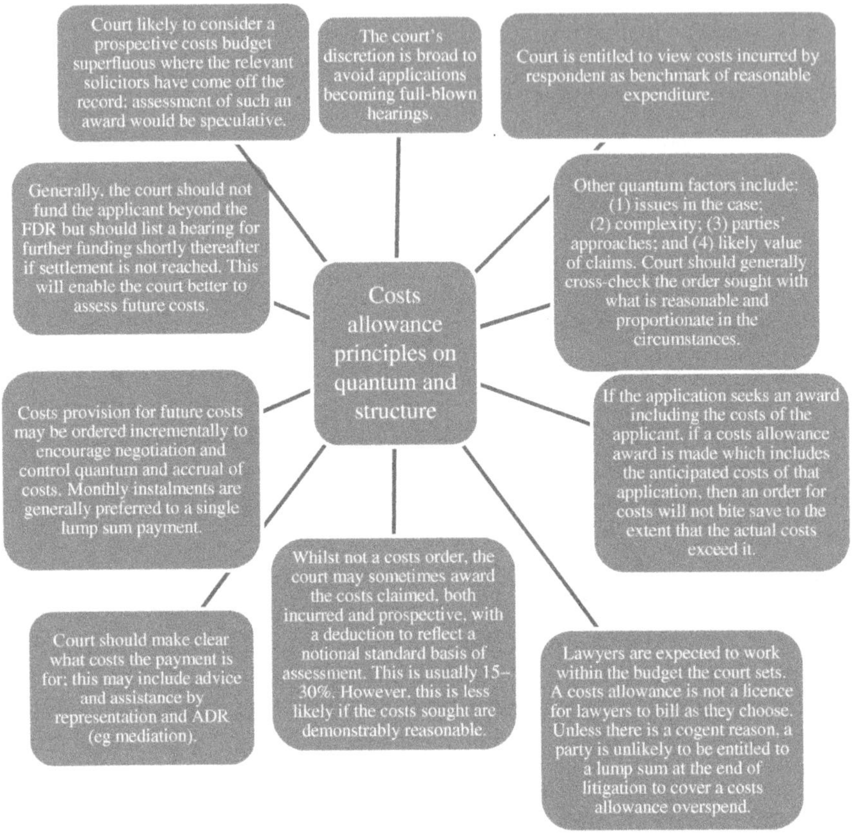

Case Summary: Re Z (No 2) (Schedule 1: Further Legal Costs Funding Order: Further Interim Financial Provision)[26]

Facts:

This judgment follows Cobb J's earlier judgment, *Re Z (No 1) (Schedule 1: Legal Costs Funding Order; Interim Financial Provision)* [2020] EWFC 80.

By the time of this hearing (a First Appointment), Z was aged eight months old. M applied for further costs provision for:

– M's costs shortfall following a private law children hearing concerning Z's welfare/medical issues (where F was successful). M had already

26 Also reported as *X v Y* [2021] EWFC 72, [2022] 3 FCR 419.

been granted an award by Cobb J albeit solely to cover negotiation and correspondence. Before and pending this hearing, Mostyn J had made awards to part-fund the children hearing (on the basis that M's solicitors would deploy the balance of the funds which Cobb J had earlier awarded for the main Sch 1 proceedings as well as rely upon a loan from M's father) and further private law children issues;

- the work within the Sch 1 proceedings to cover the period up to a private FDR. M had already been granted an award by Cobb J up to FDR but a not insignificant part of this, as held in M's solicitors' client account, was commandeered by Mostyn J for the private law children hearing as above. Mostyn J made a further award to fund M's representation to the First Appointment (but M had overspent);
- M's future costs for private law children proceedings for the next six months (including covering a possible wardship issue);
- an interim lump sum to reimburse M's father in respect of an alleged loan used to fund the private law children hearing.

Held by Cobb J:

Applications partially allowed.

Whilst it was reiterated that legal services providers, including solicitors and barristers, are neither charities nor credit-agents and should not be expected to offer unsecured credit in order to undertake their work, Cobb J expressed dismay that M's solicitors had billed M significantly in excess of the amounts which were awarded by both Cobb J and Mostyn J to cover the costs of the Sch 1 proceedings and the private law children litigation respectively. M's solicitors were not entitled to the assumption that the overspend would be retrospectively authorised. Legal service providers are expected to work conscientiously within set budgets.

Despite Cobb J's concern about the spiralling legal costs, some of M's overspend was retrospectively authorised not least as F's costs (which were the benchmark to which M's previous award was made) had also substantially increased from projected levels and additional unforeseen work had been required for the private law children proceedings.

M was awarded two thirds of the sum claimed by way of overspending but then this was reduced by 30% for a notional standard assessment. M was further awarded costs to the conclusion of the private FDR and a much smaller sum than claimed in respect of future welfare issues. M was found to have deliberately misled the court in respect of the loan (both as to provenance and quantum) from her father and M's claim was accordingly refused: in fact, in the later *Re Z (No 3) (Schedule 1: Further Orders)* [2021] EWFC 85, when Cobb J was considering costs, a small part of M's previous award for her overspend was disallowed.

PROCEDURE

9.15 The application can be made expressly within Form A or Form A1 (as applicable). In default, the application should be made using Form D11 as Family Procedure Rules 2010 ('FPR 2010'), Part 18 applies: FPR 2010, r 9.7(2).

9.16 An application can be made at any stage of the proceedings: FPR 2010, r 9.7(1). However, applications should nonetheless be made at an early stage or otherwise promptly where required, particularly to avoid:

- the complicating factor of historic costs: *LP v AE*[27];
- the vacation and sidetracking of hearings. In this context, realistic time estimates should be provided or otherwise there is a high risk of adjournment: see *O'Dwyer v O'Dwyer*[28]; *E v B (Inaccurate Time Estimates)*[29].

9.17 An application must be served in accordance with FPR 2010, Part 6 and as soon as is practical after it is filed and, in any event, at least 14 days before the court is to deal with the application: FPR 2010, r 18.8(1)(b)(i).

9.18 The application must be supported by written evidence: FPR 2010, r 18.8(2). In this context and beyond explaining why the order is necessary:

- it should include a detailed estimate of the costs both incurred and to be incurred: *Rubin v Rubin*[30];
- where the applicant has not yet provided a financial statement, the written evidence in support must give up to date information about that party's financial circumstances: FPR 2010, r 9.7(3).

9.19 Unless the respondent to the application has filed a financial statement, the respondent must, at least seven days before the court is to deal with the application, file and serve a statement of their means: FPR 2010, r 9.7(4).

9.20 *Calderbank* offers are permissible within these applications as they are within CA 1989, Sch 1 proceedings generally: Civil Procedure Rules, r 44.2(4)(c).

27 [2020] EWHC 1668 (Fam), [2021] 1 FCR 353.
28 [2019] EWHC 1838 (Fam), [2019] 3 FCR 176, [2019] 2 FLR 1020.
29 [2021] EWFC B90.
30 [2014] EWHC 611 (Fam), [2014] 1 WLR 3289, [2014] 2 FLR 1018.

CHAPTER 10

Claims for Capital: Housing

Content at a glance:

Introduction

Schedule 1 of the Children Act 1989 – capital orders to provide housing for the benefit of the child

Quantum: the court's exercise of its discretion

Capital orders under Schedule 1 where the court has made capital orders under the Matrimonial Causes Act 1973

Practical considerations

INTRODUCTION

The scope of this chapter

10.1 This Chapter will focus on the court's approach to orders designed to secure housing for the benefit of a subject child under the jurisdiction of the Children Act 1989, Sch 1 ('CA 1989'). In particular, this Chapter addresses claims made by an applicant under CA 1989, Sch 1 for orders making *capital* provision. Such orders commonly provide for the transfer of a property or alternatively the payment of a sum of money sufficient to enable the purchase of a suitable property (irrespective of how that property is ultimately legally and beneficially held[1]).

10.2 Needless to say, if there are insufficient capital resources to enable the purchase of a property, the court may have to consider alternative means of housing the applicant and the relevant child. This might mean the transfer of a council tenancy[2]; it might mean provision for capital payments to cover rental costs[3]; and it might mean consideration of a mortgage capacity[4]. However, where

1 See **10.4** onwards below.
2 *K v K (Minors: Property Transfer)* [1992] 1 WLR 530, [1992] 2 FCR 253, [1992] 2 FLR 220, CA.
3 *Stacey v McNicholas* [2022] EWHC 278 (Fam), [2022] 4 WLR 109, [2023] 1 FCR 247, [2023] 2 FLR 321. Although please note that this case is only authority for the court's ability to make an order for a series of monthly lump sums equivalent to rent in the interim period pending a respondent paying a larger capital sum to enable accommodation to be purchased.
4 *ZU v LT* [2024] EWHC 778 (Fam), [2024] 2 FCR 815.

the court has no power to make orders related to income needs in excess of a calculation by the Child Maintenance Service ('CMS')[5] the scarcity of capital resources can put a court in real practical difficulty in meeting the housing needs of an applicant, however sympathetic their plight might be. To this extent, in a case with limited assets and income below the CMS maximum threshold[6], practitioners would be well advised to read this Chapter in conjunction with **Chapters 3, 11 and 12**, because it will be essential to establish before making an application under CA 1989, Sch 1 whether or not the court can and/or is likely to exercise its discretion to make substantive orders.

Inheritance (Provision for Family and Dependants) Act 1975

10.3 If a child's parent has died, a minor child may have a claim for housing (and other) provision against the estate of that parent, in the event that he or she has died without making reasonable financial provision for the child in a will[7]. A proper discussion of the scope of such applications is beyond the remit of this book, which instead addresses claims as between living parties, but there are certain parallels between the court's discretionary exercise under CA 1989, Sch 1 and the court's assessment of the meaning of 'reasonable financial provision' under the Inheritance (Provision for Family and Dependants) Act 1975 ('I(PD) A 1975'). The interrelationship (but clear distinction) between the two statutory regimes were discussed in detail by Master Shuman in *Ubbi v Ubbi (Deceased)*[8]:

Case Summary: *Ubbi v Ubbi (Deceased)*[9]

Facts:

- The deceased Mr Ubbi built up a business with his wife and child. He started an affair with Bianca which led to two children.
- Mr Ubbi maintained Bianca and their children in rental accommodation jointly owned with his wife. He died suddenly.
- Mr Ubbi's will (which long predated the affair) made no provision for Bianca and their children together.
- Bianca made a claim under the I(PD)A 1975 on behalf of her children for reasonable financial provision, which encompassed the purchase of a property and income provision.

5 Child Support Act 1991, s 8(3); *Dickson v Rennie* [2014] EWHC 4306 (Fam), [2015] 2 FLR 978. See **Chapter 3**.
6 At the time of writing £3,000 gross per week.
7 Inheritance (Provision for Family and Dependants) Act 1975, s 2.
8 *Ubbi v Ubbi (Deceased)* [2018] EWHC 1396 (Ch).
9 [2018] EWHC 1396 (Ch).

Decision:

- The Master found there to be some parallels with the court's exercise under CA 1989, Sch 1 but that authorities under that statutory regime offered only guidance as to a possible approach in each case (paras 22–25).
- The needs of an applicant minor child are not elevated to first or paramount consideration under the I(PD)A 1975.
- The claim for housing allowed for a capitalised sum to fund a rental property for the remainder of the children's minority, but not for an outright purchase of a property: the purpose of the 1975 Act was to provide maintenance, not outright capital to the children (para 68).
- There does not appear in the judgment a discussion as to whether or not the court might have settled a property on trust for the children, to revert to Mr Ubbi's estate on their reaching majority as is common in CA 1989, Sch 1 proceedings[10].

SCHEDULE 1 OF THE CHILDREN ACT 1989 – CAPITAL ORDERS TO PROVIDE HOUSING FOR THE BENEFIT OF THE CHILD

The available orders

10.4 An overview of the statutory regime has been provided elsewhere in this book[11]. Under CA 1989, Sch 1, para 1(2) the court can make the following capital orders:

(c) a lump sum order, payable:

- to the applicant for the benefit of the child, or
- to the child

(d) an order requiring a settlement of property to be made for the benefit of the child

(e) an order for the transfer of property

- to the applicant for the benefit of the child, or
- to the child

10 But such provision would seem consistent with the decision of the Supreme Court in *Ilott v The Blue Cross* [2017] UKSC 17, [2018] AC 545, [2017] 2 WLR 979, [2017] 1 FLR 1717, which concerned a claim by an independent adult child.

11 **Chapter 2**.

'One-time only': property adjustment orders

10.5 It is essential to note that, while CA 1989, Sch 1, para 1(3) provides that these powers may be exercised 'at any time', para 1(5)(b) restricts the court's power to make property adjustment orders under para 1(2)(d) and (e):

> **Children Act 1989, Sch 1, para 1(5)**
>
> 'Where a court makes an order under this paragraph –
>
> (a) …
>
> (b) it may not make more than one order under sub-paragraph (2)(d) or (e) against the same person in respect of the same child.'

In other words, while the court may make as many lump sum orders as it considers appropriate[12], **it may only make one property adjustment order**[13] and, having made one, cannot make another[14]. It has moreover been held that the court cannot circumvent the restriction on making multiple property adjustment orders by making a lump sum order intended for the purchase of housing[15].

10.6 This restriction on repeat property adjustment orders is not as simple as it might first appear, and it has been held not to prevent a court from achieving its substantive aim of meeting housing provision for the benefit of a child, even where the structure and mechanics of the order made under CA 1989, Sch 1 would – on the face of the order – contravene this 'one-time only' rule[16].

10.7 In *MT v OT*[17], Sir Jonathan Cohen held that provision in a settlement for a future replacement (substitute) property to be acquired for the benefit of the child during his or her minority does not offend provision in CA 1989, Sch 1, para 1(5):

12 Including a series of lump sum orders over a long period of time (subject to any prohibition on orders concerning income under the Child Support Act 1991, s 8(3)): see *Stacey v McNicholas* [2022] EWHC 278 (Fam), [2022] 4 WLR 109, [2023] 1 FCR 247, [2023] 2 FLR 321 and its reference to *R v R (Lump Sum Repayments)* [2003] EWHC 3197 (Fam), [2004] 1 FLR 928.

13 Either a settlement of property order or a transfer of property order.

14 *Phillips v Peace* [2014] EWHC 3180 (Fam), [2005] 1 WLR 3246, [2005] 2 FCR 265, [2005] 2 FLR 1212, per Singer J.

15 *Phillips v Peace* [2014] EWHC 3180 (Fam), [2005] 1 WLR 3246, [2005] 2 FCR 265, [2005] 2 FLR 1212.

16 See *MT v OT* [2018] EWHC 868 (Fam), [2018] 3 FCR 621, [2019] 1 FLR 9 and *ZU v LT* [2024] EWHC 778 (Fam), [2024] 2 FCR 815.

17 *MT v OT* [2018] EWHC 868 (Fam), [2018] 3 FCR 621, [2019] 1 FLR 93 at paras 18–19.

Key citation: *MT v OT*[18]

Sir Jonathan Cohen:

> 'The replacement of one property by another does not amount to a new settlement of property. It is simply the substitution of one property for another.'

10.8 In *ZU v LT*[19], Cobb J considered *MT v OT*[20] and other cases in considerable detail as part of his analysis of the extent of the court's powers to give effect to the 'essential purpose' of CA 1989, Sch 1, namely to provide a secure home for the child during his minority[21]. He held that this purpose allowed the court routinely to make or encourage orders which were not provided for in the wording of CA 1989, Sch 1 itself[22]:

Key citation: *ZU v LT*[23]

Cobb J:

> '[102] It is undeniable that there is no express power within Schedule 1(1) to order a sale of property (ie, to assemble the sum to settle); nor is there express power to direct that a new property be purchased on trust. But that is overwhelmingly the way in which Schedule 1 housing provision is interpreted and routinely carried into effect – that is to say, a sum of money is paid over from one party to the other (usually in one tranche) to purchase a property on trust terms; after the property is purchased – at the point when the payer is then "entitled" to the property "in possession or reversion" – it is settled on Schedule 1 terms.'

10.9 Cobb J held further that the court has the power to make an order which would compel a party to raise a mortgage to supplement a capital sum to be used as a deposit to purchase a property, the equity in which would then be settled on

18 *MT v OT* [2018] EWHC 868 (Fam), [2018] 3 FCR 621, [2019] 1 FLR 93 at paras 18–19.
19 *ZU v LT* [2024] EWHC 778 (Fam), [2024] 2 FCR 815.
20 *MT v OT* [2018] EWHC 868 (Fam), [2018] 3 FCR 621, [2019] 1 FLR 93 at paras 18–19.
21 At paras 102 to 105.
22 At para 102.
23 *ZU v LT* [2024] EWHC 778 (Fam), [2024] 2 FCR 815.

trust in the usual way, and that this applies not just to an existing property, but also to a new property and any future replacement property[24].

10.10 The reason these multi-step orders do not offend the CA 1989, Sch 1, para 1(5) prohibition on multiple property adjustment orders is that 'the steps taken to achieve the settlement is a matter of form not substance …'[25]. In other words, the structure and mechanics of an order are there to enable a court to put into effect the essential purpose of CA 1989, Sch 1: to house the child.

10.11 Thus, the various orders a court might make to meet a party's housing needs on behalf of a child are extremely broad-ranging[26]:

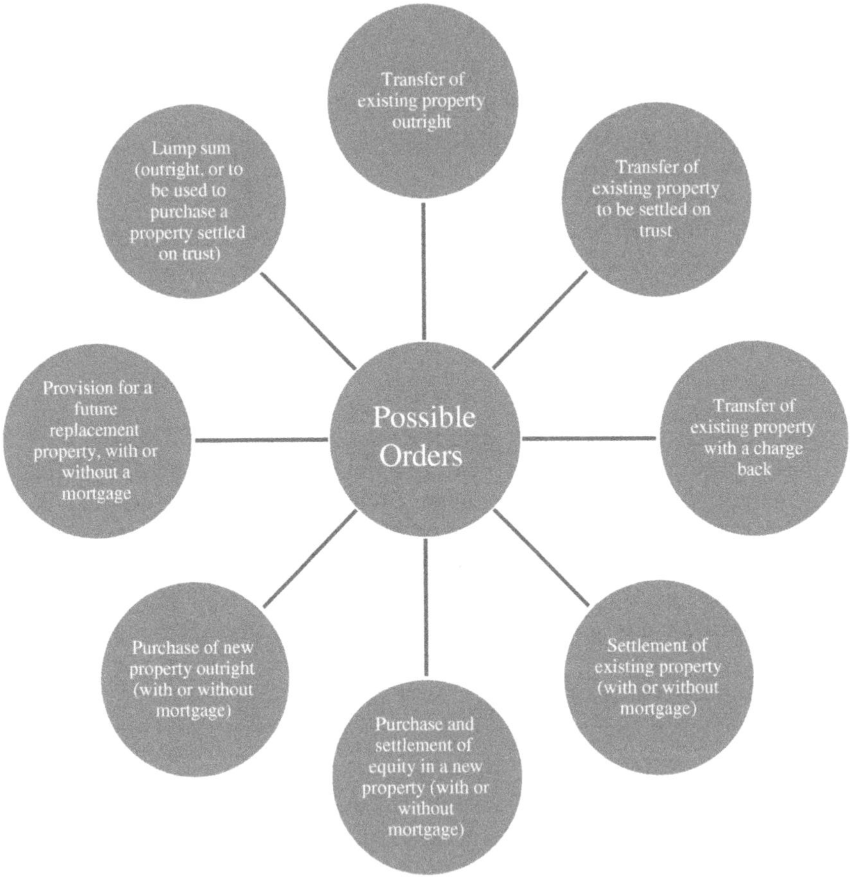

24 At paras 104 to 106. See also Baron J in *DE v AB* [2010] EWHC 3792 (Fam), [2012] 2 FLR 1396 at para 42.

25 *ZU v LT* [2024] EWHC 778 (Fam), [2024] 2 FCR 815 at para 122(v); para. 122 contains an extremely helpful summary of the judge's conclusions as to the breadth of the court's powers under CA 1989, Sch 1.

26 By way of a useful example, see the Standard Orders Template (Order 2.2) approved by the President of the Family Division and referred to by Cobb J in *ZU v LT* [2024] EWHC 778 (Fam), [2024] 2 FCR 815.

Outright provision or settled in trust?

10.12 Paragraphs **10.24** to **10.27** below address the issue of the duration of capital orders under CA 1989, Sch 1. Practitioners should note that a Schedule 1 capital award to meet an applicant's housing needs is for the benefit of the subject child, not the applicant parent. Therefore, when the child reaches adulthood (subject to any continuing education and absent any 'special circumstances') the justification underpinning the housing award is removed:

Key citation: *DE v AB*[27]

Baron J:

> '[42] … After all, this sum is, in reality, a long-term loan which will be recovered in due time and will provide this child with a secure house from which to reach his full potential as he grows towards adulthood.'

10.13 As a result, the 'standard' capital order for housing provision under CA 1989, Sch 1 is for the settlement of property into trust, which property will then revert to the paying parent at the end of the trust as follows[28]:

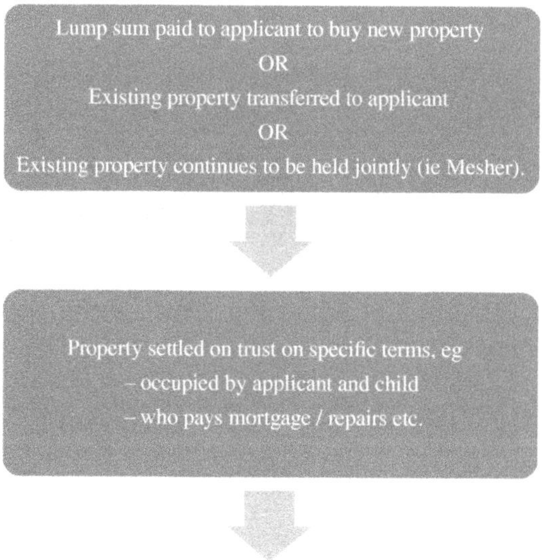

27 *DE v AB* [2010] EWHC 3792 (Fam), [2012] 2 FLR 1396.

28 *Re P (A Child) (Financial Provision)* [2003] EWCA Civ 837, [2003] 2 FCR 481, [2003] 2 FLR 865; *MT v OT* [2008] EWHC 868 (Fam), [2018] 3 FCR 621, [2019] 1 FLR 93; *DN v UD (Sch 1)* [2021] EWCA Civ 1947, [2022] Fam 289, [2022] 2 WLR 1047, [2022] 2 FLR 308; *TK v LK* [2024] EWFC 71.

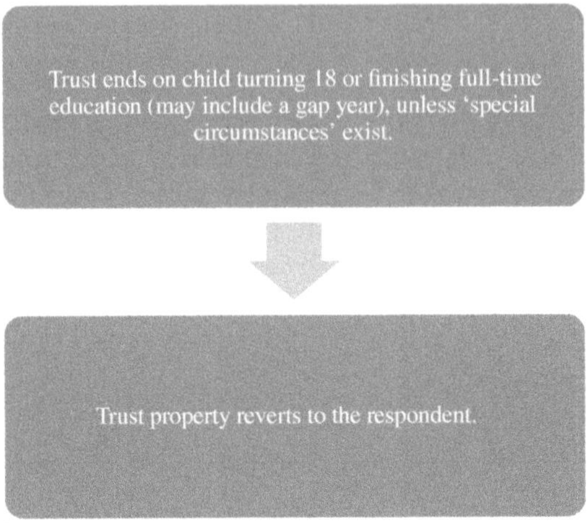

10.14 The circumstances in which a court will award outright capital housing provision to a child are vanishingly rare[29].

The meaning of 'property'

10.15 As has been discussed above, CA 1989, Sch 1, para 1(2)(d) and (e) respectively permit an order for the transfer of property or the settlement of property. 'Property' is not defined in Sch 1[30], but both sub-paragraphs refer to 'property':

to which either parent is 'entitled (either in possession or reversion)'

OR

as may be 'specified in the order'

10.16 'Property' has therefore been given a broad interpretation and can refer to any number of things[31].

29 Such an order was overturned by the Court of Appeal in *DN v UD (Sch 1)* [2021] EWCA Civ 1947, [2022] Fam 289, [2022] 2 WLR 1047, [2022] 2 FLR 308. An outright award *was* made by Recorder Allen QC in *TK v LK* [2024] EWFC 71, but the circumstances of this case were so extreme as to act as a good example of how unlikely such an order will be.

30 Nor is 'property' defined in the Matrimonial Causes Act 1973.

31 See the discussion by Cobb J in *ZU v LT* [2024] EWHC 778 (Fam), [2024] 2 FCR 815 at para 88; *Pearson v Franklin* [1994] 1 WLR 370, [1994] 2 FCR 545, [1994] 1 FLR 246, CA; *K v K (Minors: Property Transfer)* [1992] 1 WLR 530, [1992] 2 FCR 253, [1992] 2 FLR 220, CA; *Re P (A Child) (Financial Provision)* [2003] EWCA Civ 837, [2003] 2 FCR 481, [2003] 2 FLR 865; *MT v OT* [2018] EWHC 868 (Fam), [2018] 3 FCR 621, [2019] 1 FLR 93.

The right to occupy (eg a tenancy)

- *Pearson v Franklin*
- *K v K (Minors: Property Transfer)*

The net equity in a property with a mortgage

- *ZU v LT*

A new property without a mortgage

- *Re P (and many other subsequent authorities)*

A future replacement property (with or without mortgage)

- *MT v OT*

10.17 It will be apparent, therefore, that careful consideration should be given as to what 'property' is to be settled in trust under a CA 1989, Sch 1 order. In a 'big money' case it will be simple, because it will likely be a new unencumbered property. But in many other cases, care will need to be taken. For example (as in *ZU v LT*[32]), if a new house is to be bought with a mortgage raised by the applicant and some of her own cash, with the balance of the deposit to be paid by the respondent as a lump sum, then the 'property' held in trust is likely to be the percentage of the **net equity of the new property** as is represented by the respondent's lump sum, and account might need to be taken for any capital payments made towards the mortgage by the applicant over the lifetime of the trust[33].

Who can seek an order?

10.18 An application can be made for an order under CA 1989, Sch 1 by the following persons:

A parent

A guardian or special guardian

Any person named in a child arrangements order as a person with whom a child is to live

32 *ZU v LT* [2024] EWHC 778 (Fam), [2024] 2 FCR 815.

33 Such issues will be familiar to practitioners in matrimonial finance proceedings, as they are akin to 'Mesher' orders under the Matrimonial Causes Act 1973; see *Mesher v Mesher* [1980] 1 All ER 126.

10.19 It is therefore not necessary for the applicant seeking capital housing provision under CA 1989, Sch 1 to be the parent with whom the subject child lives pursuant to an order. That said, applications are far more commonly made by a parent with de facto primary caregiving responsibilities for a child (whether under a sole or a joint 'lives with' child arrangements order). Applications by a parent who does not have any day-to-day caregiving responsibilities are rare and, if made, more difficult to pursue successfully[34]:

Case Summary: N v C *(Financial Provision: Schedule 1 Claims Dismissed)*[35]

Facts:

- 12-year-old child ('P'). Following the parties' separation, P lived with M in property A owned by F.
- P then moved to live with F in a different property. She continued to spend time with M, but not overnight.
- M made a CA 1989, Sch 1 application seeking, inter alia: an order settling Property A on trust until P finished her education, and a lump sum order to refurbish the property.

Held by HHJ Hayward Smith QC sitting as a judge of the High Court:

- This was a substantial claim for housing and maintenance by a 'non-resident parent' (para 9). This was 'unusual' but not impermissible in law (paras 11 and 70).
- The concepts of 'residence' and 'non-residence' were relevant; it was important to look at the underlying reality (para 7).
- There was no jurisdiction to make a maintenance order in favour of a non-resident parent (para 67).
- F had no legal obligation to provide a home for M under CA 1989, Sch 1, his obligations related only to those for the benefit of the child. F was already providing a home for P. P lived with F and would continue to have contact with M wherever she resided.
- M was not to be permitted to remain in the property (para 72).

34 Almost all of the authorities referred to in this chapter are premised on the need for the applicant primary caregiver parent for a home for the child, but see the exceptional cases of *N v C (Financial Provision: Schedule 1 Claims Dismissed)* [2013] EWHC 399 (Fam); *MacLeod v MacLeod* [2008] UKPC 64, [2010] 1 AC 298, [2009] 3 WLR 437, [2009] 1 FCR 523, [2009] 1 FLR 641.

35 *N v C (Financial Provision: Schedule 1 Claims Dismissed)* [2013] EWHC 399 (Fam).

10.20 It is important to note that an application under CA 1989, Sch 1 cannot be made by a parent on behalf of a child who is over 18 at the time the application is made, but if the child turns 18 during the proceedings, orders can be made[36]. Orders made on the application of an adult child are discussed at **10.22** to **10.23** below.

10.21 The court can make a financial order under CA 1989, Sch 1 of its own volition, even if no application has been made for an order by one of the relevant parties[37]:

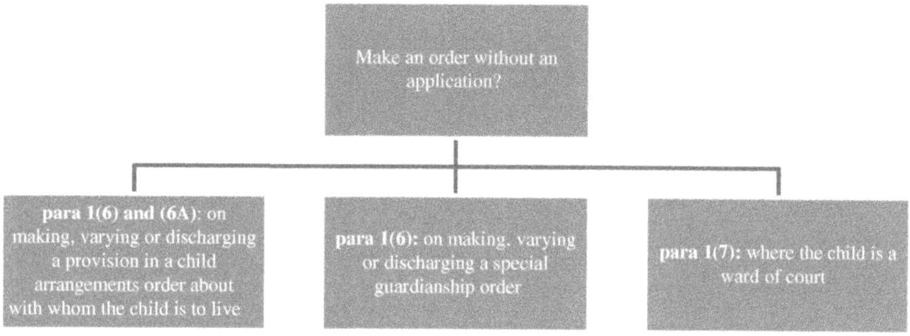

Applications by adult children

10.22 As set out in **10.20** above, a parent cannot make an application for an order in relation to an adult child. An adult child can, however, make an application for financial provision against one or both of the parents only on two bases[38] but even then, the only capital order that the court can make is a lump sum order[39]:

Adult child can make an application if (para 2(1)):

- in education (or will be)
- undergoing training for a trade, profession or vocation (where or not in gainful employment)
- special circumstances

Orders permitted (para 2(2)):

- Income: periodical payments
- Capital: lump sum

Cannot apply if (para 2(4)):

- the parents are living with each other in the same household

36 *DN v UD (Sch 1)* [2021] EWCA Civ 1947, [2022] Fam 289, [2022] 2 WLR 1047, [2022] 2 FLR 308.

37 CA 1989, Sch 1, paras 1(6) to (7).

38 CA 1989, Sch 1, para 2(1). In *Siddiqui v Siddiqui* [2021] EWCA Civ 1572, [2022] 1 FLR 840, the Court of Appeal rejected an argument by an adult child that the restriction on applications for financial relief was discriminatory against other adult children who did not come within the category of 'special circumstances'.

39 CA 1989, Sch 1, para 2(2). Note that the court can make a periodical payments order under para 2(2)(a), subject to the prohibition in para 2(3) and the right to vary a pre-existing periodical payments order in para 2(5).

10.23 Claims by adult children are comparatively rare. Even rarer still if they are made under the heading of special circumstances to justify making an order[40]. The meaning of 'special circumstances' is discussed immediately below at **10.24–10.27** and considered further in **Chapter 13**.

The duration of capital orders for financial relief under Schedule 1

10.24 CA 1989, Sch 1, para 3 expressly limits the duration of orders for periodical payments for the benefit of children[41]. No statutory limitation is imposed on capital orders for the benefit of a child. It is therefore, in principle, permissible for a court to make an outright capital order for housing for the benefit of the child which does not revert to the paying respondent. In practice, however, the authorities make very clear that the power to make such an outright order is limited[42]:

Key citation: Re N *(A Child)*[43]

Munby J:

> '[78] In my judgment, "special" or "exceptional" cases apart, "dependency" ceases at majority. So, "special" or "exceptional" cases apart, **any capital settlement under Schedule 1 should be expressed as terminating upon the child attaining the age of 18 or completing tertiary education.**' (emphasis added)

10.25 Since *Re N*[44], where this conclusion was based upon a number of preceding authorities including the seminal judgment of the Court of Appeal in *Re P*[45] (discussed below), this restriction on the court's power to make capital orders for housing a child has become entirely commonplace, culminating in the judgment of the Court of Appeal in *UD v DN*[46].

40 CA 1989, Sch 1, para 2(1)(b).
41 CA 1989, Sch 1, para 3(1) and (2).
42 See *Re P (Child: Financial Provision)* [2003] EWCA Civ 837, [2003] 2 FCR 481, [2003] 2 FLR 865; *MT v OT* [2018] EWHC 868 (Fam), [2018] 3 FCR 621, [2019] 1 FLR 93; *Re N (A Child)* [2009] EWHC 11 (Fam), [2009] 1 WLR 1621, [2009] 1 FCR 606, [2009] 1 FLR 1442.
43 *Re N (A Child)* [2009] EWHC 11 (Fam), [2009] 1 WLR 1621, [2009] 1 FCR 606, [2009] 1 FLR 1442, per Munby J at [78].
44 *Re N (A Child)* [2009] EWHC 11 (Fam), [2009] 1 WLR 1621, [2009] 1 FCR 606, [2009] 1 FLR 1442.
45 *Re P (Child: Financial Provision)* [2003] EWCA Civ 837, [2003] 2 FCR 481, [2003] 2 FLR 865.
46 *UD v DN (Sch 1)* [2021] EWCA Civ 1947, [2022] Fam 289, [2022] 2 WLR 1047, [2022] 2 FLR 308.

Case Summary: *UD v DN*[47]

Facts:

- Trial judge ordered F to settle a property in London in trust for the benefit of two children.
- At the end of the trust period (ordinary Sch 1 terms) the judge ordered that the trust property would be held 'on trust for the benefit of the children … absolutely'.

Held by the Court of Appeal:

- Appeal allowed:

  > '**such power as there is to order financial provision in favour of an adult child who is not in education or training is limited to 'special' or 'exceptional' circumstances.**'[48]

- In the circumstances of the case, seeking to protect the children from potential future manipulation or pressure did 'not begin to come within the scope of a "special" or "exceptional" circumstance which would justify the outright capital award.'[49]

10.26 If, therefore, any capital award to meet housing need must end at 18 or the completion of education **absent special or exceptional circumstances**, what are such circumstances[50]?

They must be circumstances 'relating to the children'[51].

They must be 'circumstances, such as a physical or mental disability, which create a financial need'[52].

They cannot be premised on a parent's 'prospective behaviour'[53].

Any assessment must 'focus on dependency rather than vulnerability'[54].

47 *UD v DN (Sch 1)* [2021] EWCA Civ 1947, [2022] Fam 289, [2022] 2 WLR 1047, [2022] 2 FLR 308.
48 Moylan LJ at para [76].
49 Moylan LJ at para [80].
50 See also **Chapter 13**.
51 *Kiely v Kiely* [1988] 1 FLR 248, per Booth J. Cited by the Court of Appeal in *UD v DN* (above). In this context, it has been held that one party's 'extreme wealth' (and thus ability to bear an outright order financially) is not a circumstance which comes close to 'special' or 'exceptional': *MT v OT* [2018] EWHC 868 (Fam), [2018] 3 FCR 621, [2019] 1 FLR 93.
52 *UD v DN* (above) per Moylan LJ at para [76].
53 *UD v DN* (above) per Moylan LJ at para [80].
54 Recorder Allen KC (sitting as a Deputy High Court Judge) in *TK v LK* [2024] EWFC 71 at para [87].

10.27 What does 'dependency' mean as opposed to 'vulnerability'?

Key citation: *TK v LK*[55]

Recorder Allen KC (sitting as a DHCJ):

> 'Whilst they are likely to overlap, they are not one and the same as "vulnerability" is a much broader category than "dependency". Whilst "dependent" children may well also be "vulnerable", dependency in my view implies some continuing and quantifiable financial need. Vulnerability is a broad spectrum on which many people fall, but not everyone with a vulnerability is "dependent" in the sense of requiring financial support.'

QUANTUM: THE COURT'S EXERCISE OF ITS DISCRETION

General

10.28 CA 1989, Sch 1, para 4(1) provides that the court must have regard to 'all the circumstances' of a case, including the following:

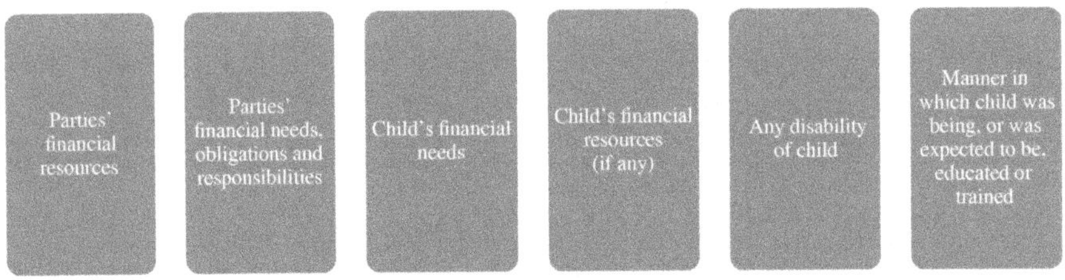

It is apparent from this list of relevant factors that the court in CA 1989, Sch 1 proceedings is focused exclusively on needs and the financial resources of the parties available to meet those needs. There is no place for arguments as to sharing or compensation; the justification for the claim begins and ends with 'needs':

55 [2024] EWFC 71 at para [87].

Key citation: *Re A (A Child)*[56]

Macur LJ:

> '[19] The literal or purposive interpretation of Sch 1 does not permit of the concept of sharing or compensation for the benefit of the child, nor, by the back door, financial provision and compensation for the carer beyond that element attributable to the care of the child during his minority, or other determined duration of dependency. There is no established authority to the contrary.'

10.29 It is further apparent that the wording of CA 1989, Sch 1, para 4 differs in some notable ways from its 'equivalent' provision under the Matrimonial Causes Act 1973 ('MCA 1973'), s 25. For example, there is **no reference to the following** in the text of Sch 1:

- the standard of living enjoyed by the family[57];
- the age of the parties[58];
- the duration of the relationship[59]; or
- the conduct of the parties if inequitable to disregard it[60].

10.30 That said, there are obvious parallels to be drawn between the court's discretionary approach to an assessment of needs in all the circumstances under both CA 1989, Sch 1 and the MCA 1973:

Key citation: *Re M-M (A Child)*[61]

McFarlane LJ:

> '[33] It is recognised that the exercise of this jurisdiction is highly discretionary and involves, in the words of Thorpe LJ in *Re P*[62] "an essentially broad-brush assessment to be taken by Family judges with much expertise and experience in the specialist field of ancillary

56 *Re A (A Child)* [2014] EWCA Civ 1577, [2015] Fam 277, [2015] 3 WLR 48, [2015] 2 FLR 625. See also *Re Z (No 2) (Schedule 1: Further Legal Costs Funding Order; Further Interim Financial Provision)* [2021] EWFC 72, [2022] 3 FCR 419.
57 MCA 1973, s 25(2)(c).
58 MCA 1973, s 25(2)(d).
59 MCA 1973, s 25(2)(d).
60 MCA 1973, s 25(2)(g).
61 [2014] EWCA Civ 276, [2014] 2 FCR 412, [2014] 2 FLR 1391.
62 *Re P (Child: Financial Provision)* [2003] EWCA Civ 837, [2003] 2 FCR 481, [2003] 2 FLR 865.

> relief." In that context this court will pay due respect both to the scope of judicial discretion and the experience of the judges who are called upon to exercise it.'

10.31 Each case will therefore turn on its facts. In some cases a respondent may be so wealthy as to justify housing provision of many millions[63], in others there may be a scarcity of resources which requires a court to take into account limited equity in one property to meet two lots of housing needs[64] and the mortgage capacity of the recipient parent[65].

Re P

10.32 The leading case as to the approach to be adopted under CA 1989, Sch 1 continues to be *Re P*[66] and the judgments of Thorpe LJ and Bodey J respectively.

10.33 Thorpe LJ held that the approach of the court should be as follows in a case involving a parent who lies 'somewhere on the spectrum from affluent to fabulously rich'[67]:

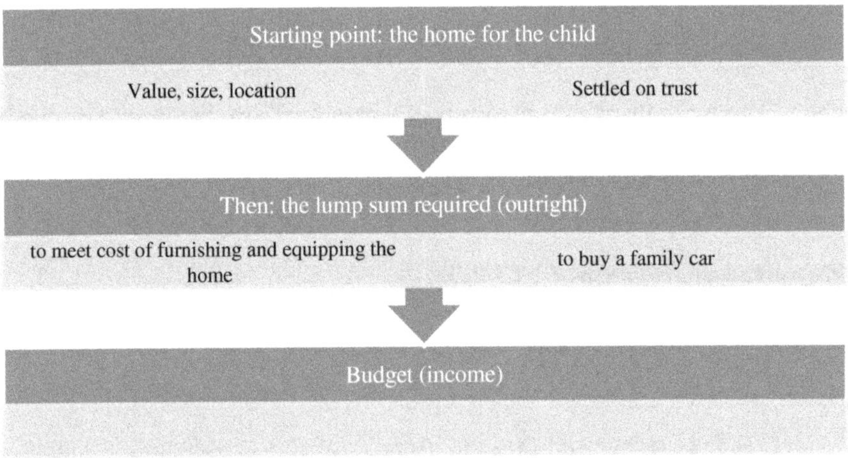

10.34 The judgment of Bodey J addresses the relevance or otherwise of specific factors which may not be contained in CA 1989, Sch 1, para 4. They are considered below in turn.

63 See *Re P (Child: Financial Provision)* [2003] EWCA Civ 837, [2003] 2 FCR 481, [2003] 2 FLR 865 and, for example, *Re Z (No 4)* [2023] EWFC 25, [2023] 2 FLR 955 (£3.65m housing fund) and *Y v Z* [2024] EWFC 4, [2024] 1 FCR 894 ($5m housing fund).
64 *DE v AB* [2010] EWHC 3792 (Fam), [2012] 2 FLR 1396.
65 *ZU v LT* [2024] EWHC 778 (Fam), [2024] 2 FCR 815.
66 *Re P (Child: Financial Provision)* [2003] EWCA Civ 837, [2003] 2 FCR 481, [2003] 2 FLR 865.
67 Per Thorpe LJ at paras 45–47.

The welfare of the child

10.35 The principle that the child's welfare is paramount[68] does not apply to applications under CA 1989, Sch 1. However,

> 'The welfare of the child while a minor, ..., is naturally a very relevant consideration as one of "... all the circumstances ..." of the case.' (Bodey J in *Re P*)[69]

Thorpe LJ went further:

> 'I would only wish to amplify by saying that welfare must be not just "one of the relevant circumstances" but, in the generality of cases, a constant influence on the discretionary outcome.' (Thorpe J in *Re P*)[70]

The length and nature of the parents' relationship

10.36 The length and nature of the parents' relationship generally has little relevance to an application under CA 1989, Sch 1, in that a child's needs are the same regardless[71]. That said, the length of the relationship between the parents is not necessarily irrelevant:

> '[23] ... The length of the relationship, however, is relevant here, I believe, in relation to the way S has been brought up and has become accustomed to be cared for. She has always been independently educated and has had, to her parents' credit, generally a comfortable lifestyle. This is linked too to standard of living.'[72]

Standard of living

10.37 While CA 1989, Sch 1 does not refer directly to the standard of living of one or both of the parties, it does refer to the financial resources of each of them[73]. It was said in *J v C (Child: Financial Provision)*[74] that:

68 Children Act 1989, s 1(1).
69 *Re P* [2003] EWCA Civ 837, [2003] 2 FCR 481, [2003] 2 FLR 865, per Bodey J at para 76(i).
70 *Re P* [2003] EWCA Civ 837, [2003] 2 FCR 481, [2003] 2 FLR 865, per Thorpe LJ at para 44.
71 *J v C (Child: Financial Provision)* [1998] 3 FCR 79, [1999] 1 FLR 152, per Hale J; cited with approval by Bodey J in *Re P (above)* at para 76(ii).
72 *N v D* [2008] 1 FLR 1629.
73 CA 1989, Sch 1, para 4(1)(a) and (b).
74 *J v C (Child: Financial Provision)* [1999] 1 FLR 152, [1998] 3 FCR 79 at p 160. Cited with approval by Bodey J in *Re P* (above) at paras 76(iii) and (iv) and by Thorpe LJ. See also: *F v G (Child: Financial Provision)* [2004] EWHC 1848 (Fam), [2005] 1 FLR 261; *MT v OT (Financial Provision: Costs)* [2007] EWHC 838 (Fam), [2008] 2 FLR 1311; *H v C* [2009] EWHC 1527 (Fam), [2009] 2 FLR 1540.

'… the child is entitled to be brought up in circumstances which bear some sort of relationship with the father's current resources and the father's present standard of living …'

10.38 In *Hussein v Makhtoum*[75], Moor J said the following in the context of proceedings under the MCA 1973 (this has subsequently been cited with approval in CA 1989, Sch 1 proceedings)[76]:

Key citation: *Hussein v Makhtoum*[77]

Moor J:

> '… the children should be able to have a lifestyle that is not entirely out of kilter with that enjoyed by them in Dubai and that enjoyed by [the father] and his family. I accept, of course, that it will be quite impossible to replicate, pound for pound, the standard of living they enjoyed before their parents separated but I am going to be generous and accept many of the figures put forward by [the mother].'

10.39 What this means in practice is dependent on the facts of each case and whether the resources of the paying party are sufficient to maintain that standard of living across two households[78]. By way of two examples from opposite ends of the spectrum[79]:

DE v AB

- Judge at first instance ordered lump sum of £85k to house M and child.
- Overturned on appeal as F would have been unable to have a deposit to house himself with a mortgage.

Re Z (No 4)

- M awarded £3.65M for a property to be settled on the child.
- Plus costs of purchase and c £100k for renovation costs.

75 *Hussein v Makhtoum* [2021] EWFC 94, [2022] 2 FLR 1185.
76 *Re Z (No 4)* [2023] EWFC 25, [2023] 2 FLR 955, per Cobb J at para [18].
77 [2021] EWFC 94, [2022] 2 FLR 1185.
78 *N v D* [2008] 1 FLR 1629 at para [23]: 'the parties will not have the standard of living, now they have separated, that they would have had had they remained together.'
79 *DE v AB* [2010] EWHC 3792 (Fam), [2012] 2 FLR 1396; *Re Z (No.4)* [2023] EWFC 25, [2023] 2 FLR 955.

Conduct inequitable to disregard

10.40 This is a factor which does not feature in CA 1989, Sch 1, para 4, nor in the analysis of the Court of Appeal in *Re P*. It has been held to be material only as a 'hazard light'[80]. The very fact that CA 1989, Sch 1 focuses on the needs of the child, rather than the parents per se, renders conduct less relevant than it may or may not be under the MCA 1973, s 25(2)(g).

10.41 That is not to say, however, that it is not a relevant feature in some cases. It is clear from the authorities that 'particularly egregious' conduct can be taken into account[81], and it has been held that the authorities on conduct in proceedings under the MCA 1973 are relevant to the court's exercise of discretion in CA 1989, Sch 1 proceedings:

Key citation: *TK v LK*[82]

Recorder Allen KC (sitting as a DHCJ):

> '[71] I do not have to consider further the question whether conduct – assuming it passes the high/exceptional threshold – may only be reflected where there is a measurable financial consequence. For reasons that I shall set out later I am wholly satisfied that in this case there is both conduct that passes this threshold and such a causative link.'

CAPITAL ORDERS UNDER SCHEDULE 1 WHERE THE COURT HAS MADE CAPITAL ORDERS UNDER THE MATRIMONIAL CAUSES ACT 1973

10.42 There is an obvious distinction between an application 'for the benefit of the child' under CA 1989, Sch 1 and an application by a former spouse for financial relief under the MCA 1973. That said, there may be some degree of crossover. In MCA 1973 cases involving children the court must give first consideration to the welfare of any minor child of the family when exercising its discretion[83].

80 *A v A (Minor: Financial Provision)* [1995] 1 FCR 309, [1994] 1 FLR 657, p 664. See also *Re S (A Child) (Unmarried Parents: Financial Provision)* [2006] EWCA Civ 479, [2006] 2 FLR 950 at para 15, where the Court of Appeal was critical of the trial judge for too much focus on M's conduct.

81 *TK v LK* [2024] EWFC 71 at para 60. See also *O v P (No 2) (Sch 1 Application)* [2014] EWHC 2225 (Fam), [2015] 2 FLR 77, per Baker J at para 132.

82 *TK v LK* [2024] EWFC 71 at para.71. The judgment of Recorder Allen KC contains a very helpful summary of the law on conduct, in both CA 1989, Sch 1 and proceedings under the MCA 1973, from paras 59 to 76.

83 MCA 1973, s 25(1).

10.43 The fact that the court has made substantive capital (and income) orders for financial relief under the MCA 1973 does not, therefore, preclude in law an application for financial orders for the benefit of a child under CA 1989, Sch 1[84], but pursuing such an application can be very difficult.

10.44 Moor J considered the relevance of financial remedy proceedings under the MCA 1973 to a subsequent application under CA 1989, Sch 1 in *PK v BC*[85].

Case Summary: *PK v BC*[86]

Facts:

- The parties were married for eight years. Their child was aged eight.
- In financial remedy proceedings after the divorce, M received £950k on a clean break basis intended to meet housing and income needs.
- F reduced his child maintenance payments and fell beneath the threshold.
- M applied under CA 1989, Sch 1 for orders, including a lump sum order to improve her housing position.

Held by Moor J:

The court had jurisdiction to deal with an application for lump sum provision for housing, notwithstanding the existence of a clean break in divorce proceedings:

> 'However, I do take the view that **the circumstances have to be exceptional** … It is, in my view, **a very high hurdle that has to be overcome** for a mother to then bring a further application for financial provision by way of housing. If it was to occur it would of course be for a settlement of property order …' (emphasis added).

10.45 The characterisation of such an application as requiring 'exceptional circumstances' was doubted by Cobb J in *MG v FG*[87], who warned[88]:

84 In *MB v KB* [2007] EWHC 789 (Fam), [2007] 2 FLR 586, the applicant mother was not 'estopped' from applying for a settlement of property order and a lump sum under CA 1989, Sch 1 notwithstanding that the court had made orders in relation to her housing need in MCA 1973 proceedings.

85 *PK v BC* [2012] EWHC 1382 (Fam), [2012] 2 FLR 1426.

86 *PK v BC* [2012] EWHC 1382 (Fam), [2012] 2 FLR 1426.

87 *MG v FG (Schedule 1: Application to strike out; Estoppel; Legal Costs Funding)* [2016] EWHC 1964 (Fam), [2016] 3 FCR 480.

88 At para 28. This was cited in *TK v LK* [2024] EWFC 71 by Recorder Allen KC (sitting as a Deputy High Court Judge), but in that case he did not consider whether the proceedings have to be

Key citation: *MG v FG*[89]

Cobb J:

> '[28] There is a danger that focusing on the particular language of a given judgment may obstruct the proper exercise of the relevant jurisdiction, and I must guard against doing so … That said, **I do regard the cases in which a second bite would be permitted as few and far between – they will indeed, in my view, be the exception rather than the rule.**'

PRACTICAL CONSIDERATIONS

10.46 Practitioners should give proper thought to the drafting of any final order in CA 1989, Sch 1 proceedings and to whether or not it is necessary to have a separate deed of trust governing the trust property. In the vast majority of straightforward cases (ie a single property to be held in trust to revert to the settlor) there will be no need for a separate deed of trust at all and, in fact, such a document can be more trouble than it is worth[90].

10.47 Careful consideration should be given to the issue of enforcement of any CA 1989, Sch 1 order in the event of a payer's non-compliance. Enforcement has been addressed more generally in **Chapter 15**, but some thought should be given to what the order *actually* provides for the parties to do and whether/how it will be enforceable in the future.

10.48 In *Re N*[91], one of the fundamental problems with enforcement had been created by the terminology of the order, which provided for the father 'to settle on the mother for the benefit of the child the sum of £220,000'. It had neglected to include any lump sum order, by which the mother could easily enforce the non-satisfaction by the father of this paragraph, which led to numerous cross-applications in enforcement proceedings[92].

10.49 The Standard Orders Template (Order 2.2) approved by the President of the Family Division and referred to by Cobb J in *ZU v LT*[93] contains wording

'exceptional' because, on the unique facts of that case, they indisputably were within that category (M had subsequently been sent to prison for a lengthy period for crimes committed against the subject child).

89 *MG v FG (Schedule 1: Application to strike out; Estoppel; Legal Costs Funding)* [2016] EWHC 1964 (Fam), [2016] 3 FCR 480.

90 See the *G v A* litigation, starting with *G v A* [2011] EWHC 2380 (Fam), [2012] 1 FLR 389.

91 *Re N (A Child) (Financial Provision: Dependency)* [2009] EWHC 11 (Fam), [2009] 1 WLR 1621, [2009] 1 FCR 606, [2009] 1 FLR 1442, per Munby J.

92 *Re N* (above), at para [11].

93 [2023] EWFC 179.

that is helpful in this regard, and which has been discussed in **10.4** to **10.11** above. The following is a non-exhaustive list of things to consider as part of the drafting process in relation to capital orders making housing provision under CA 1989, Sch 1:

- Is the respondent in the jurisdiction?
- Where is the source of the money to fund any settlement?
- Where is the trust property to be?
- Who will be the trustees? One or both of the parents? Professional trustees? Nominated individuals?
- How will the trust be managed?
- Will there be tax implications to the structure now or in the future? In this jurisdiction or another?
- What happens when the trust ends? Date for leaving? Is it to be sold?
- Is there a right to buy out the respondent's interest? If so, on what terms and when?
- Definition of continuing education? Only one degree? Gap year?
- Are there any other terms on which the trust may end?
- Who pays for what during the course of the trust?
- Is borrowing permitted or anticipated against the trust property?

CHAPTER 11

Capital Provision: Non-Housing

Content at a glance:

INTRODUCTION

11.1 As a matter of practice, and following the Court of Appeal's guidance in *Re P*[1] and *Re A*[2], a court entertaining a standalone application for financial provision in respect of a child[3] will ordinarily follow a sequence whereby findings are first made in relation to *housing need*, after which the court will turn to assess the merit and quantum of claims for *specific capital items*. Income needs and maintenance claims are typically decided last. Such standalone applications are almost invariably brought under CA 1989, Sch 1 and within this chapter, reference will be made primarily to that statute. Practitioners should, however, bear in mind that claims may also be brought under different statutory provisions including in cases where the jurisdictional requirements under CA 1989, Sch 1 are not met[4].

1 *Re P (Child: Financial Provision)* [2003] EWCA Civ 837, [2003] 2 FLR 865, CA per Thorpe LJ at para 45.
2 *Re A* [2014] EWCA Civ 1577, [2015] Fam 277, [2015] 2 FLR 625, CA at para 22.
3 Whether under the Children Act 1989 ('CA 1989'), Sch 1, the Matrimonial Causes Act 1973 ('MCA 1973') or the Civil Partnership Act 2004 ('CPA 2004').
4 For an overview of the different statutory provisions see **Chapter 2**; for jurisdiction see **Chapter 4**.

11.2 Accordingly the usual sequence for quantification of CA 1989, Sch 1 claims will be:

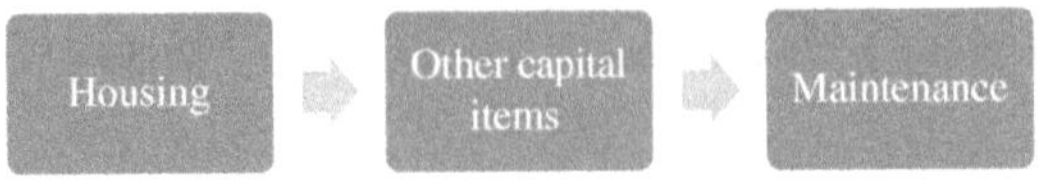

11.3 This linear approach is not set out in the statute, but flows from the practical reality that the majority of capital expenditure will be informed (if not determined) by the value, size and location of the home. The most significant items of capital expenditure usually relate to the cost of purchasing, furnishing and equipping a property, including whether any adaptations are required for security or to meet a child's health or educational needs. Similarly, the need for a car may be informed by the location of the home and the availability of other transport.

11.4 This sequence is no less applicable in a matrimonial/civil partnership context. In cases brought under the Matrimonial Causes Act 1973 ('MCA 1973') or the Civil Partnership Act 2004 ('CPA 2004'), however, the child's needs will be considered alongside (and may be subsumed by) those of the spouse or civil partner. A needs assessment is likely to follow a determination of any sharing claim[5].

11.5 Housing provision is considered in **Chapter 10**. Child maintenance is considered in **Chapter 12**. This chapter addresses the various types of award that may be made for non-housing items of capital expenditure, ie the 'second stage' above.

WHAT TYPES OF CAPITAL AWARD ARE AVAILABLE TO BENEFIT A CHILD?

11.6 The availability of orders for capital provision depends on the statutory basis of the claim for financial relief. Below is a summary of each 'menu' of capital orders by type of claim[6].

5 *Scatliffe v Scatliffe* [2016] UKPC 36, [2017] AC 93, [2017] 2 FLR 933 at para 25(x).

6 Note, the MCA 1973 powers are also available if an application is brought by an ex-spouse for financial relief after an overseas divorce pursuant to the Matrimonial and Family Proceedings Act 1984 ('MFPA 1984'), Part III. If jurisdiction is conferred only by virtue of the former matrimonial home being in England, not all of the MCA 1973 powers are available. Otherwise, the court on hearing a MFPA 1984, Part III claim can exercise any of the powers under MCA 1973, Part II. Equivalent claims may also be brought with the leave of the court in respect of civil partnerships which have been dissolved overseas, pursuant to CPA 2004, Sch 7.

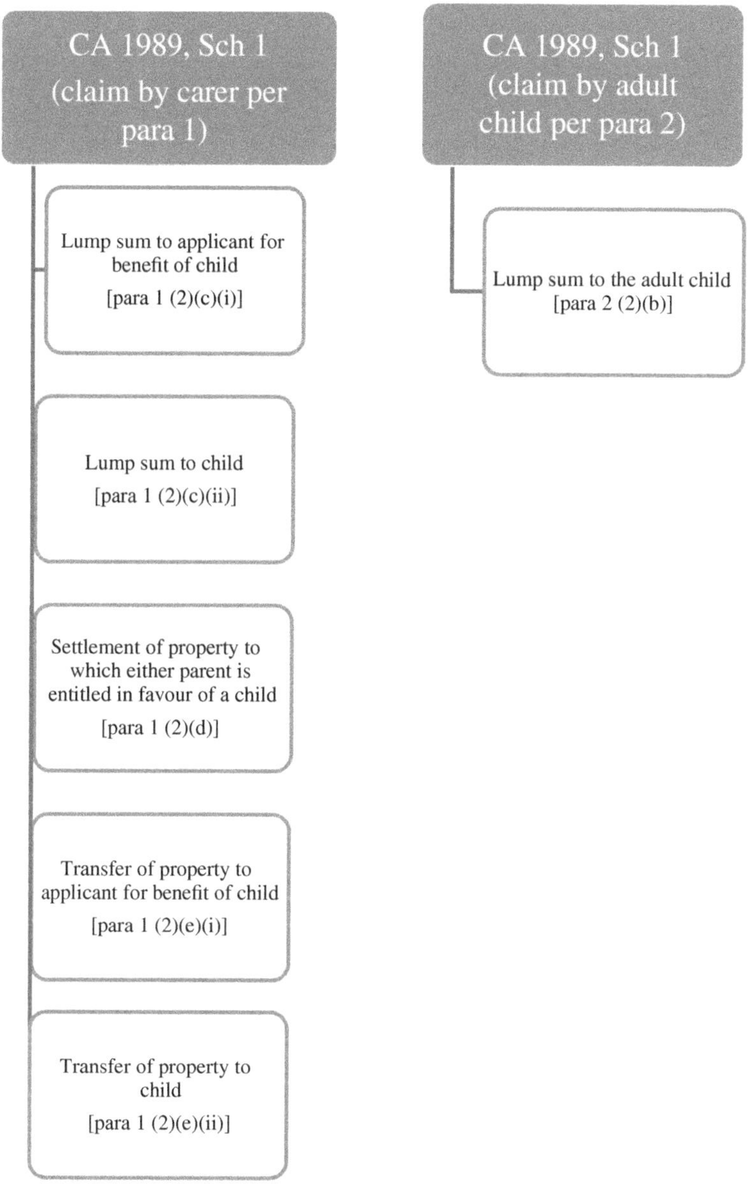
CA 1989, Sch 1 (claim by carer per para 1)
Lump sum to applicant for benefit of child [para 1 (2)(c)(i)]
Lump sum to child [para 1 (2)(c)(ii)]
Settlement of property to which either parent is entitled in favour of a child [para 1 (2)(d)]
Transfer of property to applicant for benefit of child [para 1 (2)(e)(i)]
Transfer of property to child [para 1 (2)(e)(ii)]
CA 1989, Sch 1 (claim by adult child per para 2)
Lump sum to the adult child [para 2 (2)(b)]

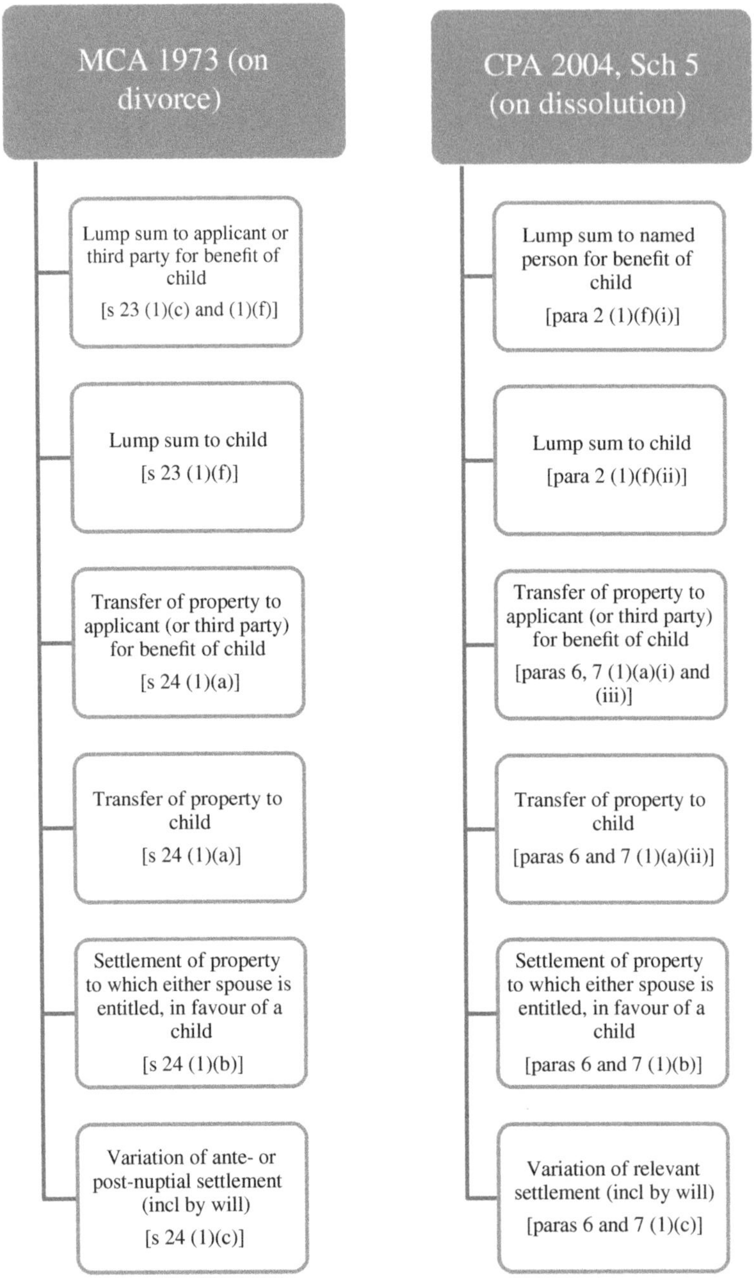
MCA 1973 (on divorce)
Lump sum to applicant or third party for benefit of child [s 23 (1)(c) and (1)(f)]
Lump sum to child [s 23 (1)(f)]
Transfer of property to applicant (or third party) for benefit of child [s 24 (1)(a)]
Transfer of property to child [s 24 (1)(a)]
Settlement of property to which either spouse is entitled, in favour of a child [s 24 (1)(b)]
Variation of ante- or post-nuptial settlement (incl by will) [s 24 (1)(c)]
CPA 2004, Sch 5 (on dissolution)
Lump sum to named person for benefit of child [para 2 (1)(f)(i)]
Lump sum to child [para 2 (1)(f)(ii)]
Transfer of property to applicant (or third party) for benefit of child [paras 6, 7 (1)(a)(i) and (iii)]
Transfer of property to child [paras 6 and 7 (1)(a)(ii)]
Settlement of property to which either spouse is entitled, in favour of a child [paras 6 and 7 (1)(b)]
Variation of relevant settlement (incl by will) [paras 6 and 7 (1)(c)]

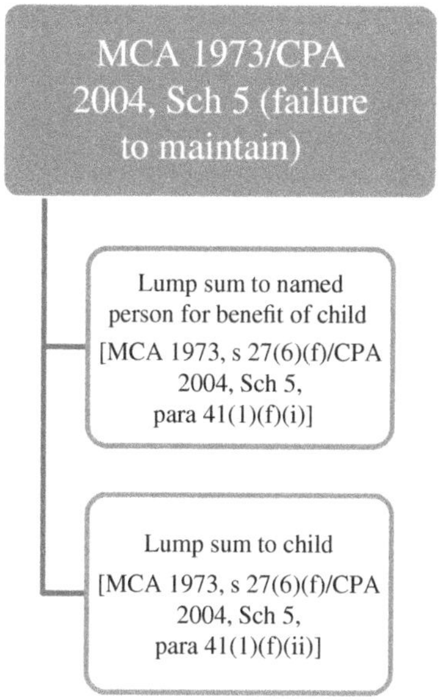

TRANSFERS AND SETTLEMENT OF PROPERTY (NON-HOUSING) AND VARIATION OF SETTLEMENTS

Overview

11.7 In the majority of cases, applications for a settlement of property (or, in a rarer case, a transfer of property) will relate to a settlement of real property or the transfer of an estate of land, eg a leasehold, for the purpose of housing. The principles applying to such orders are considered in **Chapter 10**.

11.8 It is possible, however, to transfer or settle *any* property to which either parent (in CA 1989, Sch 1 cases) or party to the marriage or civil partnership (in MCA 1973 or CPA 2004 cases) is entitled, for the benefit of the child.

11.9 In CA 1989, Sch 1 cases, applicants must be conscious of the prohibition (not contained in either MCA 1973 or CPA 2004) against more than one transfer or settlement of property being ordered against the same respondent in respect of the same child. Thus, the effect of seeking a transfer or settlement of (non-housing) property pursuant to CA 1989, Sch 1 may be to dispose of the claim for such orders, and thus preclude a further transfer or settlement of property (whether for housing or to meet some other need) should that be sought in future. This is not an issue if the claim is brought under MCA 1973 or CPA 2004, where multiple transfers or settlements of property may be made to the same child at once or in successive applications. Nor does a previous MCA 1973 or CPA 2004 settlement of property preclude a single further settlement from being made under CA 1989, Sch 1. The prohibition is against using the Sch 1 power more than once.

Settlements of property: associated property may form part of one settlement

11.10 Notwithstanding the prohibition against multiple settlements of property being made against the same respondent in respect of the same child in CA 1989, Sch 1 proceedings, the settlement of related property might properly be construed as being so closely linked in substance as properly to be defined as a single settlement.

Key citation: *DN v UD*[7]

Williams J:

> 'I do not consider that a settlement of property within the meaning of Sch 1, para 1(2)(d) connotes settlement of only one item of property. This property and its fixtures, fittings and contents are essentially indivisible ...'.

11.11 The costs of sale or purchase of substitute properties may be more appropriately dealt with as lump sum payments than as part of a settlement of property order. These are not sums that will be returned to the paying parent at a future date, so they are more akin to a lump sum than a settlement[8].

Variations of settlements under MCA 1973 and CPA 2004

11.12 If the parties to the financial claim were married or in a civil partnership, and if a settlement was made upon them that falls within the definition a nuptial settlement for the purposes of either MCA 1973, s 24 or CPA 2004, Sch 5, para 7 then the court has the power to vary that settlement on the pronouncement of a decree of divorce, nullity or judicial separation or upon the dissolution of the civil partnership[9]. This power may be exercised for the benefit of a child of the family. Under both statutes, the court has the power to extinguish the interests of the spouses or civil partners under the settlement, but not those of the child.

11.13 Where a financial claim is brought on behalf of a child in the context of parties who have been married or in a civil partnership, it is worth bearing in mind the court's power to vary settlements if there are substantive trusts which

7 [2020] EWHC 627 (Fam), [2021] 1 FLR 497. NB the Court of Appeal allowed the appeal against Williams J's orders but did not overturn this aspect of his decision. The CA judgment is reported at *UD v DN (Schedule 1, Children Act 1989: Capital Provision)* [2021] EWCA Civ 1947, [2022] Fam 289, [2022] 2 WLR 1047, [2022] 2 FLR 308 and is considered in **Chapter 13** at **13.35** onwards.

8 See *LT v ZU* [2023] EWFC 179, per HHJ Evans-Gordon at para 33.

9 The law relating to nuptial settlements was considered in **Chapter 8** of *1KBW on Trusts in Matrimonial Proceedings* (2019, Bloomsbury Professional). A detailed review of those principles is beyond the scope of this book.

may be nuptial in nature, as this may provide a further means by which capital provision can be made for the benefit of the child.

LUMP SUM ORDERS

Powers of the court to award lump sums

11.14 The most commonly used power to meet non-housing capital needs for children is a lump sum order. The court may exercise its power to order a lump sum on repeated occasions, whether the claim is brought under CA 1989, Sch 1[10], MCA 1973[11] or CPA 2004, Sch 5[12].

11.15 Although (unlike orders for settlement or transfer of property) multiple lump sum orders can be made on successive applications, it has been held that a lump sum which is intended to house a child during his or her minority should not be made on more than one occasion, or after a transfer or settlement of property has been made, to prevent the lump sum order being used to circumvent the prohibition in CA 1989, Sch 1, para 1(5)(b)[13].

11.16 Under each statute, the court has a power to order the payment of lump sum by instalments[14]. Where such an order is made, there is a further power to vary the number, quantum and date for payment of instalments[15].

11.17 The purposes for which lump sums may be sought are diverse, and courts have been creative in applying this remedy to meet need. Lump sums for the purposes of litigation funding are addressed in **Chapter 9**.

Lump sums: what is *not* a permitted purpose for the sum?

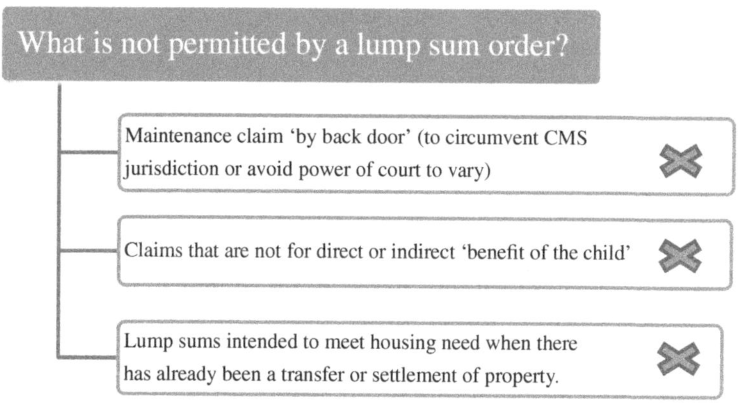

10 CA 1989, Sch 1, para 1(5).
11 MCA 1973, s 23(4).
12 CPA 2004, Sch 5, para 1(3).
13 *Phillips v Peace* [2004] EWHC 3180 (Fam), [2005] 2 FLR 1212.
14 CA 1989, Sch 1, para 5(5) and (6); MCA 1973, s 23(3)(c) and (6); CPA 2004, Sch 5, para 3(3) and (5).
15 CA 1989, Sch 1, para 5(6); MCA 1973, s 31(2)(d); CPA 2004, Sch 5, para 50(1)(e).

11.18 The power to make lump sum orders must not be used to circumvent the restrictions under the Child Support Act 1991 ('CSA 1991') on the jurisdiction of the courts to make orders for maintenance (these are considered in **Chapters 3 and 12**). It follows that lump sums may only be awarded to meet items of capital expenditure, not regular or routine outgoings or expenditure, which must be covered by periodical payments.

Case summary: *Phillips v Peace*[16]

Facts:

A wealthy father, living in a house worth £2.6 m, had no income, only capital. On M's application to the Child Support Agency, F's liability was assessed at zero. It followed that the court had no jurisdiction to make an order for periodical payments for the benefit of the child, none of the other CSA exemptions being in place.

M applied to the court for a lump sum order. She sought to use part of it to provide regular support for the child.

Held by Johnson J:

The court should not exercise its jurisdiction so as to make provision designed to avoid the terms of CSA 1991, s 8(3).

Where the CSA 1991 conferred jurisdiction as to maintenance to the CMS, the court should exercise its powers under CA 1989, Sch 1 in order to meet the need of the child in respect of *capital expenditure*[17] only.

M was awarded £90,000 for a house and lump sums for furniture, birth expenses and other capital needs. No sum was awarded towards regular outgoings/maintenance needs.

11.19 *Phillips v Peace*[18] was followed in *Dickson v Rennie*[19], where the mother's application for 'top-up' maintenance failed for lack of jurisdiction on the grounds that the CMS maintenance calculation was not a 'maximum assessment'; the court refused to order a lump sum in order to make up the shortfall in her maintenance.

16 [1996] 2 FLR 230, [1996] 2 FCR 237. NB the case has been misreported as *Phillips v Pearce*, the father's surname was in fact 'Peace'.

17 Cf *V v V (Ancillary Relief: Power to Order Child Maintenance)* [2001] 2 FLR 799, in which a lump sum was ordered when the court lost jurisdiction to order child maintenance. The court considered *Phillips v Peace* to have been correctly decided but distinguishable on its facts.

18 [1996] 2 FLR 230, [1996] 2 FCR 237 (NB the case has been misreported as *Phillips v Pearce*, the father's surname was in fact 'Peace').

19 *Dickson v Rennie* [2014] EWHC 4306 (Fam), [2015] 2 FLR 978.

Key citation: *Dickson v Rennie*[20]

Holman J at para 38:

> '... [the lump sum sought] is frankly no more than seeking to recoup or recover the difference between the ordered maintenance and the CMS calculated maintenance by means of a lump sum. I simply cannot entertain that limb of this application. To do so would be very blatantly to flout what I have described as the barrier or shutter erected by Parliament between the functions of the CMS and the court. For the reasons that I have already explained, the court order has totally ceased to have effect. For the reasons that I have also already explained, there is absolutely no power in this court to make some form of "top up" order. If I were now to order a lump sum to reflect those amounts, I would be very obviously flouting the will of Parliament and, indeed, not acting as a court of law.'

11.20 In *Green v Adams*[21] Mostyn J summarised the principle as follows:

> '... the court does not have jurisdiction to make an award to meet the quotidian expenses of living; to meet, if you like, the cost of one's daily bread. It can only make an award for genuinely capital expenditure of a singular nature.'

Similarly, in *G v W*[22] it was held by Sir Jonathan Cohen that regular outgoings should ordinarily be met through orders for periodical payments.

Case summary: *G v W*[23]

Facts:

M appealed against a CA 1989, Sch 1 order. The parties had a two year old child, who lived with her. M had a negligible income as a social influencer; F was a successful sportsman.

The parties agreed the major elements of the order: the housing fund (£1.35m); a furnishing fund; periodical payments at a rate of £8,000 pm; a car; nursery and school fees to be paid by F.

20 *Dickson v Rennie* [2014] EWHC 4306 (Fam), [2015] 2 FLR 978.
21 *Green v Adams* [2017] EWFC 24, [2017] 2 FLR 1413, Mostyn J.
22 [2022] EWHC 1101 (Fam), [2022] 3 FCR 248, Cohen J.
23 [2022] EWHC 1101 (Fam), [2022] 3 FCR 248, Cohen J.

Five issues were left for the trial judge to decide, namely whether F should pay: (i) a lump sum to clear M's debts; (ii) additional financial provision to cover the costs of a nanny to age 18; (iii) a lump sum to pay for M to undergo remedial gynaecological surgery; (iv) a lump sum to pay for the M's moving costs and security in her new home; plus (v) the date for the periodical payments to start.

M was successful only in relation to her claim for sums to clear her debts and moving costs. She appealed.

Held by Sir Jonathan Cohen:

Appeal allowed in part.

- Additional provision made for a period of nine years by way of enhanced periodical payments to cover the costs of a nanny.
- Lump sum allowed for limited degree of backdating allowed for past expenses incurred on childcare (taking into account that M had incurred some of these expenses after the court had ruled against interim funding for them at interlocutory stages, and also that some of the 'debts' were incurred to family members for this purpose).
- No additional provision for the payment of other debts which the mother had incurred by 'reckless over-expenditure'[24].
- No lump sum for M's surgical treatment, she having not provided any evidence of its necessity nor urgency, and the evidence suggesting it was likely to be performed on the NHS the following year.
- No award for home security, as the housing fund of £1.35m was sufficient to include any adaptations required.

Nanny costs should be met by periodical payments as there would be no accountability to F if the order were framed as a lump sum. Such costs were likely to be a regular outgoing, and should be subject to variation if in fact no nanny was engaged.

11.21 As *G v W*[25] illustrates, the boundary between a 'capital' need and an 'income' need is not always clearly defined. For example, a lump sum to provide a maintenance fund for the mother's home was permitted in *A v A*[26], but expressly excluded on the basis it should not form part of a capital award in *J v C*[27]. The distinction between capital and income needs is less important where the court has jurisdiction to make a full range of financial orders.

24 At para 29.
25 [2022] EWHC 1101 (Fam), [2022] 3 FCR 248, Cohen J.
26 *A v A (A Minor: Financial Provision)* [1994] 1 FLR 657.
27 *J v C (Child: Financial Provision)* [1999] 1 FLR 152, Hale J.

In *J v C*, the court did not have jurisdiction to make orders for maintenance, as the father's maintenance obligation were subject to the jurisdiction of the CSA; by contrast in both *G v W* (due to the scale of the father's income) and *A v A* (the father being overseas) the court did have jurisdiction to make orders for maintenance. Where jurisdiction is limited, the court must be particularly cautious not to award a lump sum which circumvents the statutory prohibition on making a maintenance award.

11.22 In *S v M*[28] Moor J dismissed an appeal against a series of lump sums for the purpose of interim housing by way of rent, pending receipt of a larger lump sum for a property purchase. The father argued that recurring expenses for rent were disguised maintenance payments, which was prohibited by the Child Support Act 1991, s 8(3). Moor J held that the court had addressed the need for long-term housing by capital award, and so was entitled to meet interim housing the same way.

Case summary: *S v M*[29]

Facts:

In CA 1989, Sch 1 proceedings, F was ordered to pay a lump sum of £350,000 to M outright and a further £50,000 to her on reversionary terms by way of housing provision for her and the child.

Pending payment of the lump sum, F was ordered to make monthly payments to M to fund her rent. Since the court did not have jurisdiction to make orders for maintenance due to CSA 1991, s 8(3), this provision was directed to be paid as a series of lump sums. The judge concluded there was a clear distinction between housing provision and routine maintenance expenses, and therefore that this cost could be met via lump sums without offending the limitation on jurisdiction to order maintenance payments.

F appealed.

Held by Moor J:

Appeal dismissed, although the judge had 'not found this an easy case to decide' (para 35).

The court *had* jurisdiction to order rental payments before the capital sum was paid.

28 *S v M* [2022] EWHC 278 (Fam), [2022] 4 WLR 109.
29 *S v M* [2022] EWHC 278 (Fam), [2022] 4 WLR 109.

- '… I entirely accept that the decision in Dickson v Rennie is correct. The court cannot "top up" a CMS assessment unless there is a maximum assessment …' (para 35).
- 'I have been struck by the admitted fact that this court does, despite the existence of the CSA, retain jurisdiction to provide for the housing costs of the child and the parent with care by way of a capital sum. It has never been suggested that this falls foul of the provisions of the CSA. Capital awards are regularly made in large sums to enable a property to be purchased, even though the property is, almost always, held on trust for the payer. The courts have therefore clearly accepted that such provision does not fall within the maintenance provisions where the CSA has exclusive jurisdiction.' (para 36).
- 'If the court has jurisdiction to provide a capital fund for housing, it is difficult to see why it does not have jurisdiction to provide for the costs of such housing prior to the property being acquired. It would be completely illogical if one was not maintenance provision but the other was.' (para 37).
- 'I accept entirely that [making an award to cover rent] has to be done by way of lump sums. There is no question that there is jurisdiction to make more than one lump sum. The provision of past payments of rent can easily be covered, as here, by a crystallised figure. I was slightly more troubled about the ongoing monthly lump sums. I take some comfort from the decision of Wilson J in R v R [(Lump Sum Repayments) [2004] 1 FLR 928], where the overall lump sum was not quantified but there were monthly lump sums payable for a further twenty years.' (para 40).
- '… I simply cannot see why [responsibility for providing housing for the mother and the child during the child's dependency] only applies after the father pays the capital lump sum. The obligation applies both before and after he pays the lump sum. The CSA legislation does not mean it can only be his responsibility after he pays the lump sum. To so determine would be illogical and would encourage delay in payment to the huge detriment of [the child] or any other child in a similar situation.' (para 42).

11.23 In *SP v QR*[30] HHJ Hess held that the court could not order ongoing monthly lump sums to discharge mortgage interest payments when the Child Maintenance Service had jurisdiction for maintenance. He distinguished *S v M*[31] chiefly by reference to the duration of the proposed order – had the order sought been made the obligation would have been in place for more than a decade.

30 *SP v QR* [2024] EWFC 57.
31 *S v M* [2022] EWHC 278 (Fam), [2022] 4 WLR 109, [2023] 1 FCR 247, [2023] 2 FLR 321.

Lump sums for capitalised child maintenance

11.24 There is no jurisdictional bar to capitalising child maintenance obligations with payment of a lump sum, albeit in practice such orders will be exceptionally rare. When such an order came before Mostyn J on appeal in *AZ v FM*[32], he commented that he had no memory of encountering such an order despite being in full-time practice since 1981. Capitalisation of child maintenance is addressed further in **Chapter 12** at **12.39** onwards and **Chapter 14** at **14.25** onwards.

Lump sums: illustrations in practice

11.25 A lump sum paid to a child or for their benefit (under any of the available statutory powers) must be for the benefit of the child. This requirement may not defeat an otherwise meritorious claim in an MCA 1973 or CPA 2004 context, because the absence of benefit to a child will not preclude legitimate claims by the applicant in their own right. However, in a CA 1989, Sch 1 context, where the parent or carer has no independent claim of their own, such benefit is a pre-requisite of any lump sum.

11.26 The courts have exercised the power in a wide range of circumstances. Below are some examples from past cases:

Purpose of lump sum	Case examples
A family car (or cars), sometimes including index linked future lump sums for replacement vehicles at prescribed intervals.	*H v C*[33] *Re P*[34] *PG v TW (No 2)*[35] *MT v OT*[36] *A v V*[37]
A car for a child (who was learning to drive) or nanny.	*H v C*[38] *Y v Z*[39]

32 *AZ v FM* [2021] EWFC 2, [2021] 2 FCR 729, [2021] 2 FLR 1371, Mostyn J.
33 *H v C* [2009] EWHC 1527, [2009] 2 FLR 1540, Judge Kevin Barnett.
34 *Re P (Child: Financial Provision)* [2003] EWCA Civ 837, [2003] 2 FCR 481, [2003] 2 FLR 865, CA.
35 *PG v TW (No 2)* [2014] 1 FLR 923, HHJ Horowitz QC.
36 *MT v OT* [2018] EWHC 868, [2019] 1 FLR 93, Cohen J.
37 *A v V* [2022] EWHC 3501 (Fam), Francis J.
38 *H v C* [2009] EWHC 1527, [2009] 2 FLR 1540, Judge Kevin Barnett.
39 *Y v Z (Schedule 1)* [2024] EWFC 4, [2024] 1 FCR 894, Peel J.

Discharge of carer's debts (not necessarily related to child's expenses)[40].	*MT v OT*[41] *Morgan v Hill*[42] *Re M-M*[43] *Y v Z*[44] *Re Z (A Child) (No 4)*[45]
Costs of installing security in a new home.	*Y v Z*[46] *Al Maktoum*[47]
Building work on a property.	*A v V*[48]
Future school fees fund.	*Tracey v Tracey*[49]
Decorating and furnishing a home.	*Re P*[50] *Phillips v Peace*[51] *Y v Z*[52] *A v V*[53] *Re Z (A Child) (No 4) (Schedule 1 Award)*[54] *Al Maktoum*[55]
The costs of pets/horses.	*Y v Z*[56] *Al Maktoum*[57]

40 Although see *G v W* [2022] EWHC 1101 (Fam), [2022] 3 FCR 248, as a recent example where not all debts incurred by the carer were discharged. Specifically, debts the mother had incurred in defiance of an interim order which did not make provision for them could not be recovered. The mother was also left with debts she had incurred to family members that had been 'caused by reckless over-expenditure.' Cobb J followed this approach in *Re Z (A Child) (No 4) (Schedule 1 Award)* [2023] EWFC 25, [2023] 2 FLR 955.

41 *MT v OT* [2018] EWHC 868, [2018] 3 FCR 621, [2019] 1 FLR 93.

42 *Morgan v Hill* [2006] EWCA Civ 1602, [2007] 1 WLR 855, [2006] 3 FCR 620, [2007] 1 FLR 1480.

43 *Re M-M (Schedule 1 Provision)* [2014] EWCA Civ 276, [2014] 2 FCR 412, [2014] 2 FLR 1391.

44 *Y v Z (Schedule 1)* [2024] EWFC 4, [2024] 1 FCR 894.

45 *Re Z (A Child) (No 4) (Schedule 1 Award)* [2023] EWFC 25, [2023] 2 FLR 955.

46 *Y v Z (Schedule 1)* [2024] EWFC 4, [2024] 1 FCR 894.

47 *Her Royal Highness Haya bint al Hussein v His Highness Mohammed bin Rashid Al Maktoum* [2021] EWFC 94, [2022] 2 FLR 1185 – albeit note this was an MCA 1973 claim and the 'need' for security was established both for the claimant wife and for the children of the family.

48 *A v V* [2022] EWHC 3501 (Fam).

49 *Tracey v Tracey* [2006] EWCA Civ 734, [2006] 2 FCR 481, [2007] 1 FLR 196. Sometimes school fees will be more appropriately addressed by way of ongoing maintenance. In *Tracey v Tracey*, Thorpe LJ considered the relative advantages of making a secured periodical payments order (which would have been more flexible, and capable of future variation) over a lump sum (which would be more final). The merits will depend on the facts of the specific case.

50 *Re P (Child: Financial Provision)* [2003] EWCA Civ 837, [2003] 2 FCR 481, [2003] 2 FLR 865.

51 *Phillips v Peace* [1996] 2 FLR 230, [1996] 2 FCR 237.

52 *Y v Z (Schedule 1)* [2024] EWFC 4, [2024] 1 FCR 894.

53 *A v V* [2022] EWHC 3501 (Fam).

54 *Re Z (A Child) (No 4) (Schedule 1 Award)* [2023] 2 FLR 955.

55 *Her Royal Highness Haya bint al Hussein v His Highness Mohammed bin Rashid Al Maktoum* [2021] EWFC 94, [2022] 2 FLR 1185.

56 *Y v Z (Schedule 1)* [2024] EWFC 4, [2024] 1 FCR 894.

57 *Her Royal Highness Haya bint al Hussein v His Highness Mohammed bin Rashid Al Maktoum* [2021] EWFC 94, [2022] 2 FLR 1185.

Removal costs (and associated expenses).	*Re N*[58] *Re Z (A Child) (No 4)*[59]
The costs of shipping pets and belongings to another jurisdiction.	*Y v Z*[60]
Payment of a lump sum into a trust to provide trustees with a contingency fund from which to meet their costs, buildings insurances and various unspecified expenditure over the lifetime of a settlement, so requests do not need to be made of the father.	*A v V*[61]
Deposit on a rental flat (as an interim award).	*Re Z (Sch 1)*[62]
Reimbursement of costs in other proceedings and future legal fees.	*R v F*[63] *UD v DN*[64]
Medical, nursing and hospital costs.	*Phillips v Peace*[65]
Clothing and baby equipment.	*Phillips v Peace*[66]

58 *Re N (Payments for Benefit of Child)* [2009] EWHC 11 (Fam), [2009] 1 WLR 1621, [2009] 1 FLR 1442.
59 *Re Z (A Child) (No 4) (Schedule 1 Award)* [2023] EWFC 25, [2023] 2 FLR 955.
60 *Y v Z (Schedule 1)* [2024] EWFC 4, [2024] 1 FCR 894.
61 *A v V* [2022] EWHC 3501 (Fam).
62 *Re Z (Schedule One: Legal Costs Funding order; Interim financial provision)* [2020] EWFC 80, [2021] 2 FLR 727.
63 *R v F (Schedule One; Child Maintenance: Mother's Costs of Contact Proceedings)* [2011] 2 FLR 991.
64 *UD v DN (Schedule 1, Children Act 1989: Capital Provision)* [2021] EWCA Civ 1947, [2022] Fam 289, [2022] 2 WLR 1047, [2022] 2 FLR 308.
65 *Phillips v Peace* [1996] 2 FLR 230, [1996] 2 FCR 237.
66 *Phillips v Peace* [1996] 2 FLR 230, [1996] 2 FCR 237.

CHAPTER 12

Child Maintenance in Non-CSA Cases

Content at a glance:

INTRODUCTION

12.1 The child support legislation – and the associated formulae for determining the extent of any child maintenance obligation – will apply in the very large majority of cases [see **Chapter 3** for Child Support Act 1991 ('CSA 1991') cases dealt with by the Child Maintenance Service].

12.2 The family court has jurisdiction to determine an application for child maintenance:

- in cases that fall outside the jurisdiction of the CSA scheme (because, for example, either the parent with care or the non-resident parent lives abroad);
- where the parties have concluded a maintenance agreement [see **Chapter 3** at **3.15**];
- where the application relates to education or concerns a child with a disability [see **Chapter 13**];

- in so-called 'top up' cases where a maximum assessment is in force [see **Chapter 3** at **3.15**].

12.3 In the case of married parents, Matrimonial Causes Act 1973 ('MCA 1973'), s 23(1)(d)–(e) enables the court to make orders for periodical payments and secured periodical payments for a child's benefit in the context of the divorce or nullity proceedings or in proceedings for judicial separation. In the case of parents who are civil partners, equivalent provisions are contained in the Civil Partnership Act 2004 (CPA 2004), Sch 5, para 2(1)(d)–(e). These can be invoked within proceedings for the dissolution of the civil partnership, nullity or separation.

12.4 Where the child's parents were not married or civil partners, Children Act 1989 ('CA 1989'), s 15 and Sch 1, para 1 provide a similar mechanism through which the court can make periodical payments orders for the benefit of children.

12.5 This chapter examines the approach of the family court to the assessment of child periodical payments under the MCA 1973 and the CPA 2004[1] and CA 1989, Sch 1. The jurisdiction to make such orders is dealt with in **Chapter 4**. The detailed procedural requirements for bringing a claim are considered in **Chapter 5**. Applications for capital payments for housing and otherwise are addressed in **Chapters 10 and 11**.

12.6 Whilst the jurisdictional frameworks under MCA 1973 (and CPA 2004) and CA 1989 are different, the approach of the court to determining applications under each of those statutes is similar. The overarching theme that unites applications determined outside of the CSA 1991 scheme is that the court has a broad *discretion* both in terms of whether or not to make an order, and the quantum of the order, and that the key criterion is 'reasonableness'.

12.7 This is considerable overlap in the principles applied by the court in cases which involve the children of married parents and unmarried parents. The court approaches all such applications in a similar way, namely by examining competing budgets and determining what it is 'reasonable' for the payer to pay, having regard in particular to affordability, need and lifestyle factors.

12.8 Irrespective of which Act the application is brought under, an important consideration for the court is ensuring that the maintenance order is for the benefit of *the child* and not 'back door' financial provision for the parent.

12.9 This said, as will be seen in this chapter the case law which has developed in CA 1989, Sch 1 cases (where a parent has no ability to claim spousal maintenance) demonstrates that the courts are prepared to take a broad

1 CPA 2004, Sch 5, paras 20 and 21 set out the matters to which the court is required to have regard on an application for financial remedies under the Act; they essentially replicate the provisions of MCA 1973, s 25.

view as to the concept of maintenance 'for the benefit of a child'. This may include costs associated with being a carer for the child (sometimes referred to as 'carer's allowance') that go beyond that which most people would consider strictly referrable to the child themselves.

12.10 For this reason, in the authors' experience proposed budgets in CA 1989, Sch 1 applications are often more extensive than the 'children's budget' element of a matrimonial or civil partnership claim. Such budgets may be crafted to reflect additional costs indirectly associated with bringing up a child in a lifestyle that bears some resemblance to that of the other parent.

MARRIED PARENTS AND CIVIL PARTNERS – POWER TO MAKE ORDERS UNDER THE MATRIMONIAL CAUSES ACT 1973 AND THE CIVIL PARTNERSHIP ACT 2004

12.11 Section 23 of the MCA 1973(1) provides:

> **Matrimonial Causes Act 1973, s 23**
>
> '(1) On making a divorce, nullity of marriage or judicial separation order or at any time after making such an order (whether, in the case of a divorce or nullity of marriage order, before or after the order is made final), the court may make any one or more of the following orders, that is to say …
>
> …
>
> (d) an order that a party to the marriage shall make to such person as may be specified in the order for the benefit of a child of the family, or to such a child, such periodical payments, for such term, as may be so specified;
>
> (e) an order that a party to the marriage shall secure to such person as may be so specified for the benefit of such a child, or to such a child, to the satisfaction of the court, such periodical payments, for such term, as may be so specified …'.

The same power exists under CPA 2004, Sch 5, para 2(1)(d) and (e).

12.12 It should be noted that under the MCA 1973 and CPA 2004, where child periodical payments (and lump sums for children) are concerned, the court also has the power to make orders:

- *before* the making of the order for divorce/nullity/judicial separation or the order for dissolution of the civil partnership/nullity/separation (MCA 1973, s 23(2)(a); CPA 2004, Sch 5, para 1(2)(a)); and

- following a *dismissal* of such an application after the beginning of the trial either forthwith or within a 'reasonable period' after the dismissal (MCA 1973, s 23(2)(b); CPA 2004, Sch 5, para 1(2)(b)).

12.13 An order for child periodical payments/secured periodical payments under MCA 1973 and CPA 2004 can be made in favour of either:

(i) 'such person as may be specified in the order' (in theory the order could stipulate that the payments are made to a third party looking after the child and not to one of the divorcing couple); or

(ii) the child themselves.

In either case the order must be 'for the benefit' of a child who is 'a child of the family'. The expression 'child of the family' has a statutory definition[2]. It has been held that whether a child is a child of the family is an objective test: *Re A (Child of the family)*[3].

12.14 It is also possible to order payments to be made partly to the child directly and partly to the parent for the child's benefit[4].

PARENTS WHO ARE NOT MARRIED OR CIVIL PARTNERS – POWER TO MAKE ORDERS UNDER CHILDREN ACT 1989, SCH 1

12.15 The CA 1989, Sch 1, para 1 empowers the court to make, inter alia, child periodical payments orders and secured periodical payments orders for children (ie those under 18) on an application by their parent or guardian. The jurisdiction under CA 1989, Sch 1, para 1 extends, in cases where the parents are or were married or civil partners, to a child who is 'a child of the family': CA 1989, Sch 1, para 16(2) (see **12.13** above).

12.16 The CA 1989, Sch 1, para 2 enables applications for child periodical payments (but, interestingly, *not* for *secured* periodical payments) to be made directly against a parent by an adult child (ie a person aged over the age of 18), provided that:

(i) the applicant either is in or will be in education or training (including professional or vocational training) [see **Chapter 13**]; or

(ii) there are 'special circumstances' that apply (an example of special circumstances being the adult child's disability) [see **Chapter 13**].

2 See MCA 1973, s 52(1), CPA 2004, Sch 5, para 80(2) and CA 1989, s 105(1). These virtually identical statutory provisions are set out in **Chapter 5** at **5.23**.

3 [1998] 1 FLR 347; see also *D v D (Child of the Family)* (1981) 2 FLR 93.

4 *G v G (Periodical Payments: Jurisdiction to Vary)* [1998] Fam 1, [1997] 2 WLR 614, [1997] 1 FCR 441, [1997] 1 FLR 368, per Ward LJ.

By contrast with CA 1989, Sch 1, para 1, applications under para 2 cannot be made on the basis that the adult child concerned was 'a child of the family': CA 1989, Sch 1, para 16(2).

12.17 A child periodical payments order (and, in the case of orders in respect of children under the age of 18, *secured* periodical payments order) can be made against either one of the child's parents, or against *both* parents.

12.18 The distinction between 'non-resident parents' and 'parents with care' that applies in the case of the statutory scheme for CSA 1991 claims does not apply under CA 1989, Sch 1 (although, in practice, it is likely to be the parent with whom the child lives for most of the time that is the one making an application).

MARRIED PARENTS AND CIVIL PARTNERS – STATUTORY FACTORS TO BE APPLIED WHEN THE COURT DECIDES WHETHER OR NOT TO MAKE AN ORDER

12.19 In deciding whether or not to exercise its discretion to make financial orders for the benefit of a child of the family, the court must give *first* consideration to the welfare while a minor, of any child of the family who has not attained the age of 18 (MCA 1973, s 25(1); CPA 2004, Sch 5, para 20).

12.20 First (as opposed to paramount) consideration means that the court must consider the welfare of the child before any other relevant matter and that the welfare of the child will be more important than any other single factor, but the child's welfare can still be outweighed by a combination of other relevant factors[5].

12.21 As well as the requirement to consider 'all the circumstances', MCA 1973, s 25 requires the court to have regard in particular to:

(i) certain factors in the standard checklists of factors contained in MCA 1973, s 25(2) (married parents) and CPA 2004, Sch 5, para 21(2) (civil partners); the full checklists apply when financial claims are made by spouses or civil partners in their own right;

(ii) the additional checklist of factors contained in MCA 1973, s 25(3) and CPA 2004, Sch 5, para 22(2) which apply in relation to claims for provision in relation to a child; and

(iii) where a child of the family is not the child of the party against whom an order may be made, the further factors contained in MCA 1973, s 25(4) and CPA 2004, Sch 5, para 22(3).

5 See *N v N (Consent Order: Variation)* [1993] 2 FLR 868, per Roche LJ.

Matrimonial Causes Act 1973, s 25(2) standard checklist applicable in children cases

'(2) … the court shall in particular have regard to the following matters—

(a) the income, earning capacity, property and other financial resources which each of the parties to the marriage has or is likely to have in the foreseeable future, including in the case of earning capacity any increase in that capacity which it would in the opinion of the court be reasonable to expect a party to the marriage to take steps to acquire;

(b) the financial needs, obligations and responsibilities which each of the parties to the marriage has or is likely to have in the foreseeable future;

(c) the standard of living enjoyed by the family before the breakdown of the marriage;

…

(e) any physical or mental disability of either of the parties to the marriage;

…'

These provisions are replicated in CPA 2004, Sch 5, para 21. MCA 1973, s 25(3)(e) (see below) and CPA 2004, Sch 5, para 22(3)(e) specify those matters within the standard checklist to which court must have particular regard when dealing with a claim for financial provision for a child.

Matrimonial Causes Act 1973, s 25(3) additional checklist in children cases

'(3) As regards the exercise of the powers of the court under section 23(1)(d), (e) or (f), (2) or (4), 24 or 24A above in relation to a child of the family, the court shall in particular have regard to the following matters—

(a) the financial needs of the child;

(b) the income, earning capacity (if any), property and other financial resources of the child;

> (c) any physical or mental disability of the child;
>
> (d) the manner in which he was being and in which the parties to the marriage expected him to be educated or trained;
>
> (e) the considerations mentioned in relation to the parties to the marriage in paragraphs (a), (b), (c) and (e) of subsection (2) above.'

These provisions are essentially replicated in CPA 2004, Sch 5, para 22(2).

> **Matrimonial Causes Act 1973, s 25(4) further checklist where 'child of the family' is not child of the party**
>
> '(4) As regards the exercise of the powers of the court under section 23(1)(d), (e) or (f), (2) or (4), 24 or 24A above against a party to a marriage in favour of a child of the family who is not the child of that party, the court shall also have regard—
>
> (a) to whether that party assumed any responsibility for the child's maintenance, and, if so, to the extent to which, and the basis upon which, that party assumed such responsibility and to the length of time for which that party discharged such responsibility;
>
> (b) to whether in assuming and discharging such responsibility that party did so knowing that the child was not his or her own;
>
> (c) to the liability of any other person to maintain the child.'

These provisions are essentially replicated in CPA 2004, Sch 5, para 22(3).

PARENTS WHO ARE NOT MARRIED OR CIVIL PARTNERS – PRINCIPLES APPLIED WHEN THE COURT DECIDES WHETHER OR NOT TO MAKE AN ORDER

12.22 In deciding whether to exercise its powers and, if so, in what manner CA 1989, Sch 1, para 4 requires the court to have regard to 'all the circumstances' of the case including a list of specified factors.

Children Act 1989, Sch 1, para 4(1)

> 'In deciding whether to exercise its powers under paragraph 1 or 2, and if so in what manner, the court shall have regard to all the circumstances including—
>
> (a) the income, earning capacity, property and other financial resources which [any parent, the applicant and any other person in whose favour the court proposes to make the order] has or is likely to have in the foreseeable future;
>
> (b) the financial needs, obligations and responsibilities which [any parent, the applicant and any other person in whose favour the court proposes to make the order] has or is likely to have in the foreseeable future;
>
> (c) the financial needs of the child;
>
> (d) the income, earning capacity (if any), property and other financial resources of the child;
>
> (e) any physical or mental disability of the child; and
>
> (f) the manner in which the child was being, or was expected to be, educated or trained.'

12.23 Whilst the 'welfare' of the subject child is not a factor specifically identified within the paragraph 4 checklist (and the paramountcy principle does not apply to orders for financial provision under CA 1989, Sch 1[6]), unsurprisingly the courts have approached applications under CA 1989, Sch 1 on the basis that the child's welfare is a very important consideration.

For example, in *Re P (a child) (financial provision)*[7] Thorpe LJ held that the child's welfare will be '… in the generality of cases, a constant influence on the discretionary outcome'.

12.24 The parties' 'standard of living', which is listed as a specific factor to which the court must have regard at MCA 1973, s 25(2)(c) and CPA 2004, Sch 5, para 21(2)(c) but does *not* feature in the checklist in CA 1989, Sch 1, para 4, is an important factor that the court will take into account when determining the fair level of child periodical payments, including in applications under CA 1989, Sch 1: *F v G (Child: Financial Provision)*[8].

6 Section 105(1) of the Children Act 1989 provides that the term 'upbringing', to which the paramountcy principle at s 1(1) of the Act applies, does not include applications for a child's maintenance.

7 [2003] EWCA Civ 837, [2003] 2 FCR 481, [2003] 2 FLR 865 at [44].

8 [2004] EWHC 1848 (Fam), [2005] 1 FLR 261.

EXERCISING DISCRETION

12.25 Whether determining child maintenance applications under CA 1989, Sch 1 or the MCA 1973/CPA 2004, the family court will carry out a discretionary balancing exercise in which it will consider 'all the circumstances of the case' paying particular regard to the relevant statutory checklists referred to above.

12.26 The exercise of the court's powers has been described as 'highly discretionary': *Re M-M (Schedule 1 Provision)*[9]. It involves '... an essentially broad-brush assessment to be taken by family judges with much expertise and experience in the specialist field of ancillary relief ...': *Re P (Child: Financial Provision)*[10]. The assessment must be 'fair, just and reasonable taking into account all the circumstances ...': *Re P (Child: Financial Provision)*[11].

12.27 The judgment of Thorpe LJ at [45]–[49] in *Re P (Child: Financial Provision)*[12] remains the leading authority as to the proper approach to determining an application under CA 1989, Sch 1.

Case summary: *Re P (Child: Financial Provision)*[13]

Facts:

The parents had an 'on/off' relationship for around four years and towards the end of the relationship M gave birth to their daughter. F described himself as 'fabulously rich'. M applied for financial provision for their child and at first instance the judge had awarded (inter alia) a sum of £450,000 for the purchase of a house (and £30,000 for its furnishings); £20,000 for a car to be replaced every four years at the F's expense; and periodical payments of £35,360 per annum. The judge accepted F's undertaking to meet the costs of the child's education. He also awarded £7,500 to compensate the M for the shortfall between the date of her application and the implementation of the order. M appealed on the basis that the award did not properly reflect the scale of F's wealth.

Held by the Court of Appeal:

The appeal was allowed and the award increased to: £1m for housing (with an additional £100,000 for furnishings); periodical payments of

9 [2014] EWCA Civ 276, [2014] 2 FCR 412, [2014] 2 FLR 1391, per McFarlane LJ at [33].
10 [2003] EWCA Civ 837, [2003] 2 FCR 481, [2003] 2 FLR 865, per Thorpe LJ at [43].
11 [2003] EWCA Civ 837, [2003] 2 FCR 481, [2003] 2 FLR 865, per Bodey J at [76](viii).
12 [2003] EWCA Civ 837, [2003] 2 FCR 481, [2003] 2 FLR 865.
13 [2003] EWCA Civ 837, [2003] 2 FCR 481, [2003] 2 FLR 865.

£70,000 pa; and backdated payments of £40,000 after giving credit for voluntary payments received.

Thorpe LJ held that, logically, the court will ordinarily start by determining the level/nature of any home that the respondent must provide for the child [see **Chapter 10**]. His Lordship observed that the court decision in respect of housing is likely to provide useful boundaries assisting the court to go on to determine the amount of any lump sum order [see **Chapter 11**] to be made for the child's benefit (which in most cases, he held, should include the cost of furnishing and equipping the home and the cost of a family car).

Once issues of housing and lump sum have been settled the court will be in much a better position to determine what budget the applicant will reasonably require to fund their expenditure in maintaining the home and its contents and in meeting other expenditure external to the home, such as school fees, holidays, routine travel expenses, entertainments, presents etc.

Thorpe LJ proposed a broad and practical approach to rival budgets produced by the parties and reminded practitioners that as periodical payments for children are variable:

> '… the court should discourage undue bickering over budgets. What is required is a broad commonsense assessment. What the court first ordains may have a comparatively brief life before a review is claimed by one or other party …'.

12.28 Although the judgment in *Re P (Child: Financial Provision)*[14] states that it is intended to apply in cases where '… one or both of the parents lie somewhere on the spectrum from affluent to fabulously rich'[15], as HHJ Hess observed in *SP v QR*[16] at [13] '… it does not follow from this … that awards cannot properly be made (if justified on the merits) against paying parents of more modest wealth, even where all or most of the available capital is needed to provide a home for a child'.

12.29 The following table summarises the provision for child periodical payments which have been made in some of the high net worth/ultra high net worth reported cases since *Re P*[17] was decided:

14 [2003] EWCA Civ 837, [2003] 2 FCR 481, [2003] 2 FLR 865.
15 Per Thorpe LJ at [45].
16 [2024] EWFC 57 (B).
17 [2003] EWCA Civ 837, [2003] 2 FCR 481, [2003] 2 FLR 865.

Case Name	Summary of payer's wealth	Award
Re A (A Child: Financial Provision)[18]	F was an extremely wealthy member of a Middle Eastern royal family and asserted the 'millionaire's defence' – ie giving only limited financial disclosure on the basis he accepted that he could afford to pay any order the court might reasonably make.	£204,000 pa in addition to the payment of school fees and a car allowance and additional costs referable to the upkeep of the home.
Hussein v Maktoum[19]	H was the ruler of the Emirate of Dubai and W was the sister of the King of Jordan. H adopted the 'millionaire's defence'.	£5,600,000 pa per child to the later of the end of tertiary education or four years after they have finished their degree (during this post tertiary education period the maintenance to be paid to the children directly), CPI index linked and secured by an HSBC Bank Guarantee in the sum of £290 million.
Collardeau-Fuchs v Fuchs[20]	The husband was a billionaire (there was some debate about the extent of his net worth but Mostyn J held (§13 of his judgment) that the result of the case '… does not differ depending on whether the husband is worth $700 million or $1 billion or $1.7 billion.'	£277,200 pa per child to completion of tertiary education, CPI index linked. (the wife also had her own *Duxbury* income of c £1.1m pa and in fact the overall household maintenance budget was set at £1.664m and the amount H was to pay – £550k pa in total – was the sum required to meet the shortfall between W's *Duxbury* fund and household needs).
Re Z (No 4) (Schedule 1 Award)[21]	F was an 'immensely wealthy' investment manager based in the USA. M previously worked in fashion and interior design. She lived in London with the child, who suffered from a rare genetic disorder and had significant care needs.	M was awarded £148,250 pa general maintenance plus £71,533 nanny cost (until age 9), school fees (including 1:1 support), health and medical insurance, interim rent and flight costs to the USA.

18 [2014] EWCA Civ 1577, [2015] 3 WLR 48, [2015] 2 FLR 625.
19 [2022] EWFC 94.
20 [2022] EWFC 135, [2023] 2 FLR 345.
21 [2023] EWFC 25, [2023] 2 FLR 955.

Y v Z[22]	F was a member of a Middle Eastern Royal family who relied upon the 'millionaire's defence'. M was a former professional equestrian.	F was ordered to pay a total of USD $500,000 pa for two children plus school fees, tuition and life insurance.
Lauryn Goodman v Kyle Walker[23]	F was a professional footballer with capital wealth of, broadly, £27m and income of £3.5–£5m net pa.	£150,000 pa in total for the two children in addition to school fees and reasonable extras and the costs of a nanny.

The 'Household Expenditure Child Support Award'

12.30

Case summary: *Collardeau-Fuchs v Fuchs*[24]

Facts:

H (aged 62) was of German origin and was a real estate investor who owned a substantial portfolio of prime Manhattan real estate. W was aged 47 and of French origin. They had married in 2012 and had two children aged six and four.

The husband's net worth totalled over $1bn and the standard of living during the marriage was extremely high with the family spending almost £5m each year.

Six weeks before their marriage the husband and wife had signed a prenuptial agreement (PNA) in accordance with New York law; it was later modified in March 2014. Under the PNA the parties created a separation of property regime, and W relinquished her claim to spousal maintenance on divorce. Both parties had been represented by experienced lawyers and W accepted the binding nature of the modified PNA, however the parties disagreed as to the correct interpretation of its terms or on the quantum of child maintenance that should be paid for the benefit of the children (W sought £1.3m per annum).

Held by Mostyn J:

At para 129 of his judgment[25] Mostyn J drew together the strands from earlier authorities and summarised the approach to be adopted

22 [2024] EWFC 4, [2024] 1 FCR 894.
23 [2024] EWFC 212 (B).
24 [2022] EWFC 135, [2023] 2 FLR 345.
25 [2022] EWFC 135, [2023] 2 FLR 345.

in quantifying the appropriate level of child maintenance as follows:

(a) when determining a child maintenance application, the welfare of the child must be a constant influence;

(b) a child maintenance award can extend beyond the **direct** expenses of the children. It can additionally meet the expenses of the mother's household, to the extent that the mother cannot cover, or contribute to, those expenses from her own means. Such an award might be referred to as a **Household Expenditure Child Support Award** ('a HECSA'). The essential principle is that **it is permissible to support the child by supporting the mother**;

(c) a HECSA cannot meet those expenses of the mother which are directly personal to her and have no reference to her role as carer of the child. An example might be a subscription to a nightclub. However, the award can meet the expenses of the mother which are personal to her provided that they are connected to her role as a carer. Examples given by Mostyn J were the provision of a car or designer clothing;

(d) the reasonable level of the mother's household expenses should be judged by reference not only to the present standard of living of the respondent but also, if applicable, to the standard of living enjoyed by the family prior to the breakdown of the relationship. The object of a HECSA is not to replicate either such standard, but to ensure that the child's circumstances 'bears some sort of relationship' to them. The standard of living in the parties' home prior to the breakdown of the relationship is 'as good a baseline' as any other;

(e) the HECSA must be set at such a level that the mother is not burdened by unnecessary financial anxiety;

(f) when assessing the mother's budget, the court should paint with a broad brush and not get bogged down in detailed analyses. Rather, the court should achieve a fair and realistic outcome by the application of broad common-sense to the overall circumstances of the particular case.

W was awarded child maintenance of £554,494 pa, the judge having assessed her HECSA at £1,664,810 pa of which she was able to contribute £1,110,316 pa from her own income to be derived from a *Duxbury* fund.

12.31 The guidance in *Re P* and subsequent cases was helpfully distilled by Peel J in *Y v Z (Schedule 1)*[26] as follows:

Key citation: *Y v Z (Schedule 1)*[27]

Peel J:

'[35] I have been referred to a number of authorities. From these I draw the following principles:

i) The main orders which Schedule 1 entitles me to make are:

a. Settlement of property …

b. Lump sum or sums …

c. Child maintenance (secured or unsecured).

ii) Each such order, by the wording of the statute must be "for the benefit of the child", or made direct to the child (which will be very rare).

iii) The court shall have regard to the matters set out at para 4 of Schedule 1 in the exercise of its discretion.

iv) Although para 4 does not expressly refer to the welfare of the child, in the generality of cases welfare will be a constant influence on the discretionary outcome; *Re P*[28].

v) Nor does para 4 refer expressly to standard of living, although in my judgment that is likely to be a highly material factor in many cases, particularly those which fall into the so-called "big money" category.

vi) In *Al Maktoum* (supra)[29] at para 91, Moor J suggested that "… the children should be able to have a lifestyle that is not entirely out of kilter with that enjoyed by them in Dubai and that enjoyed by [the father] and his family". In *Collardeau-Fuchs v Fuchs*[30], Mostyn J observed that standard of living before breakdown of the relationship "… should not however be allowed to dominate the picture as there will be many children, particularly children dealt with under Sch 1, who will not have experienced a standard of living within a functioning relationship either because the liaison between the parents was very brief, or

26 [2024] EWFC 4, [2024] 1 FCR 894.
27 [2024] EWFC 4, [2024] 1 FCR 894.
28 [2003] EWCA Civ 837, [2003] 2 FCR 481, [2003] 2 FLR 865 at para 44.
29 [2021] EWFC 94, [2022] 2 FLR 1185.
30 [2022] EWFC 135, [2023] 2 FLR 345 at para 119.

because the child was born after the relationship had come to an end". In my judgment the relevance of the standard of living during the relationship, and the standard of living of each party after the end of the relationship, will vary from case to case, and, as was said at para 21 of *Re A*[31], will have to be seen in context.

vii) The court will ordinarily determine the claims in sequence as to (a) property, (b) lump sum or sums, and (c) child maintenance; *Re P* (supra) at para 45.

viii) The court deals with property first because, as stated at para 22 of Re A (supra), "The nature of the child's home environment provides the obvious base line from which to consider commensurate levels of maintenance and is as good as any other".

ix) Child maintenance can be interpreted sufficiently broadly to include elements referable to the claimant in his/her capacity as the child's carer; *Re P* (supra) at paras 48–49. For many years this proposition, or concept, was known as the carer's allowance. More recently, at para 129 of *Fuchs* (supra) Mostyn J has suggested referring to it as a Household Expenditure Child Support Award [HECSA]. Whatever terminology is applied, the principle is clear, although its application is highly discretionary. It is not always easy to draw a bright line between budgetary items to which the claimant has no entitlement as being exclusively personal to him/her, and personal items which may reasonably be claimed as being necessary to discharge the carer's duties, including items which help sustain the carer's physical/emotional welfare; *Re P* (supra) at para 81. The court "... has to guard against unreasonable claims made on the child's behalf but with the disguised element of providing for the mother's benefit rather than for the child"; *J v C* (supra) at 159H.

x) The court should "not generally attach weight to the risk that the father may reduce or withdraw his support when the child comes of age (or ceases education or training) thereby obliging the child to adapt to a lower lifestyle at that time"; *Re P* (supra) at para 77 (iii).

xi) In general (and particularly in the bigger money cases), the court is entitled to paint with a broad brush and will not ordinarily need to descend into a line-by-line budgetary analysis; *Re P* (supra) at para 77(i) and *Fuchs* (supra) at para 129(f).

xi) Ultimately, "the overall result ... should be fair, just and reasonable taking into account all of the circumstances"; *Re P* (supra) at para 76(viii).'

31 [2014] EWCA Civ 1577, [2015] Fam 277, [2015] 3 WLR 48, [2015] 2 FLR 625.

RELEVANCE OF THE CMS FORMULA TO THE EXERCISE OF DISCRETION AS TO QUANTUM OF PERIODICAL PAYMENTS

12.32 Whilst the family court has a wide discretion, the amount a payer would have been required to pay if applying the CSA 1991 arithmetical formula to the payer's gross income (see **Chapter 3**) remains a relevant and informative consideration: *Re M-M (Schedule 1 Provision)*[32].

In *James v Seymour*[33] Mostyn J referred to the CMS formula as a 'useful starting point' where the payer has an income up to £650,000. He also observed that strict application of percentage-based formulae can lead to anomalous outcomes, which he illustrated as follows:

Key citation: *James v Seymour*[34]

Mostyn J:

> '[34] … While the [CMS] formula does make adjustments for the number of children, its primary driver is the percentage of F's adjusted gross income to be paid in child support maintenance. This leads to [anomalies]. The amount that would be payable under the formula where the father's income is £650,000 (and there is no shared care, and no other child living with him) is (when rounded to the nearest £1,000) £60,000 for a single child, £40,000 for each of two children, and £33,000 for each of three children. While it is true that there will be economies of scale where there is more than one child in a family unit, it is obvious, at least to me, that a single child does not cost anything like 50% more to rear than each of a pair of children, let alone 80% more than each of a trio of children.'

12.33 Such anomalies (and the potential for an unfair outcome with a strict application of an unadjusted CMS formula) had already been observed by Moor J in *CMX v EJX (French Marriage Contract)*[35] in which he had declined to apply the CMS formula.

12.34 In an effort to address perceived difficulties with a strict application of percentage-based formula, Mostyn J has developed an adjusted 'CMS' formula tabulated at the end of his judgment [see the Appendix 1 where the table is replicated]. Mostyn J's intention was to harness the simplicity of a formula whilst mitigating the risk of a formula producing an anomalous result.

32 [2014] EWCA Civ 276, [2014] 2 FCR 412, [2014] 2 FLR 1391.
33 [2023] EWHC 844 (Fam), [2023] 4 WLR 53, [2023] 2 FCR 582, [2024] 1 FLR 614.
34 [2023] EWHC 844 (Fam), [2023] 4 WLR 53, [2023] 2 FCR 582, [2024] 1 FLR 614 at para 34.
35 [2022] EWFC 136, [2023] 1 FCR 344, [2023] 2 FLR 14.

12.35 Mostyn J's approach of applying an adjusted formula was endorsed by Cobb J in *De Renée v Galbraith-Marten*[36].

Case summary: *De Renée v Galbraith-Marten*[37]

Facts:

At a final hearing before Mostyn J, F consented to an order for periodical payments on the basis of guidance he had been given by the judge in court as to the application of a formula based upon the CSA formula in cases which exceeded the CSA maximum. A few months later, Mostyn J decided *James v Seymour*[38] revising his previous guidance and held that it was appropriate to make certain adjustments to the CSA formula.

F applied to set aside the order.

Held by Cobb J:

The order was set aside on the basis that it would be unfair to hold F to his consent to an order based upon a guideline that was, unforeseeably, abandoned by Mostyn J very shortly thereafter by his later decision.

12.36 It is important to emphasise that the decision in *James v Seymour*[39], whilst providing important guidance, does not fetter the court's wide discretion as to the amount which it ultimately considers fair and reasonable.

12.37 In practice judges may be more willing to apply the *James v Seymour*[40] adjusted formula in cases where the payer's income is relatively modest and:

- it only slightly exceeds the maximum amount of income to which the CSA formula is applicable; or
- it would have by subject to the CSA formula but falls outside its jurisdiction as a result of one of the parties residing overseas.

12.38 In cases where the payer has a very high income judges may prefer to start from a clean sheet and a formulaic approach may be less attractive. Mostyn J observed in *James v Seymour*[41] that where the payer's income is over £650,000 gross pa the adjusted formula does not apply and the court will

36 [2023] EWFC 141, [2023] 3 FCR 738, [2024] 1 FLR 589.
37 [2023] EWFC 141, [2023] 3 FCR 738, [2024] 1 FLR 589.
38 [2023] EWHC 844 (Fam), [2023] 4 WLR 53, [2023] 2 FCR 582, [2024] 1 FLR 614 at para 34.
39 [2023] EWHC 844 (Fam), [2023] 4 WLR 53, [2023] 2 FCR 582, [2024] 1 FLR 614.
40 [2023] EWHC 844 (Fam), [2023] 4 WLR 53, [2023] 2 FCR 582, [2024] 1 FLR 614.
41 [2023] EWHC 844 (Fam), [2023] 4 WLR 53, [2023] 2 FCR 582, [2024] 1 FLR 614.

exercise its broad discretion considering the statutory checklist and all the circumstances of the case. The rationale for the £650,000 ceiling is not clear.

CAPITALISATION OF CHILD PERIODICAL PAYMENTS ORDERS

12.39 Although there is no 'clean break' provision when determining child periodical payments, the court does have the ability to capitalise child periodical payments by way of awarding a lump sum on an application to vary or discharge a child periodical payments order: CA 1989, Sch 1, para 5(3); MCA 1973, s 31(5); and CPA 2004, Sch 5, para 53[42].

12.40 Orders for capitalisation of child periodical payments will be rare. However, it may be a useful tool for cases involving unreliable or reluctant payers or where there has been protracted litigation and a number of applications to vary: see, for example, *AZ v FM (Capitalisation of Child Maintenance)*[43]; see also **Chapter 14** at **14.25** onwards.

Case summary: *AZ v FM (Capitalisation of Child Maintenance)*[44]

Facts:

The parties separated after a long marriage and thereafter engaged in lengthy and costly family court litigation as well as proceedings in the Chancery Division. After a final hearing in the family proceedings H was ordered to pay maintenance to W for the benefit of their child (then aged 19 and at university) at a rate of £1,700 per month until the end of tertiary education.

H moved abroad, remarried, did not pay consistently, and arrears built up necessitating enforcement proceedings. A few months later H applied to vary the maintenance. H's application to vary was refused and the court at first instance made an order capitalising child maintenance instead. H appealed.

Held by Mostyn J:

Under MCA 1973, s 31(5), where a variation application related to a periodical payments order made in favour of a child of the family, the court had the power to discharge the order and to order instead a commutation ('capitalisation') payment.

42 *MT v OT (Schedule 1 Order)* [2018] EWHC 868 (Fam), [2018] 3 FCR 621, [2019] 1 FLR 93.
43 [2021] EWFC 2, [2021] 2 FCR 729, [2021] 2 FLR 1371; see also *Re C (A Chid) (Financial Provision: Non-disclosure)* [2024] EWFC 115; see also **Chapter 14** at **14.25–14.28**.
44 [2021] EWFC 2, [2021] 2 FCR 729, [2021] 2 FLR 1371.

Where the court capitalised an order for child maintenance it would need a future change of circumstances of 'exceptional magnitude' before the court would later augment (eg by making a new order for child periodical payments or a further lump sum) what had been intended to be a one-off commutation payment. However, capitalisation of child maintenance will be 'a very rare bird indeed' given the risks and uncertainties inherent in capitalisation in most cases.

In the present case, the incessant litigation between the parents and the short term left to run on the maintenance order strongly militated in favour of capitalisation.

CHAPTER 13

Claims Arising from Education, Disability, Health and Special Circumstances

Content at a glance:

INTRODUCTION

13.1 This chapter considers applications for financial provision related to a child's education or a disability. Such issues are often relevant when the court is considering whether to make orders in favour of or for the benefit of adult children over the age of 18. The circumstances in which such claims can be made have been circumscribed by statute and case law. They are essentially limited to situations in which adult children remain in some form of education or training or there exist 'special circumstances'.

13.2 The principle that children are entitled to be maintained and educated but that, in the absence of disability or other special circumstances, they have no claim on their parents' resources after attaining their

independence pre-dates the Children Act 1989 ('CA 1989'). It was articulated in the successive cases of:

Chamberlain v Chamberlain
[1973] 1 WLR 1557

Lilford v Glynn
[1979] 1 WLR 78

Kiely v Kiely
[1988] 1 FLR 248

Key citation: *Kiely v Kiely*[1]

Booth J:

> 'I agree with the submission of Mr Gordon that the provisions of the 1973 Act make it clear that the statutory scheme is to enable the court to make proper financial provision for children as children or dependants.
>
> This view is supported by dicta in a number of reported decisions: see, for example, *Chamberlain v Chamberlain*[2] per Lord Scarman LJ at p 38; *Lord Lilford v Glynn*[3] per Orr LJ at p 447.'

13.3 The historic authorities were referred to by Hale J in *J v C*[4], where she briefly traced the legislative history of CA 1989, Sch 1 and the Family Law Reform Act 1987 ('FLRA 1987'), its near-identical predecessor. She stated that:

Key citation: *J v C*[5]

Hale J:

> '[FLRA 1987] implemented two Law Commission reports on illegitimacy. The object of those reports was to remove the difference in

1 *Kiely v Kiely* [1988] 1 FLR 248 at 252.
2 [1974] 1 All ER 33.
3 [1979] 1 All ER 441.
4 *J v C (Child: Financial Provision)* [1999] 1 FLR 152 at 155.
5 *J v C (Child: Financial Provision)* [1999] 1 FLR 152 at 155.

> legal positions of children. The underlying principle was that children should not suffer just because their parents had, for whatever reason, not been married to one another. Equally of course they should not get more. There is a long line of authority, beginning with *Chamberlain v Chamberlain*[6], and continuing with *Lilford (Lord) v Glynn*[7] and *Kiely v Kiely*[8], that children are entitled to provision during their dependency and for their educations, but they are not entitled to a settlement beyond that, unless there are exceptional circumstances such as a disability, however rich their parents may be'.

13.4 In *T v S*[9] Johnson J reaffirmed the principle that support for children extends to the end of their minority or education, but in the absence of disability or other special circumstances, not beyond that. More recently, the principle has been re-emphasised by the Court of Appeal in *UD v DN*[10] (see para **13.34** below).

SCHEDULE 1 OF THE CHILDREN ACT 1989

13.5 The court's powers under CA 1989 to make orders for financial provision for children are contained in CA 1989, Sch 1, paras 1 and 2.

13.6 The CA 1989, Sch 1, para 1 sets out the court's power to make a range of orders including periodical payments, secured periodical payments, lump sums, settlement of property orders and transfer of property orders. Paragraph 1(5)(a) suggests that the court's powers to make orders under this provision are generally restricted to children under the age of 18. In the case of orders for periodical payments and secured periodical payments, this is reinforced by the terms of paragraph 3[11].

13.7 The CA 1989, Sch 1, para 2 contains the court's power to make orders for financial provision in favour of a person over the age 18. The court has power to make a periodical payments order[12] or a lump sum order[13] against that person's parents provided that:

- the child is or will be (or would be if an order were made) receiving instruction at an education establishment or undergoing training

6 [1973] 1 WLR 1557.
7 [1979] 1 WLR 78, (1978) FLR 427.
8 [1988] 1 FLR 248.
9 *T v S (Financial Provision for Children)* [1994] 1 FCR 743, [1994] 2 FLR 883.
10 *UD v DN (Schedule 1, Children Act 1989; Capital Provision)* [2021] EWCA Civ 1947, [2022] Fam 289, [2022] 2 FLR 308.
11 See **13.8** below.
12 CA 1989, Sch 1, para 2(2)(a).
13 CA 1989, Sch 1, para 2(2)(b).

for a trade, profession or vocation, whether or not while in gainful employment, or

- there are special circumstances which justify the making of an order.

13.8 The CA 1989, Sch 1, para 3 deals with the *duration* of orders for periodical payments and secured periodical payments made pursuant to para 1. In the first instance such orders should not extend beyond the child's 17th birthday 'unless the court thinks it right in the circumstances of the case to specify a later date'[14]. The court is in any event enjoined from extending periodical payments orders beyond a child's 18th birthday[15], subject to exceptions[16] where:

- the child is or will be (or would be if an order were made) receiving instruction at an education establishment or undergoing training for a trade, profession or vocation, whether or not while in gainful employment; or
- there are special circumstances which justify the making of an order.

13.9 For the purposes of CA 1989, Sch 1, paras 2 and 3, 'special circumstances' may include any physical or other disability of the child or young person: *C v F*[17] and *T v S*[18].

MATRIMONIAL CAUSES ACT 1973 AND CIVIL PARTNERSHIP ACT 2004

13.10 The Matrimonial Causes Act 1973 ('MCA 1973') contains similar provisions to those in CA 1989, Sch 1 in relation to the circumstances in which a court can make financial provision for a child beyond the age of 18 including the potential to do so where 'special circumstances' are present. The case law and guidance in relation to MCA 1973 is thus relevant to applications under CA 1989, Sch 1 and vice versa. Equivalent provisions are also contained in the Civil Partnership Act 2004 ('CPA 2004'), Sch 5.

13.11 Section 29 of the MCA 1973 sets out the restrictions upon making an order for financial provision for a child beyond that child's 18th birthday:

Matrimonial Causes Act 1973, s 29

> **'Duration of continuing financial provision orders in favour of children, and age limit on making certain orders in their favour.**

14 CA 1989, Sch 1, para 3(1)(a).
15 CA 1989, Sch 1, para 3(1)(b).
16 CA 1989, Sch 1, para 3(2).
17 *C v F (Disabled Child: Maintenance Orders)* [1999] 1 FCR 39, [1998] 2 FLR 1.
18 *T v S (Financial Provision for Children)* [1994] 1 FCR 743, [1994] 2 FLR 883.

> (1) **Subject to subsection (3) below, no financial provision order** and no order for a transfer of property under section 24(1)(a) above **shall be made in favour of a child who has attained the age of eighteen**.
>
> (2) **The term** to be specified in a periodical payments or secured periodical payments order in favour of a child may begin with the date of the making of an application for the order in question or any later date or a date ascertained in accordance with subsection (5) or (6) below but—
>
> (a) **shall not in the first instance extend beyond the date of the birthday of the child next following his attaining the upper limit of the compulsory school age** … unless the court considers that in the circumstances of the case the welfare of the child requires that it should extend to a later date; and
>
> (b) **shall not in any event, subject to subsection (3) below, extend beyond the date of the child's eighteenth birthday**.
>
> (3) Subsection (1) above, and paragraph (b) of subsection (2), shall not apply in the case of a child, if it appears to the court that—
>
> (a) **the child is, or will be**, or if an order were made without complying with either or both of those provisions would be, **receiving instruction at an educational establishment or undergoing training for a trade, profession or vocation**, whether or not he is also, or will also be, in gainful employment; **or**
>
> (b) **there are special circumstances** which justify the making of an order without complying with either or both of those provisions.'

Equivalent provisions are to be found in CPA 2004, Sch 5, paras 5, 9 and 49.

EDUCATION

13.12 Where parents are separated, a 'non-resident parent' will normally be expected to pay child maintenance to the 'resident parent' until the later of a child attaining 18 or finishing secondary education[19].

19 Child Support Act 1991, s 1.

13.13 The provisions of the Child Support Act 1991 ('CSA 1991') mean that, absent exceptions, the court does not have the power to make orders for periodical payments for a child unless the parent against whom an order has been made is the subject of a 'maximum assessment' by the Child Maintenance Service ('CMS'), which requires that parent to have a gross income of at least £156,000[20]. One exception is contained in CSA 1991, s 8(7).

Child Support Act 1991, s 8(7)

> 'This section shall not prevent a court from exercising any power which it has to make a maintenance order in relation to a child if—
>
> (a) the child is, will be or (if the order were to be made) would be receiving instruction at an educational establishment or undergoing training for a trade, profession or vocation (whether or not while in gainful employment); and
>
> (b) the order is made solely for the purposes of requiring the person making or securing the making of periodical payments fixed by the order to meet some or all of the expenses incurred in connection with the provision of the instruction or training.'

13.14 Periodical payments orders can be made to meet the costs of a child's education, whether or not the court's more general power to order child maintenance is precluded by CSA 1991. The terms of CSA 1991, s 8(7) are relatively wide. In addition to enabling the court to make orders for the payment of any fees charged by an educational establishment (eg school fees), the subsection permits orders which relate to expenses incurred 'in connection' with the child's instruction or training. This could include:

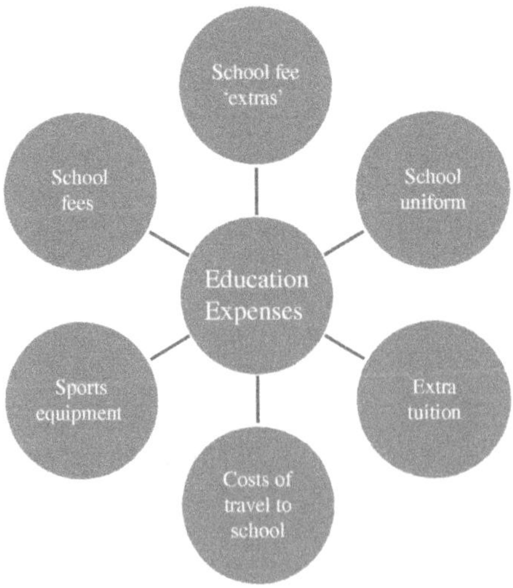

20 See **Chapter 3** for cases dealt with by the CMS.

13.15 For the purposes of CSA 1991, s 8(7) any instruction must take place at 'an educational establishment'. Section 55(3) of the CSA 1991 states that a 'recognised educational establishment' means an establishment recognised by the Secretary of State for the purposes of the section as being, or as comparable to, a university, college or school. There is no authority defining 'educational establishment' for these purposes, but the term could give rise to anomalies:

- an educational pre-school nursery would be covered, but possibly not a day-care nursery;
- a private childminder would not be covered;
- tuition by a private tutor may not be covered unless the tuition is 'in connection with' the education provided by the child's school. Conversely, tuition provided by a language centre would be covered;
- music lessons at school would be covered but private music lessons outside school may not be.

13.16 It is not uncommon for there to be disputes between parties in respect of the educational establishment a child should attend. Parties might disagree about whether a private education or state education is most appropriate, or whether the child should attend one school over another. The decision as to which school a child should attend will usually be a welfare based decision and very often it will be necessary for a party to apply for a specific issue order to deal with schooling under CA 1989, s 8; such an application may be dealt with prior to or in conjunction with the financial application.

13.17 In *James v Seymour*[21] Mostyn J factored the payer's responsibility for paying school fees into his so-called Adjusted Formular Methodology ('AFM') which was held by him to apply in cases where the paying party has a gross income which exceeds £156,000 and which, for that reason fall outside the jurisdiction of the CMS. By contrast, for cases which fall within the CMS's remit, the CMS will establish the paying parent's gross income, deduct the amount paid into any pension savings and then work out, from the number of nights the child stays with the paying parent, how much should be paid each week; in general, no account is taken of school fees being paid although boarding fees may be taken into account in part (see **Chapter 3** at **3.42**).

13.18 In the absence of agreement between the parents, the court has the power to make financial orders for the maintenance of an adult child during

21 *James v Seymour* [2023] EWHC 844 (Fam). This case is considered in more detail in **Chapter 12** at **12.32–12.38**.

the period of that person's tertiary education (including training for a trade, profession or vocation). Orders can be made in relation to the following:

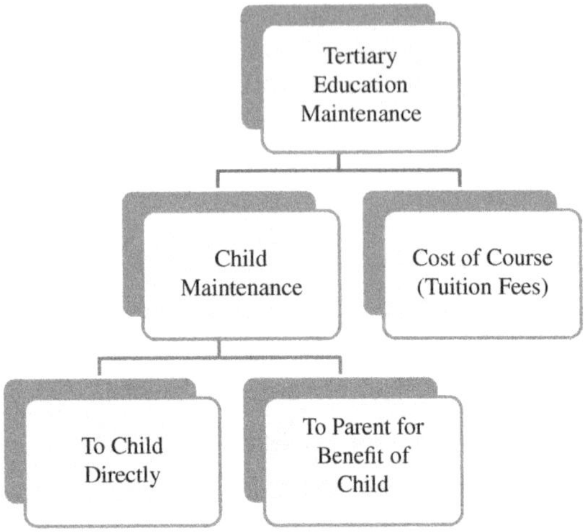

13.19 Where a parent is expected to continue to provide a child with a home while the child is at university it is common for a maintenance order to apportion the overall sum for maintenance between the parent and the child. For example, a maintenance order might state that from the date of commencement by the child of tertiary education, the maintenance will be divided as to X% which will be paid to the parent and Y% which will be paid to the child. The sum to be paid to the parent with whom a child lives outside term time is sometimes referred to as a 'roofing allowance'.

13.20 There is no authority providing guidance as to the percentage of maintenance to be paid directly to a child upon commencement of tertiary education. Typically, this varies between one third and two thirds, although in some cases all of it may be paid to the child whilst in others the whole sum may continue to be paid to the child's parent. Often these arrangements are enshrined in orders which are made years before a child actually attends university. Practitioners should, in those circumstances, bear in mind that:

- the actual costs of university attendance will be unknown at that stage (tuition fees are likely to increase and the cost of renting accommodation will be unknown);
- allocating a large proportion of the maintenance to be paid to the child directly may cause economic hardship to the caring parent if the majority of the maintenance is used to meet fixed outgoings such as housing costs;
- conversely, if the amount of maintenance to be paid directly to the child is too small, this may be insufficient to cover the child's accommodation and other costs at university;

- where the amount of child maintenance is very large, allocating a fixed percentage to be paid to the child directly will result in the child receiving a very large income whilst a student which the parents may regard as inappropriate.

13.21 Whether a court will order maintenance for an adult child will ultimately depend upon the specific circumstances of the family. For example, if a younger sibling was about to attend university – the court would consider the context of the family and whether provision had been made for the child's older siblings or whether they had been expected to 'pay their way'. All relevant circumstances will be taken into account including the financial resources and needs of the parents. When practitioners are considering the question of maintenance for tertiary education which will not occur for a number of years, it may be preferable to defer the issue until it becomes relevant or at least record that the question may be reviewed at the relevant time.

13.22 If the child maintenance has been paid under a CMS assessment then the rules[22] specify that the maintenance is paid until the child is 16 years of age, or until 20 if the child continues in full time education to the end of 'A' levels or the equivalent. This means that once the adult child has finished 'A' levels, the child maintenance ends. Some parents do agree provisions for child maintenance that provide for university, frequently set out as being maintenance to the age of 18 or the child completing their first (undergraduate) degree whichever shall be the later – sometimes with provision for a gap year[23]. Given that there is jurisdiction under CA 1989, Sch 1 for payments to be made while a child is 'undergoing training for a trade, profession or vocation'[24] then arguably maintenance could also cover a period when the child was undergoing post-graduate vocational training.

13.23 While a gap year does not itself constitute full time education or training, it is open to parties to agree that payments should continue while the gap year is undertaken – as in reality it will often represent a necessary (and uncontroversial) transition period between secondary and tertiary education during which the child in question may be unlikely to earn their own income sufficient to be self-supporting. If the gap year is spent doing an internship (ie 'training' for a future career) it might be arguable that it constitutes training for a trade or profession, whereas a gap year spent travelling or working in a shop is unlikely to fit within that definition. If the parents do not agree about funding for a gap year, the authorities suggest that maintenance during a gap year before or after tertiary education may be permissible: see *Re N*[25],

22 Child Benefit (General) Regulations 2006, regs 2–7.

23 See **13.23** below.

24 See **13.7** above.

25 *Re N (Payments for Benefit of Child)* [2009] EWHC 11, [2009] 1 WLR 1621, [2009] 1 FCR 606, [2009] 1 FLR 1442.

following *A v A*[26] and *Phillips v Peace*[27]. The rationale appears to be that during a gap year the child remains in education or training, which has not ceased.

13.24 In *Re N (Payments for Benefit of Child)*[28], Munby J considered the appropriate term for the termination of a trust holding a property provided to house a child and which was to revert to the father.

Case Summary: Re N (Payments for Benefit of Child)[29]

Facts:

M applied for financial provision in respect of the parties' child. A district judge made various orders including an order requiring F to settle on M the sum of £220,000 to be used to purchase a home of the child until he attained the age of 21 or completed full time tertiary education, *whichever was the later.*

Following a convoluted process, the case came to be considered in the High Court by Munby J who reviewed various earlier authorities in which different views had been expressed as to the time when a settlement of property should come to an end.

Held by Munby J:

There is a long-established general principle that, absent 'special' or 'exceptional' circumstances, children are not entitled to financial provision except during their dependency or for their education.

In the absence of 'special' or 'exceptional' circumstances, a child's dependency ceases when they attain their majority. Accordingly, any capital settlement should be expressed as terminating upon the child attaining the age of 18 or completing tertiary education (para 78).

It will often be appropriate also to allow for the child to have a gap year either before or after they have concluded their first degree course (para 81).

The evidence must establish any special circumstances relied upon. It is not sufficient for the court to have regard to the fact that increasing numbers of adult children continue to live at home rent-free with their parents (para 79).

26 *A v A (A Minor: Financial Provision)* [1995] 1 FCR 309, [1994] 1 FLR 657.
27 *Phillips v Peace* [1996] 2 FCR 237, [1996] 2 FLR 230.
28 *Re N (Payments for Benefit of Child)* [2009] EWHC 11, [2009] 1 WLR 1621, [2009] 1 FCR 606, [2009] 1 FLR 1442.
29 *Re N (Payments for Benefit of Child)* [2009] EWHC 11, [2009] 1 WLR 1621, [2009] 1 FCR 606, [2009] 1 FLR 1442.

DISABILITY AND HEALTH

13.25 A further exception to the statutory restriction under CSA 1991 against the court making maintenance orders for children[30] is contained in CSA 1991, s 8(8).

> **Child Support Act 1991, s 8(8)**
>
> This section shall not prevent a court from exercising any power which it has to make a maintenance order in relation to a child if—
>
> (a) an allowance under Part 4 of the Welfare Reform Act 2012 (personal independence payment) or a disability living allowance is paid to or in respect of him; or
>
> (b) no such allowance is paid but he is disabled,
>
> and the order is made solely for the purpose of requiring the person making or securing the making of periodical payments fixed by the order to meet some or all of any expenses attributable to the child's disability.

13.26 Section 8(9) of CSA 1991 contains a definition of the term 'disabled' for these purposes.

> **Child Support Act 1991, s 8(9): meaning of 'disabled'**
>
> For the purposes of subsection (8), a child is disabled if he is blind, deaf or dumb or is substantially and permanently handicapped by illness, injury, mental disorder or congenital deformity or such other disability as may be prescribed.

13.27 In *C v F (Disabled Child: Maintenance Orders)*[31] the Court of Appeal held that although the focus of CSA 1991, s 8(8) was upon expenses attributable to the child's disability, the court should take such expenses into account 'in the broadest sense'. By way of example, such expenses could include:

30 See **Chapter 3** for maintenance dealt with by the CMS.

31 *C v F (Disabled Child: Maintenance Orders)* [1999] 1 FCR 39, [1998] 2 FLR 1.

13.28 On an application for periodical payments in respect of a disabled child the court is required, when exercising its discretion, to have regard to the list of factors set out in CA 1989, Sch 1, para 4, although these criteria and the normal exercise of discretion are circumscribed by CSA 1991, s 8(8)[32]. Nevertheless, in *C v F (Disabled Child: Maintenance Orders)*[33], Butler-Sloss LJ suggested that in some cases the restricted terms of CSA 1991, s 8(8) would make little difference to the court's determination.

Key citations: *C v F (Disabled Child: Maintenance Orders)*[34]

Butler-Sloss LJ:

> 'The magistrates were entirely right to focus upon the expenses attributable to the child's disability. Having said that, it seems to me that it is implicit in any periodical payments application that the court will have to exercise its discretion after considering all the relevant circumstances of each individual case. That consideration will inevitably focus upon the income and assets of the parents, both applicants and potential providers, their respective obligations and

32 *C v F (Disabled Child: Maintenance Orders)* [1999] 1 FCR 39, [1998] 2 FLR 1.
33 *C v F (Disabled Child: Maintenance Orders)* [1999] 1 FCR 39, [1998] 2 FLR 1.
34 *C v F (Disabled Child: Maintenance Orders)* [1999] 1 FCR 39, [1998] 2 FLR 1.

> financial commitments, in addition to the needs of the child, the degree of disability of the child and any income or allowances paid to the child.'
>
> …
>
> 'In reality I am not sure that in the case of a child under a severe disability in respect of whom a long-term order is sought, there would be a great deal of difference in most cases between the approach provided for in the relevant subparagraphs of para 4 of Sch 1 and in s 8(8).'

13.29 There are various statutory provisions[35] which make clear that the court has jurisdiction to make orders for financial provision in respect of adult children where there exist 'special circumstances'. These can undoubtedly include health issues or disability. Such jurisdiction exists despite the definition of 'child' under CSA 1991, s 55 which prevents maintenance assessments being made under that Act in respect of adult children beyond the age of 19[36].

13.30

Key citations: *C v F (Disabled Child: Maintenance Orders)*[37]

Thorpe LJ:

> '… Thus I conclude that whether the application is by a parent in relation to a child or whether the application is by a person over the age of 18, the court's jurisdiction, provided there are special circumstances, may extend until terminated by either the death of the payer or the payee.'

Butler-Sloss LJ:

> '… There is indisputably jurisdiction in the Children Act to extend indefinitely a periodical payments order for the benefit of someone over the age of 19. It is part of the philosophy of the Children Act that a young person … with a total dependence upon others for the rest of his life should look for continuing financial support from his parents for whatever period may be necessary'.

35 CA 1989, Sch 1, para 2(1)(b); MCA 1973, s 29(3)(b).
36 *C v F (Disabled Child: Maintenance Orders)* [1999] 1 FCR 39, [1998] 2 FLR 1.
37 *C v F (Disabled Child: Maintenance Orders)* [1999] 1 FCR 39, [1998] 2 FLR 1.

SPECIAL CIRCUMSTANCES APART FROM DISABILITY

13.31 In the absence of 'special circumstances', orders for financial provision generally come to an end, at the latest, when a child attains their majority or completes tertiary education. Thus, any capital settlement under CA 1989, Sch 1 should be expressed as terminating when the child attains 18 or completes tertiary education[38].

13.32 Apart from in cases where a child has a disability, the courts have generally rejected applications for financial provision to extend beyond a child's 18th birthday on the ground of 'special circumstances'.

13.33 As well as being 'special' or 'exceptional' the circumstances should relate to the children[39].

Key citations: *T v S (Financial Provision for Children)*[40]

Johnson J:

> 'Whilst I do not think that the category of "special circumstances" should be necessarily always so limited, it does seem to me that in its reference to special circumstances in relation to the duration of periodical payments, Parliament was intending the court ordinarily to look at special circumstances related to the children – such, for example, as some physical or other handicap.'

13.34 Examples of circumstances which have been held not to qualify as 'special' for these purposes include:

- the tendency of adult children to remain living at home[41];
- the extreme wealth of the father[42];
- the possibility that the child might not inherit upon the father's death[43];
- seeking to protect children from financial pressure that may emanate from the father's prospective behaviour[44].

38 *C v F (Disabled Child: Maintenance Orders)* [1999] 1 FCR 39, [1998] 2 FLR 1.
39 *UD v DN (Schedule 1, Children Act 1989; Capital Provision)* [2021] EWCA Civ 1947, [2022] Fam 289, [2022] 2 FLR 308.
40 *T v S (Financial Provision for Children)* [1994] 2 FLR 883.
41 *Re N (Payments for Benefit of Child)* [2009] EWHC 11, [2009] 1 WLR 1621, [2009] 1 FCR 606, [2009] 1 FLR 1442.
42 *MT v OT (Financial Provision: Costs)* [2007] EWHC 838 (Fam), [2008] 2 FLR 1311.
43 *MT v OT (Financial Provision: Costs)* [2007] EWHC 838 (Fam), [2008] 2 FLR 1311.
44 *UD v DN (Schedule 1, Children Act 1989; Capital Provision)* [2021] EWCA Civ 1947, [2022] Fam 289, [2022] 2 FLR 308.

UD v DN

13.35 The Court of Appeal in *UD v DN*[45] considered the question of 'special circumstances' in the context of an application for outright capital provision to be made for children. The decision is significant both in terms of the legal principles it analyses and the practical impact it has for family practitioners specialising in this area.

13.36

Case Summary: *UD v DN (Schedule 1, Children Act 1989; Capital Provision)*[46]

Facts:

The parties had three children: DD (22), TD (19) and GD (14). M and the children moved from Russia to the UK in 2010. They lived in a home valued at c £10 million. F made plans for DD's financial future, giving him £607k to purchase a property in London.

In 2018, M issued proceedings under CA 1989, Sch 1.

Williams J made an order which required F to settle the London home and its contents in a trust for the benefit of TD and GD. The trust was to end on the first to occur of various events, including GD turning 18, or six months after GD completed full-time tertiary education. TD was aged 17 on the date of the application and 19 when the order was made. He also made an order for H to provide outright capital to the children when the trust came to an end.

F appealed. He argued that the court did not have jurisdiction to make a settlement of property order in favour of an adult child and that it was wrong to make orders for outright capital.

Held by the Court of Appeal:

Appeal allowed in part.

On an application by a parent, the court has jurisdiction to make a settlement of property order in respect of a child who was over 18 provided that the *application* had been made before they reached that age. [NB: it remains an unresolved question whether the jurisdiction exists if the parent does not make the application until after the child has turned 18.]

45 *UD v DN (Schedule 1, Children Act 1989; Capital Provision)* [2021] EWCA Civ 1947, [2022] Fam 289, [2022] 2 FLR 308.

46 *UD v DN (Schedule 1, Children Act 1989; Capital Provision)* [2021] EWCA Civ 1947, [2022] Fam 289, [2022] 2 FLR 308.

> In the absence of special circumstances, the court should not make orders for outright capital in favour of a child. Such circumstances had to relate to the child and to a consequent continuing financial need which extended into adulthood.
>
> In this case, the court had been wrong to make orders for outright capital to benefit the children when they were adults on the basis that that F might otherwise use his financial muscle to impose some form of 'financial ultimatum' on the children. F's previous physical and psychological abuse of the children and their vulnerability to being manipulated by F did not create a financial need which amounted to a special circumstance.

13.37 Following *UD v DN*[47] in assessing whether the facts of a particular case give rise to 'special circumstances' the focus must be upon a child's ongoing dependency rather than their vulnerability. Practitioners should note the following points in particular:

- in order to satisfy the court that a child has a relevant 'dependency' it is probably necessary to demonstrate some continuing and quantifiable *financial* need;
- the conduct of the paying party (in and of itself) has no role to play;
- the effects of domestic abuse are only relevant to the extent that they have created an ongoing dependency and/or financial need;
- the level of wealth of the parents will be relevant to quantum once the discretionary exercise has been engaged, but it is not (in and of itself) to be treated as an 'exceptional circumstance' for the purpose of justifying an order being made in respect of an adult child.

13.38 Whilst vulnerability and dependency are likely to overlap, they are different concepts. The former is much broader than the latter. Not everyone with a vulnerability is 'dependent' in the sense of requiring financial support. The parameters of CA 1989, Sch 1 would be stretched too far if every adult with a vulnerability could make a claim for financial provision against their parents.

47 *UD v DN (Schedule 1, Children Act 1989; Capital Provision)* [2021] EWCA Civ 1947, [2022] Fam 289, [2022] 2 FLR 308.

Key citation: *UD v DN (Schedule 1, Children Act 1989; Capital Provision)*[48]

Moylan LJ:

> 'The Judge sought … to support his decision to award the children an interest in the family home by interpreting the use of the word "dependency" in the authorities as connoting "some form of vulnerability or need continuing from childhood into adulthood which can be remedied by capital provision". In my view, this does not support his decision because it is far too broadly expressed a proposition and one which does not accurately reflect the effect of the long line of decisions dating back to *Chamberlain v Chamberlain*.'

13.39 Despite the decision in *UD v DN*[49], it may be difficult in some cases to distinguish a dependency from a vulnerability. Arguably most vulnerabilities can be ameliorated with financial support (eg to provide for medical care, therapeutic support or housing) and therefore create a dependency. *UD v DN*[50] shows that practitioners should be cautious before coming to the conclusion that even children who are very vulnerable will satisfy the 'special circumstances' test.

13.40 In cases involving serious abuse, practitioners should consider whether the children have a freestanding cause of action against the perpetrator of the abuse as an alternative to claiming outright capital under CA 1989, Sch 1.

13.41 In *TK v LK*[51] DHCJ Nicholas Allan KC considered whether the facts of the case gave rise to special circumstances in the light of *UD v DN*[52].

48 *UD v DN (Schedule 1, Children Act 1989; Capital Provision)* [2021] EWCA Civ 1947, [2022] Fam 289, [2022] 2 FLR 308.
49 *UD v DN (Schedule 1, Children Act 1989; Capital Provision)* [2021] EWCA Civ 1947, [2022] Fam 289, [2022] 2 FLR 308.
50 *UD v DN (Schedule 1, Children Act 1989; Capital Provision)* [2021] EWCA Civ 1947, [2022] Fam 289, [2022] 2 FLR 308.
51 *TK v LK* [2024] EWFC 71.
52 *UD v DN (Schedule 1, Children Act 1989; Capital Provision)* [2021] EWCA Civ 1947, [2022] Fam 289, [2022] 2 FLR 308.

Case Summary: *TK v LK*[53]

Facts:

M, who was serving a substantial sentence of imprisonment, had engaged in very serious abuse towards the child. She abducted the child to another country, made false allegations of serious sexual abuse against F and alienated the child from F.

Within care proceedings, a judge had found that M had undertaken 'the most sustained conduct of improper parental influence and manipulation I have seen for some time. It is an extreme example' which had 'very real consequences [for the child]'.

Following those proceedings, M committed a very serious offence against the child, for which she received a lengthy prison sentence. The child was diagnosed with PTSD and required ongoing psychiatric support and therapy.

Held by DHCJ Nicholas Allen KC:

Whilst 'dependent' children may well also be 'vulnerable', dependency in my view implies some continuing and quantifiable financial need. Vulnerability is a broad spectrum on which many people fall, but not everyone with a vulnerability is 'dependent' in the sense of requiring financial support (para 87).

The conduct of the paying party to the question of long-term financial provision is relevant solely to the extent it creates an ongoing dependency and/or financial need (para 88).

In this case, the effect on the child of M's abusive conduct was such that they could be considered a long-term dependant of F well beyond their minority. Accordingly, the 'special circumstances' test was satisfied.

53 *TK v LK* [2024] EWFC 71.

CHAPTER 14

Variation

Content at a glance:

INTRODUCTION

14.1 This chapter addresses the powers available to the court to vary orders making financial provision to or for the benefit of the child. The main focus of the chapter is on applications made pursuant to the Children Act 1989 ('CA 1989'), Sch 1. The same essential principles apply when the court is considering equivalent variation applications under the Matrimonial Causes Act 1973 ('MCA 1973') and the Civil Partnership Act 2004 ('CPA 2004'), even though they are subject to different statutory regimes. The chapter also considers the ability of the court to vary provisions for housing for a child and the scope for the Child Maintenance Service ('CMS') to revise its maintenance assessments (although the role of the CMS in dealing with child maintenance is dealt with more fully in **Chapter 3**).

14.2 A 'variation' or change to the level or duration of the maintenance payment order might happen:

- Automatically because it was provided for in the original order
- As a new order because a variation application is made and the court changes the amount or duration of the earlier order

Practitioners need to be cautious before issuing variation proceedings as these can sometimes become as complex and expensive as the proceedings which led to the original order.

14.3 The following table summarises the key principles on a variation application. These are considered in more detail below.

What financial orders can be varied?	Orders for child maintenance can be varied. The court can not only vary the amount (upwards or downwards) but it can also dismiss the order or change the length of the order.
What factors does the court consider on variation?	The court will consider all the circumstances of the case *including* any change in the matters to which the court was required to have regard when the original order was made.
Relevance of welfare	In MCA 1973 and CPA 2004 cases the welfare of the child is the court's 'first consideration'. In cases under CA 1989, Sch 1, welfare is not mentioned as a relevant consideration in the statute, but it has been held to be a factor of great importance[1].
Is a change of circumstances needed?	No, but any change of personal and financial factors since the original order was made may have great importance and without any material change a variation application may be difficult to pursue.

THE STATUTORY PROVISIONS

14.4 The CA 1989, Sch 1, paras 1 and 2 contain the various powers of the court to make financial orders in respect of children. CA 1989, Sch 1, para 1(4) and (5) provide the power for variation in relation to periodical payments and secured periodical payments:

1 See **14.11** below.

Children Act 1989, Sch 1, para 1(4) and (5)

(4) An order under sub-paragraph (2)(a) [*periodical payments*] or (b) [secured *periodical payments*] may be varied or discharged by a subsequent order made on the application of any person by or to whom payments were required to be made under the previous order.

(5) Where a court makes an order under this paragraph—

(a) it may at any time make a *further* such order under sub-paragraph (2)(a), (b) or (c) with respect to the child concerned if he has not reached the age of eighteen;

(b) it may not make more than one order under sub-paragraph (2)(d) [*settlement of property*] or (e) [*transfer of property*] against the same person in respect of the same child.

14.5 The CA 1989, Sch 1, para 6 provides that in exercising its powers under paras 1 or 2 to vary or discharge an order for the making or securing of periodical payments the court shall have regard to all the circumstances of the case, including any change in any of the matters to which the court was required to have when making the order. It also sets out other relevant matters:

Children Act 1989, Sch 1, para 6

(1) … the court shall have regard to **all the circumstances of the case, including any change in any of the matters to which the court was required to have regard when making the order**.

(2) The power of the court … **shall include power to suspend any provision of the order temporarily and to revive any provision so suspended**.

(3) Where … the court varies the payments …, **the court may provide that the payments as so varied shall be made from such date as the court may specify,** except that, subject to sub-paragraph (9), the date shall not be earlier than the date of the making of the application.

(4) An application for the variation of an order made under paragraph 1 … may, if the child has reached the age of sixteen, be made by the child himself.

(5) Where an order … under paragraph 1 ceases to have effect on the date on which the child reaches the age of sixteen, or at any time after that date but before or on the date on which he reaches the age of eighteen, the child may apply to the court which made the order for an order for its revival.

(6) If on such an application it appears to the court that—

(a) the child is, will be or … would be receiving [education or training]; or

(b) there are special circumstances which justify the making of an order …,

the court shall have power by order to revive the order from such date as the court may specify, not being earlier than the date of the making of the application.

(7) Any order which is revived … may be varied or discharged under that provision …

(8) An order for the making or securing of periodical payments made under paragraph 1 may be varied or discharged, after the death of either parent, on the application of a guardian or special guardian of the child concerned.

(9) [Powers of variation in CMS cases]

14.6 In considering 'all the circumstances of the case' the court will have regard to all the matters set out in CA 1989, Sch 1, para 4:

- the income, earning capacity, property and other financial resources which each person has or is likely to have in the foreseeable future
- the financial needs, obligations and responsibilities which each person has or is likely to have in the foreseeable future
- the financial needs of the child
- the income, earning capacity (if any), property and other financial resources of the child
- any physical or mental disability of the child
- the manner in which the child was being, or was expected to be, educated or trained

14.7 The CA 1989, Sch 1, para 6(1) requires the court to have regard specifically to any change in any of the circumstances to which the court was required to have regard when making the original order.

14.8 Equivalent provisions in matrimonial cases are set out in MCA 1973, s 31. This provides that in exercising its powers on a variation application, the court shall have regard to all the circumstances of the case, first consideration being given to the welfare while a minor of any child of the family who has not attained the age of 18. For the purposes of a variation application, the circumstances of the case include any change in any of the matters to which the court was required to have regard when making the order to which the application relates. This means that changes in the MCA 1973, s 25(2) factors since the order was made will be considered. The s 25 factors can be summarised as follows:

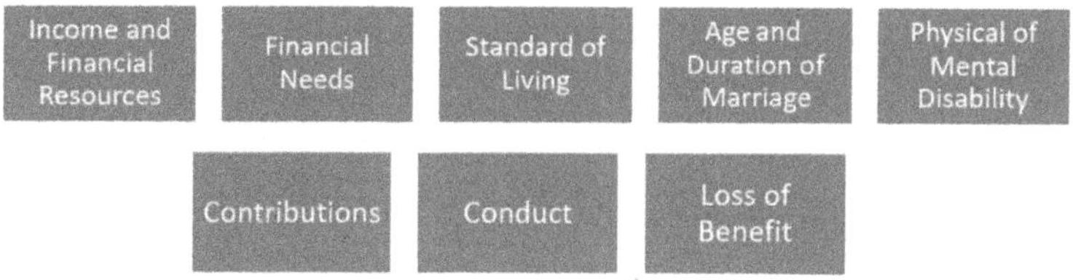

14.9 Under the Civil Partnership Act 2004 ('CPA 2004'), the relevant variation provisions are set out in CPA 2004, Sch 5, Part 11. As with the MCA 1973, the court must have regard to all the circumstances of the case, giving first consideration to the welfare of any child of the family who has not reached the age of 18 (CPA 2004, Sch 5, para 59(1)). The circumstances of the case on a variation application again include any change in any of the matters to which the court was required to have regard when making the original order (CPA 2004, s 59(2)) which are the same as those contained in MCA 1973, s 25 (corresponding provisions at CPA 2004, Sch 5, para 21(2)) – see **14.8** above.

14.10 Inevitably, on a variation application under any of the statutory regimes the primary focus of the court is likely to be on changes in relation to two circumstances in particular:

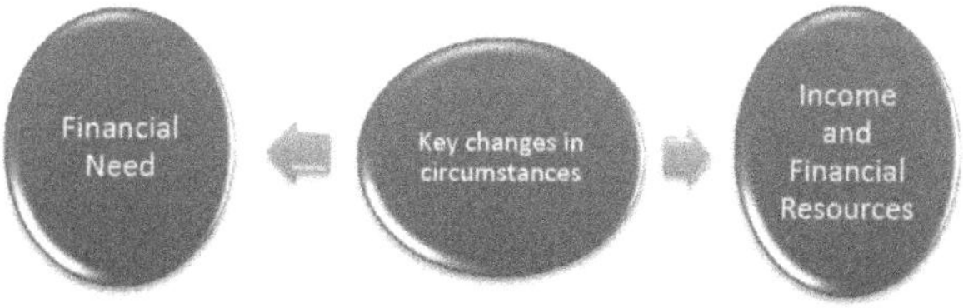

RELEVANCE OF WELFARE

14.11 When considering an application to vary an order for child maintenance under MCA 1973, CPA 2004 or CA 1989, Sch 1 the welfare of the child is a relevant consideration. For cases under the MCA 1973 and the CPA 2004, this principle that the child's welfare is the court's 'first consideration' is enshrined in statute: see MCA 1973, s 31(7) and CPA 2004, Sch 5, para 20. For cases under CA 1989, Sch 1 the principle that the child's welfare is a relevant consideration comes from case law.

14.12 In *J v C (Child: Financial Provision)*[2] Hale J held that whilst the welfare of the child is not specifically identified as a factor in CA 1989, Sch 1, para 4, it remains a relevant consideration.

Key citation: *J v C (Child: Financial Provision)*[3]

Hale J:

> 'Nevertheless, in cases under the Children Act 1989 the welfare of the child concerned, even if neither the paramount nor the first consideration, must be one of the relevant circumstances to be taken into account when assessing whether and how to order provision'.

In *Re P*[4], Thorpe LJ went further, holding that the child's welfare will be '... in the generality of cases, a constant influence on the discretionary outcome ...'.

CHANGE IN CIRCUMSTANCES

14.13 In theory, it is possible to apply for a variation of a child maintenance payment without showing that there has been a change in circumstance. In practice, however, without a change such an application would have little prospects of success; a court may treat it as an attempt to appeal the original order by the back door. Accordingly, applicants for a variation should set out each side's financial position when the original order was made and demonstrate why the position has changed materially. Variation applications do not involve an entirely 'de novo' examination; the focus will be upon what now is different.

2 *J v C (Child: Financial Provision)* [1998] 3 FCR 79, [1999] 1 FLR 152.
3 *J v C (Child: Financial Provision)* [1998] 3 FCR 79, [1999] 1 FLR 152.
4 *Re P (A child) (Financial Provision)* [2003] EWCA Civ 837, [2003] 2 FCR 481, [2003] 2 FLR 865.

14.14 A number of factors can be relied upon to demonstrate that the original order is no longer appropriate. The following diagram sets out some examples:

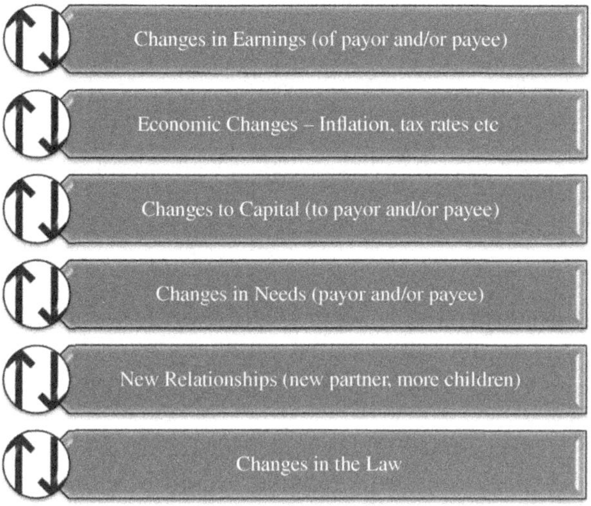

INDEXATION

14.15 Indexation orders provide for maintenance payments to vary automatically in line with inflation. The standard index of variation which features in the Financial Remedies Court ('FRC') precedent order is the Consumer Price Index ('CPI'). There is no rule of law which requires the CPI to be used in preference to the Retail Price Index ('RPI'). The CPI and the RPI each measure inflation by reference to different products. In some cases, for example where a substantial element of the maintenance is intended to cover housing costs such as the payment of a mortgage, it may be more appropriate for the RPI to be used. In cases where one of the parties lives in another jurisdiction it may be more appropriate for an overseas measure of indexation to be used.

14.16 The FRC standard precedent for an indexation clause is as follows:

> The periodical payments set out in paragraph [*para number*] [and paragraph [*para number*] above] shall be varied automatically on the 'variation date', which shall be on the date of the payment due in [*month*] and at yearly intervals afterwards. The change in the payments shall be the percentage [change] / [increase], if any, between the [consumer prices index] / [consumer prices index including owner occupiers' housing costs] for the month 15 months before the variation date (ie [*month*] in the first instance) and the [consumer prices index] / [consumer prices index including owner occupiers' housing costs] for the month 3 months before the variation date (ie [*month*] in the first instance).

14.17 Although it is common practice for periodical payments orders to contain an indexation clause, this will not necessarily be appropriate in every case. For example:

- the paying party's income may be static or decreasing;
- the payments may initially be set at a high level with an expectation of a reduction once the receiving party is able to increase their earnings.

Where, however, an order does not include an indexation clause, this may be relied upon in support of a variation application (as the original order will not have kept pace with changes in the cost of living).

COURT ORDERS AND THE CHILD MAINTENANCE SERVICE

14.18 The role of the Child Maintenance Service ('CMS') is considered in detail in **Chapter 3**.

14.19 When practitioners are negotiating orders for child maintenance it is important to consider the potential for a parent to make a future application to the CMS, despite the existence of the court order[5]. Such an application can be made any time from the date 12 months after the date of the court order. It is not possible to exclude the jurisdiction of the CMS beyond that. Unless the case falls within one of the exceptions contained in the Child Support Act 1991 ('CSA 1991') a CMS assessment will trump the court order and usually terminate it for all purposes.

14.20 Clauses are sometimes inserted into orders which are intended to prevent parties from making applications to the CMS and leave the payer's obligation within the court system. Save for cases under the MCA 1973 or CPA 2004 where orders can be made which combine periodical payments for the spouse or civil partner with the child maintenance[6], artificial attempts to oust the jurisdiction of the CMS are unlikely to be successful.

14.21 The circumstances in which the right to make an application to the CMS is likely to exist are set out in **Chapter 3**.

RELEVANCE OF CMS FORMULA TO VARIATION CASES

14.22 In *James v Seymour*[7] Mostyn J considered the principles to be applied to the determination of periodical payments in cases where the paying party

5 See **3.15** above.
6 These are known as '*Segal* Orders' and are discussed in **Chapter 3** at **3.15**; see also *Dorney-Kingdom v Dorney Kingdom* [2000] 3 FCR 20, [2000] 2 FLR 855.
7 *James v Seymour* [2023] EWHC 844 (Fam), [2023] 4 WLR 53, [2023] 2 FCR 582, [2024] 1 FLR 614. This case is considered in more detail in **Chapter 12** at **12.32**.

has a gross income in excess of £156,000 per annum[8]. Notwithstanding the broad statutory discretion, Mostyn J held that it was relevant to take account of an adjusted version of the CMS formula which applies in cases involving a paying party with income up to £156,000 pa. He termed this adjusted formula the Adjusted Formular Methodology ('AFM') and the result produced by an application of the AFM the Child Support Starting Point ('CSSP'). He held that, subject to exceptions, in cases involving income up to £650,000[9], the court should begin by applying the AFM to calculate the CSSP. The court should then go on to consider whether the CSSP required upward or downward adjustment. *James v Seymour*[10] is considered in more detail in **Chapter 12** at **12.32** onwards. A table summarising the methodology proposed by Mostyn J is included in Appendix 1.

14.23 Mostyn J held, however, that his approach involving the use of the AFM should not apply in variation cases. He emphasised instead the need to have regard to a change in circumstances since the original order was made, holding that the original order adjusted by inflation should normally be used as the CSSP.

Key citation: *James v Seymour*[11]

Mostyn J:

> '42. … The terms of [MCA 1973, s 31(7)], and of [CA 1989, Sch 1, para 6(1)], require identification of the changes of circumstances since the original order was made. This means that the value of the original order adjusted by inflation should normally be used as the CSSP.
>
> 45. This being a variation case the appropriate CSSP was the value of the current order adjusted by inflation …'

In other words, on a variation application the court should first adjust the original order to take account of inflation (in many cases this will have occurred automatically through the inclusion of an indexation clause). The court should then consider whether there is a justification to depart upwards or downwards from that adjusted figure.

8 In cases involving income below that level, the CMS generally has exclusive jurisdiction and the court does not have a role to play, although this is a simplification of the position. The role of the CMS is considered in detail in **Chapter 3**.

9 It is not clear why Mostyn J chose the figure of £650,000 as the upper limit for his adjusted formula. The same upper limit figure was identified by Mostyn J in *CB v KB* [2019] EWFC 78.

10 *James v Seymour* [2023] EWHC 844 (Fam), [2023] 4 WLR 53, [2023] 2 FCR 582, [2024] 1 FLR 614. This case is considered in more detail in **Chapter 12** at **12.32**.

11 *James v Seymour* [2023] EWHC 844 (Fam), [2023] 4 WLR 53, [2023] 2 FCR 582, [2024] 1 FLR 614. This case is considered in more detail in **Chapter 12** at **12.32**.

REASONS FOR AN INCREASE OR DECREASE OR TERMINATION OF CHILD MAINTENANCE

14.24 The list of reasons justifying an increase or decrease or termination of child maintenance is not closed. The following tables set out common examples of changes in circumstances relied upon.

Reasons for an increase	
Payer	**Recipient**
• Income gone up • Unexpected bonuses • Expenses reduced (eg the end of another obligation such as paying educational costs) • Household may have changed – for example a new relationship might mean that there are more resources for the household increasing what might be made available in payments • Decreased time with child • Change of residence so that child now living mainly with payee	• Loss of employment • Other income may have gone down • Costs may have increased (eg educational expenses) • Inflation has eroded the buying power of the original order • Increased time with the child • Change of residence so that child now living mainly with payee • Cessation of financial support from father of second child

Reasons for a Decrease or Termination	
Payer	**Recipient**
• Loss of job • Income has gone down • Income anticipated to go down • Paying additional expenses (eg school fees) • New family to support • Loss of partner's income supporting household • Spending increased time with the child • Change of residence so that child now living mainly with payor	• Return to work • Unreasonable refusal to work after period of adjustment • Promotion • Additional income or increased income • Inheritance • Unexpected windfall (eg lottery win) • Child at boarding school with decrease in household costs • Cohabitation • Financial support from father of second child • Change of residence to that child now living mainly with payor

CAPITALISATION

14.25 It not possible to achieve a 'clean break' in respect of child maintenance. Under MCA 1973, ss 25A and 31 and under CPA 2004, Sch 5, paras 23 and 53 the court has the power to dismiss claims for periodical payments by a spouse or civil partner and to direct that no such claims may in the future be brought. There is no equivalent power in relation to periodical payments for a child. It therefore remains open to a parent to make such a claim at any time (subject to the statutory restrictions upon the court dealing with applications in CMS cases). Similarly, under CA 1989, Sch 1, it is not possible to impose a clean break in relation to child maintenance.

14.26 There have been cases, however, in which the court has capitalised child maintenance by directing the payment of a single lump sum instead of ongoing periodical payments. Although for many years the jurisdiction to capitalise child maintenance had been doubted, it was held to exist by Mostyn J in *AZ v FM*[12]. Non-payment or failure to comply with a past award *can* be a ground to justify a capitalisation, although the jurisdiction will only rarely be exercised.

Key citation: *AZ v FM*[13]

Mostyn J:

> 'I am satisfied the jurisdiction [to capitalise an award of court-ordered child support] exists, and that in this case the trial judge was entitled to exercise it, it will remain a very rare bird indeed. … The combination of: (1) incessant litigation, on which the trial judge found the husband thrived, (2) repeated defaults on the part of the husband with the maintenance obligation, and (3) the age of the child and the relatively short period until the maintenance liability expired, all militated strongly in favour of a capitalisation and the ending of financial links between the parties. In the overwhelming majority of cases, however, the risks and uncertainties inherent in capitalisation will lead the court, where it has jurisdiction, to make, or continue, a traditional order for periodic payments … it seems to me that capitalisation could only properly be considered where [CSA 1991] could not apply, because, for example, one of the parents or the child is habitually resident overseas, or because the child is over 19.'

14.27 In *Re Z (No 5) (Enforcement)*[14] Cobb J made an order for capitalisation on the basis that:

- the father had, over a protracted period, shown himself unwilling to recognise the authority of the court, and had wilfully failed to submit to its orders;

12 [2021] EWFC 2, [2021] 2 FCR 729, [2021] 2 FLR 1371.
13 [2021] EWFC 2, [2021] 2 FCR 79, [2021] 2 FLR 1371.
14 [2024] EWFC 44, [2024] 2 FCR 901, [2024] 2 FLR 691.

- the father was resident abroad, and therefore out of reach of other enforcement strategies;
- the registration and enforcement process was likely to be a difficult and uncertain process in the USA.

The child had unusual and very particular health needs.

14.28 In *Re C (A Child) (Financial Provision: Non-Disclosure)*[15] Richard Harrison KC sitting as a Deputy High Court Judge made an order for capitalisation in circumstances where:

- the father had misled the court with false evidence;
- the father had failed to disclose his true financial position;
- the mother's requests for housing, maintenance, and child support were reasonable and necessary for the child's well-being;
- the court ordered the father to pay specific amounts for housing, debts, maintenance, and education costs;
- the father had been an erratic payer, had breached court orders, had previously failed to engage in the proceedings, had lied and taken steps to defeat the mother's claims, and was residing in a jurisdiction where enforcement would be difficult;
- this was accordingly a rare case in which it was appropriate to order that the future periodical payments and school fees should be commuted as a single lump sum to cover the period until the child attained the age of 18, with any surplus at that point to be used in respect of the father's maintenance obligations thereafter.

CHILD MAINTENANCE SERVICE

14.29 In the context of CMS cases the term 'variation' refers to varying the CMS's initial assessment to take account of additional income or resources of the paying party which may not have been factored into the calculation.

14.30 The CMS will take the information about the paying parent's income, which is used to calculate the amount of child maintenance to be paid, from records held by HMRC. Initially, therefore, this may only include 'earned' income (ie a salary, bonus, etc). If the paying parent is self-employed or receives dividends from a company/rental income from investment properties, this may not be taken into consideration in the initial child maintenance calculation.

15 [2024] EWFC 115.

14.31 In these circumstances, the parent receiving payments can ask the CMS for a 'variation', to take into account the paying parent's income from all sources, not just those that were included in the original calculation. To be successful in a variation application, the parent receiving payments will need to show that:

- the paying parent receives un-earned income of at least £2,500 per year (for example, rental income from properties, interest on investments, or dividends from companies)
- the paying parent is diverting their income – for example, if they have a company which is generating significant profits, but they aren't paying any of this to themselves
- the paying parent receives earned income which has not been taken into account
- the paying parent has assets apart from their primary residence in excess of £31,250 in respect of which they should be treated as having a deemed income by applying an interest rate of 8% to those assets

14.32 It is possible also for a paying parent to seek a 'variation' to take account of certain financial commitments which may not have featured in the original calculation. These are considered in **Chapter 3** at **3.43**.

14.33 Where there has been a relevant change in circumstances since a CMS assessment, it is possible for either parent to seek a 'review' or supersession of the original assessment. These applications are considered in **Chapter 3** at **3.47** and **3.51**.

14.34 If there has been a change in a child's living situation or contact arrangement since the child maintenance calculation was made, either parent can apply for a supersession, and this is likely to change the amount that should be paid. This is because the CMS takes into account how many nights (on average) per week the child stays with the paying parent, in calculating the amount of child maintenance due. There will only be a change to the child maintenance payable where there has been a change in the number of overnights the child spends with the paying parent. If the parents simply agree to swap days/nights but each retain responsibility for the child for the same number of overnights in total, there will be no change to the child maintenance payable.

14.35 If the paying parent has changed jobs or received a pay rise since the child maintenance calculation was made, this might need to be brought to the attention of the CMS. Generally, the CMS will update the child maintenance calculation on an annual basis. However, there are some situations in which the CMS will update the calculation mid-way through the year, if the paying parent's circumstances have changed significantly (by 25% or more).

14.36 The Child Support Maintenance Calculation Regulations 2012 state that the CMS must be notified of a change in income if it meets certain criteria. In addition to the annual review and the periodic income check, a paying parent or a person with care can inform the CMS of a change of income at any point – to do so is to request a 'supersession'. In some cases, a paying parent is required to inform the CMS of a change in income. If a child maintenance calculation is based on historic data from HMRC, a paying parent's current income must be at least 25% different from the HMRC historic figure for the maintenance calculation to be altered. The paying parent does not need to inform the CMS of income changes of less than 25%. The GOV.UK page on changes that need to be reported to the CMS sets out the changes parents must tell the CMS about, and whether to contact the service by phone or online[16].

What you need to report
Tell the Child Maintenance Service if: • you change who the child's main carer is • you change the agreement on how often the child stays overnight, either with the paying parent or a local authority, and this change to 'shared care' affects your child maintenance payments • you want to change how you make and get payments using Direct Pay or Collect and Pay • you move house (give your new address within 7 days of moving) • you change your bank details • you change your phone number • you want someone else to deal with your case for you • you add a child to your case • the child is being adopted by someone else • you want to close your case • the child no longer lives in the UK • someone on the case dies
There are extra things that need to be reported about the paying parent. Either parent can tell the Child Maintenance Service if the paying parent: • misses a payment when using Direct Pay • makes any voluntary payments on top of existing payments • has an income change of 25% or more, or no longer has an income • is spending more or less money in order to see the child, for example on transport costs
If your child is aged 16 to 19 • You must report certain information about your child's education after they turn 16

14.37 If the paying parent has not done this but the parent receiving payments is aware that one of these changes has taken place, they can inform the CMS of the change. The CMS will then update their calculation to take this into account.

16 See https://www.gov.uk/child-maintenance-service/change-of-circumstances.

Any change to the amount of maintenance the receiving parent receives may be backdated to the date when the paying parent's circumstances changed.

CMS: CHALLENGING AN ASSESSMENT

14.38 It is possible to challenge a CMS calculation in three main circumstances:

- if the information used in the child maintenance calculation is wrong;
- if circumstances have changed;
- if the full circumstances have not been taken into account.

14.39 The CMS has a standard way to calculate child maintenance. It is based on:

- how much the child's other parent earns;
- how many children they pay child maintenance for;
- whether the child stays overnight with their other parent;
- if there are any other children living with the child's other parent.

14.40 Either parent may want to challenge the calculation because:

- they believe the CMS has used the wrong information to calculate the child maintenance;
- either their or the child's other parent's circumstances have changed since the amount was calculated;
- they want other information about the other parent's income or circumstances taken into account.

14.41 The following table (which replicates the table at **3.41**) summarises the different processes that can be initiated to alter an assessment.

Action	When it is used
Revision (also known as Mandatory Reconsideration)	The amount was calculated using the wrong information. For example, where the CMS has: • made a mistake about the number of children the paying parent pays maintenance for; • used incorrect income figures; • not included all the days the parent receiving payments or the paying parent care for the child; • if the paying parent has not disclosed all their earnings.

Supersession	Either parent's circumstances have changed since the child maintenance was calculated. A new calculation may be needed because: • there has been a change in financial circumstances; • the contact or living arrangements for the child have changed; eg if the number of nights the child stays with the paying parent has changed.
Variation	The parent receiving payments wants additional information about the paying parent's finances to be taken into account: • the parent receiving payments believes the paying parent has income other than wages or self-employed earnings, or unearned income from capital worth over £2,500 a year; • the parent receiving payments wants other information or circumstances to be taken into account; • they can ask the CMS to look at the paying parent's income that may not have been included in the original CMS calculation; • CMS can be asked to take into account income or circumstances that it has not already considered; • the parent receiving payments believes that the paying parent's income is higher than they have declared to the CMS; • the parent receiving payments might suspect that the paying parent is using self-employment or payment by dividend to make their salary income look artificially low. The paying parent wants additional information about their financial commitments to be taken into account, including in relation to contact costs, costs relating to a disability, boarding school fees, certain debts and mortgage costs.
Appeal	The parent receiving payments wants to challenge a decision made by the CMS, such as a decision to refuse their request for a revision. A refusal to a request for a supersession or variation can also be appealed but a revision request must be made first.

VARIATION OF HOUSING PROVISION

14.42 Orders for the transfer of property or the settlement of property for the benefit of a child are generally framed on the basis that the property in question will revert to the paying party, at the latest, at a defined time (usually at the conclusion of the child's tertiary education)[17]. It is usual also to include in the order reference to other events which can trigger the reversion of the property to the paying party. One such catch-all trigger may be 'further order of the court'. Although these words might suggest that the court retains jurisdiction to revisit or vary the settlement, its ability to do so is in fact limited.

17 Under CA 1989, Sch 1 the court can only make orders in respect of housing for the benefit of a child. In cases under MCA 1973 and CPA 2004, applicants are entitled to make claims in respect of housing for their own benefit.

14.43 CA 1989, Sch 1 limits the number of orders that can be made against the same person in respect of the same child under CA 1989, para 1(2)(d) (settlement of property) or (e) (transfer of property) as pursuant to para 1(5)(b) 'it may not make more than one order under sub-paragraph (2)(d) or (e) against the same person in respect of the same child'.

14.44 In *Phillips v Peace (No 2)*[18] it was held that a court has no jurisdiction to make a further order in respect of housing in relation to the same child. The statutory limitation of making settlement of property orders could not be outflanked by seeking a lump sum order the purposes of which was to obtain further housing provision.

14.45 It is notable that the restriction in CA 1989, Sch 1 puts unmarried parents with care at a disadvantage compared to those who were previously married or subject to a civil partnership. In *MB v KB*[19] the court held it was permissible to use CA 1989, Sch 1 to make a settlement of property order, where a financial remedy order made within divorce proceedings between the same parents had included provision for housing. The justification for the decision was that the second order was being sought under a different statute.

14.46 Variations in form (rather than financial substance) are however possible. In *MT v OT (Schedule 1 Order)*[20], the court permitted an application to vary a settlement to provide for a replacement property to be purchased. The court rejected an argument that allowing the application violated the statutory prohibition upon making more than one order.

Key citation: *MT v OT (Schedule 1 Order)*[21]

Cohen J:

> '[19] … The replacement of one property by another does not amount to a new settlement of property. It is simply the substitution of one property for another.'

14.47 It should be noted that in *MT v OT (Schedule 1 Order)*[22] the court did not *increase or vary* the value/quantum available for housing generally. The mother accepted that the costs of the new purchase (eg SDLT) would come from the proceeds of sale of the prior one. Additional funds for removals and furnishing

18 [2004] EWHC 3180 (Fam), [2005] 1 WLR 3246, [2005] 2 FCR 265, [2005] 2 FLR 1212.
19 [2007] EWHC 789 (Fam), [2007] 2 FLR 586.
20 [2018] EWHC 868 (Fam), [2018] 3 FCR 621, [2018] 1 FLR 94.
21 [2018] EWHC 868 (Fam), [2018] 3 FCR 621, [2018] 1 FLR 94.
22 [2018] EWHC 868 (Fam), [2018] 3 FCR 621, [2018] 1 FLR 94.

were held to be lump sums orders *not* for a new home, but general expenses referable to the child's care.

14.48 The court's jurisdiction over any trust arrangements under which a home may be held does not cease when those arrangements are put in place; they are capable of variation.

Key citation: *G v A (Financial Remedy: Enforcement) (No 3)*[23]

Peter Jackson J:

> '[23] … I reject the submission that the jurisdiction of the family court ends when the trust deed is executed …'

And

> '[26] I find that the family court has not only the jurisdiction but the duty to consider any proper applications relating to the fulfilment of its order and to give whatever directions appear appropriate to give effect to it. Such directions may override the trust deed, which exists as an expression of the court's will and not as an obstruction to it.'

14.49 Thus, if implementation of the arrangements as originally provided for is frustrated, or it otherwise becomes necessary to vary them in order to give effect to the court's intention in making the order, the court can adjust them accordingly: *G v A (Financial Remedy: Enforcement) (No1)*[24].

14.50 In considering the terms of an order the court may expressly reserve powers of review and variation of the housing provision on future changes of circumstances (eg relocation); such an approach was adopted by Hayden J in *G v S (Children Act 1989 Schedule 1)*[25].

23 [2011] EWHC 2377 (Fam), [2012] 1 FLR 415 at para 23.
24 [2011] EWHC 2380 (Fam), [2012] 1 FLR 389 at para 67.
25 [2017] EWHC 365 (Fam), [2017] 2 FCR 307, [2017] 2 FLR 1207 at para 19.

CHAPTER 15

Enforcement and Injunctive Relief

Content at a glance:

INTRODUCTION

Scope of the chapter

15.1 This chapter will address the various domestic routes available to a litigant seeking to enforce orders making financial provision for children. This chapter can only give an overview of possible routes to enforce or to encourage compliance with orders, as a full discussion of enforcement would require an entire book. To that end, practitioners are referred to *1KBW on Enforcement in Financial Remedy Proceedings*[1] which, although focused on proceedings under the Matrimonial Causes Act 1973 ('MCA 1973'), contains a more in-depth discussion and analysis of many of the routes of enforcement discussed more summarily in this chapter.

15.2 Practitioners should also be aware of the potential to seek the recognition and enforcement of maintenance orders via the 2007 Hague Convention[2]. Full consideration of the Convention is beyond the scope of this

1 *1KBW on Enforcement in Financial Remedy Proceedings* (Bloomsbury Professional, 2023).
2 The Convention on the International Recovery of Child Support and Other Forms of Family Maintenance concluded on 23 November 2007 at The Hague.

book, although it is considered more fully in **Chapter 4** (see **4.53** to **4.63**). It does not create new enforcement remedies. It provides a procedure through which decisions about 'maintenance obligations arising from a parent-child relationship'[3] (amongst others) made in one Contracting State can be recognised and enforced in others, subject to the conditions in Article 20 being met and to limited exceptions to recognition and enforcement in Article 22. Chapter III of the Convention creates a procedural route through which applications can be transmitted via Central Authorities; it extends not only to applications for recognition and enforcement but also to modification applications.

15.3 This chapter only discusses the routes available *in court* to a litigant to enforce financial provision for children. However, in certain circumstances the court may not be the best route (or even a possible route) to enforcement. The obvious example is where the Child Maintenance Service (CMS) has issued a calculation for a parent's liability under the Child Support Act 1991[4]: any default by the payer under such a CMS calculation can only be enforced via the CMS itself, through its own internal enforcement mechanism.

15.4 Finally, this chapter will assume that any order making financial provision for a child has been made in the family court and as a result any reference to rules and/or procedure will be to the Family Procedure Rules 2010 (FPR 2010) unless otherwise indicated. That said, there may be instances where the court has made orders providing financially for a child in the county court[5]; in those circumstances the enforcement routes are confined to the county court and the application of the Civil Procedure Rules 1998 (CPR 1998). To a large extent the two courts and the two procedural regimes enable a similar enforcement process[6], but it is not always the case and care should be taken to ensure that the correct procedure is followed.

Structure of the chapter

15.5 This chapter will adopt the following structure and aim to provide an overview of the potential domestic enforcement routes available:

3 See Article 2(1)(a).

4 See **Chapter 3**.

5 See the brief discussion on claims under the Inheritance (Provision for Family and Dependents) Act 1975 in **Chapter 10**.

6 Eg, the FPR 2010 incorporate wholesale the provisions of the 'General Rules about Enforcement of Judgments and Orders' in CPR Part 70.

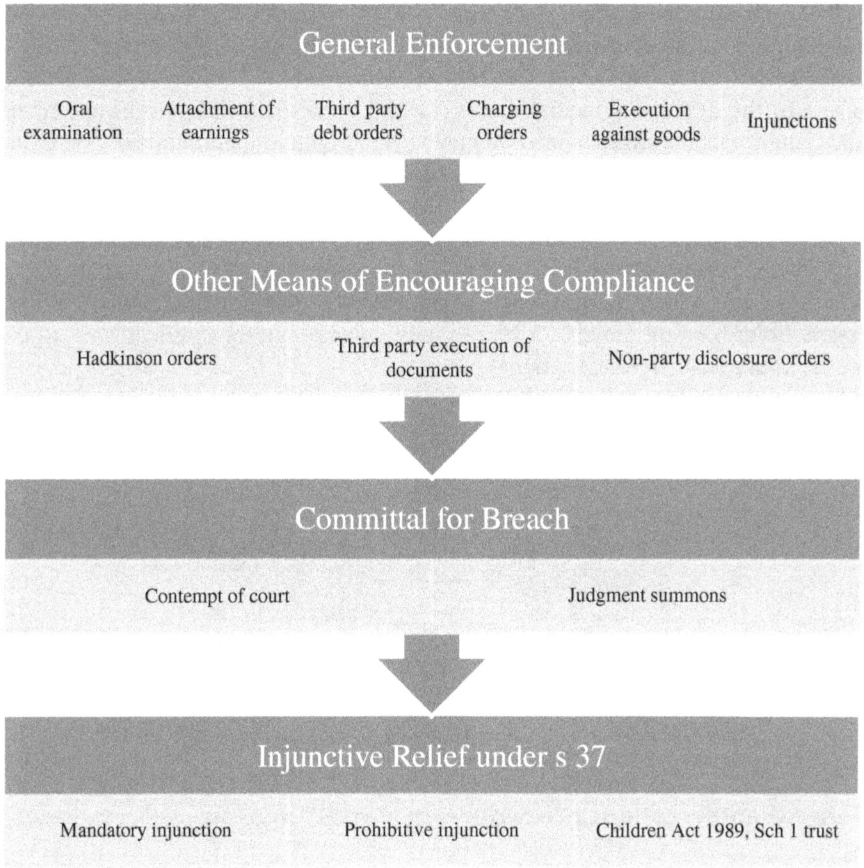

GENERAL ENFORCEMENT AND SPECIFIC REMEDIES

15.6 If a court has ordered a party (the debtor) **to pay money to another party**[7] (the creditor) for the benefit of a child, the creditor has a choice in deciding how to enforce any default under that order[8]:

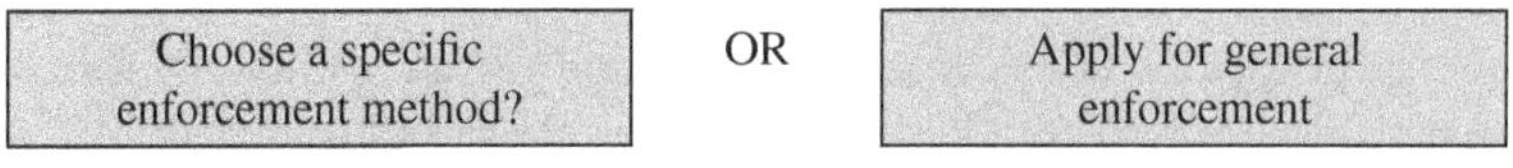

7 Practitioners should bear in mind the terms of the order which they are seeking to enforce. Eg, as is discussed in **15.38–15.46** below, a Children Act 1989, Sch 1 order for the settlement of property is not of itself an order 'for the payment of money' but an order to settle property. Of course, if the order follows the Standard Orders Template Order 2.2, it would almost always include a correlative lump sum order which *could* be enforced inter partes. There is further discussion on this topic in **Chapter 10**.

8 FPR 2010, r 33.3(2).

15.7 An application made for 'general enforcement'[9] is an application 'for such method of enforcement as the court may consider appropriate'[10]. This carries certain advantages, not least for a creditor who does not yet have a clear idea as to the debtor's financial resources and, thus, may prove to be the most expedient route of enforcement. That said, the temptation automatically to issue a general application without giving it further thought should be resisted, as there may well be a good reason not to apply via the general route. One such reason might be that the application for general enforcement is **on notice** to the other party, whereas it is permissible (and not uncommon) to make an application for a charging order and/or a third party debt order **without notice** and to obtain an interim order binding the debtor before they know about the application[11]. Such a course may have significant benefits.

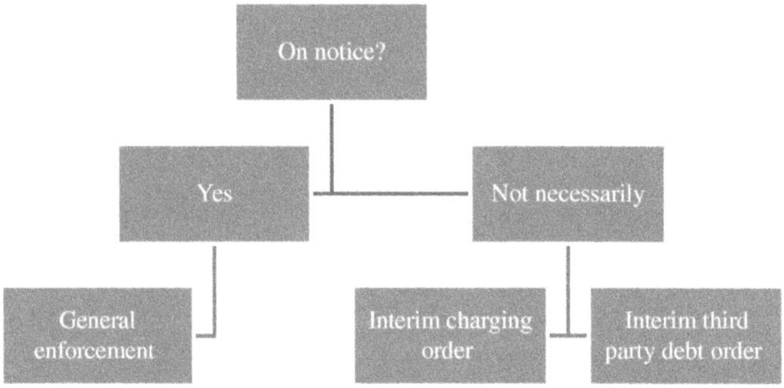

General enforcement procedure: oral examination

15.8 Nowadays it is far more common for a creditor to apply to enforce arrears under the 'general enforcement' method, not least because it does not require the applicant to specify the form of relief which they seek. However, that does not absolve the applicant creditor from an obligation to follow procedural rules relevant to a specific enforcement order[12] and it may be that the information provided in an application for general enforcement is not sufficient to enable a court automatically to make any order sought. So it is necessary to consider the points raised in the paragraphs below specific to each enforcement remedy. That said, the authors suggest that it may **not** be necessary to make separate applications for specific enforcement orders *alongside* an application for general enforcement; such a reading of FPR 2010, r 33.3(1) would seem to undermine the very purpose of the general enforcement route.

15.9 Having issued the application, the court will make an order requiring the debtor: (i) to attend court to be questioned about their means; and (ii) to produce

9 In Form D50K.
10 FPR 2010, r 33.3(2)(b).
11 See **15.15** and **15.19** below.
12 FPR 2010, r 33.3(1) qualifies Part 33 as applying 'except where a rule or practice direction applies'.

such documents as to their means as are in their control[13]; this is a parallel jurisdiction to the CPR 1998, Part 71 order to attend for 'Oral Examination'[14].

15.10 While the rules provide that the debtor will be questioned on oath by a court officer[15] the overwhelming likelihood in practice is that the family court will list a hearing *inter partes* before a judge, and whether the debtor will be questioned on oath (or permitted to be cross-examined) as to their means is often a question of whether the allocated listing time for the hearing allows it. The Standard Orders Template Order No 4.6 indicates the following directions will be issued by the court on receipt of a general enforcement application[16]:

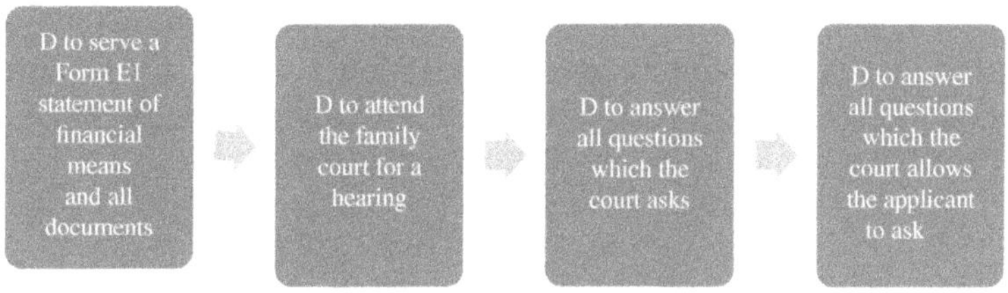

Attachment of earnings

15.11 An attachment of earnings order is an order directed to a debtor's employer, who must then make periodical deductions from the debtor's earnings and pay those amounts to the nominated collecting officer (the court), who forwards those payments to the creditor[17].

15.12 On its face this is a specific enforcement mechanism applicable only to a 'maintenance order' made by the High Court or the family court[18]. However, a 'maintenance order' is defined as including (emphasis added)[19]:

'An order for periodical **or other payments**'	Matrimonial Causes Act 1973

AND

'An order for periodical **or other payments**'	Children Act 1989, Sch 1

AND

'An order for periodical **or other payments**'	Civil Partnership Act 2004, Sch 5

13 As meaning documents in a person's possession, documents to which a person has a right to possession and documents of which a person has a right to inspect/take copies (CPR 1998, r.31.8).
14 FPR 2010, r 33.3(3) applies CPR 1998, r 71.2(6) and (7).
15 CPR 1998, r 70.6.
16 There is no obligation to use the Standard Orders Template orders, and in the event that the case demands it, it is open to an applicant to include alongside the Form D50K a draft directions order listing more specific items of financial disclosure from the debtor to assist the enforcement process.
17 Attachment of Earnings Act 1971, ss 6 and 24.
18 FPR 2010, Pt 39, r 39.1; Attachment of Earnings Act 1971, s 1.
19 Attachment of Earnings Act 1971, Sch 1.

In other words, a maintenance order can include a lump sum order and any other order for the payment of money made under those Acts, for the purposes of an attachment of earnings order. That said, depending on the scale of the debtor's income, enforcing a substantial lump sum via periodical monthly deductions from earned income is unlikely to prove a particularly efficient mechanism.

15.13 If an application has not been made for general enforcement, a separate application for an attachment of earnings order is made in a Form FE15[20] by the creditor to the family court as a 'request for an attachment of earnings order'. That application form sets out what is required in the application, including the 'Debtor's employment details'[21]. If the debtor's full employment details are not known, consideration should be given to: (i) making a general enforcement application rather than this specific application; and/or (ii) requesting that the court exercises its powers to: 'send to any person appearing to be the debtor's employer a notice requesting that person to give to the court a statement of the debtor's earnings.'[22]

15.14 The application will be heard in private (absent an order to the contrary)[23] and at a hearing[24].

Third party debt orders

15.15 A third party debt order[25] is an order addressed to a third party who owes money to or holds money on behalf of the debtor to pay the creditor some/all of that money[26]. The third party must be in the jurisdiction[27]. There is theoretically no restriction on the identity of the third party, who may be an individual or an entity. For obvious reasons, the most common target of a third party debt order is a bank which is known to hold funds on behalf of the debtor.

15.16 An application for a freestanding third party debt order is made in Form N349[28]. The content of the application is governed by CPR 1998, PD72, para 1.2 which prescribes specific information to be included in the application notice[29].

20 The application is made pursuant to FPR 2010, r 33.3(1), but the procedure is governed by FPR 2010, Pt 39.
21 Section 6 of Form FE15. Any 'general enforcement application' must include this information (or direct that the debtor provides it) in order for the court to have sufficient information to make an order at a subsequent hearing.
22 Attachment of Earnings Act 1971, s 14; FPR 2010, r 39.7–39.8.
23 FPR 2010, r 39.8.
24 FPR 2010, r 39.5(3). The notice of hearing will be served on the debtor by the court, with a Form FE17 'Reply' which must be filed eight days after being served with the application: FPR 2010, r 39.6.
25 Formerly known as a 'garnishee order'.
26 Applications are governed by CPR 1998, Pt 72, incorporated into the FPR 2010 with small amendments by FPR 2010, r 33.24.
27 CPR 1998, r 72.1.
28 Unusually there is no form specific to an application in the family court.
29 These will not all be listed here, as they are covered in the application Form 349 itself. Suffice to say, however, that if a creditor is only making a 'general enforcement' application, the court will need to have all of the information required by CPR 1998, Pt 72 in order to make a third party debt order against the debtor.

15.17 The application will initially be made without notice to the debtor and without the need for a hearing[30]. Therefore, assuming that an applicant creditor has included all of the requisite information in the application notice, the court will make an interim third party debt order and must then list an 'on notice' hearing within 28 days at which it will decide whether or not to make the order final[31].

15.18 If a creditor has made a freestanding application for a third party debt order and obtained an interim order on the papers, there are specific service requirements set out in the CPR 1998 which must be complied with (not least because the interim order only binds the third party once it has been served):

What to serve?

- Interim order, application notice and any documents in support

When to serve? (CPR 1998, r 72.5)

- On the third party: no less than 21 days before the hearing
- On the debtor: within 7 days of service on third party and no less than 7 days before the hearing
- Certificate of service is required if the creditor serves

Effect of service?

- Third party bound by the order (CPR 1998, r 72.4(4))
- Bank must conduct a search and identify all accounts held by the debtor and provide detail in 7 days (CPR 1998, r 72.6)

What does the debtor do?

- File and serve evidence setting out grounds to object to a final order (r 72.8)

At the hearing the court may (CPR 1998, r 72.8(6))

- make a final order
- discharge interim order
- decide any disputed issues
- list a trial

Charging orders

15.19 A charging order can only be obtained in respect of an **order to pay money to another person**. Of great relevance is the fact that a Children Act 1989, Sch 1 (CA 1989) settlement of property order does **not** fall within that definition and cannot be enforced by way of a charging order[32]. A charging order can be used to secure unpaid periodical payments, a lump sum, or any other direct payment from one party to another, but not a property adjustment order.

30 CPR 1998, r 72.4(1).
31 CPR 1998, r 72.4(2)–(4).
32 See Munby J in *Re N (A Child) (Payments for the Benefit of a Child)* [2009] EWHC 11 (Fam), [2009] 1 WLR 1621, [2009] 1 FCR 606, [2009] 1 FLR 1442. And see the discussion below about the drafting and enforcement of CA 1989, Sch 1 settlement of property orders at **15.38** onwards.

15.20 Where a debtor is required by court order to pay money to another person, the court may make an order:

> '... for the purpose of enforcing that [order] ... imposing on any such property of the debtor as may be specified in the order a charge for securing the payment of any money due or to become due under the [order]'[33].

15.21 'Property' encompasses broad categories of assets held beneficially by a debtor[34]:

15.22 As with third party debt orders discussed above, an application for a charging order is ordinarily dealt with on paper without a hearing, when the court may make an interim charging order and subsequently list a hearing to decide whether or not to make it final[35]. Applications may be made (and routinely are made) without notice to the debtor[36]. It should be noted that a court does have the jurisdiction to make an immediate final order – on notice to the debtor – but such orders are extremely rare[37].

33 Charging Orders Act 1979, s 1.
34 Charging Orders Act 1979, s 2. Section 6 defines 'stock' as including shares, debentures and any securities of the body concerned. Note that a beneficial interest under a trust does not include a case where a debtor is a potential beneficiary under a discretionary trust; it must be a beneficial 'interest'.
35 FPR 2010, r 40.5.
36 FPR 2010, r 40.4(1).
37 *Veluppillai v Veluppillai* [2015] EWHC 3095 (Fam), [2016] 2 FLR 681, [2016] Fam Law 19; *Green v Adams* [2017] EWFC 24, [2017] 3 FCR 79, [2017] 2 FLR 1413.

15.23 If the application is to enforce an order made in the family court[38], the application should be made to the family court using Form FE6[39] or FE7[40]. Those Forms – if completed correctly – contain the required information under the rules[41].

15.24 Having obtained an interim charging order, the applicant creditor's mind must turn to service and to the next steps before a return date hearing:

What to serve?

- Interim order, application notice and any documents in support

When to serve? (FPR 2010, r 40.6)

- No less than 21 days before the hearing

Serve on whom? (FPR, r 40.6) – as applicable to the facts of a particular case

- the debtor
- any co-owner of land/property
- other creditors identified in the application or directed (eg mortgage lender)
- trustees
- whoever keeps the register for the relevant stock (eg BoE)
- Certificate of service is needed

Effect of service?

- bound by the interim order
- debtor cannot dispose of interest in securities
- third party served must not permit a transfer of securities or pay a dividend/interest relating to them

What can the debtor do?

- File and serve evidence setting out grounds to object to a final order (r 40.8)

At the hearing the court may (FPR 2010, r 40.8(2))

- make a final order
- discharge interim order
- decide any disputed issues
- list a trial
- make any other order the court considers 'appropriate'

38 See Mostyn J in *VS v RE* [2018] EWFC 30, [2018] 1 WLR 3757, [2018] 3 FCR 294, [2018] 2 FLR 1213.
39 Application for charging order on land or property.
40 Application for charging order on securities. See also applications for 'Stop Notices' under the Charging Orders Act 1979, s 5.
41 FPR 2010, r 40.4(2) and PD40.

Warrant of control/execution against goods

15.25 In the event of a default by a debtor it is open to the applicant creditor to seek permission to issue a request for the issue of a warrant[42] of control, whereby the court authorises an enforcement officer to do the following[43]:

1.
   - Enter the debtor's property at specific times
   - For the purpose of searching for and taking control of goods chattels and other property
2.
   - Take control of goods, chattels and other property of the debtor
   - Up to the value of the debt
   - Using reasonable force if necessary
3.
   - Sell the goods, chattels and other property at a public auction
   - For the best price that can reasonably be obtained
4.
   - Apply the proceeds of sale to pay the applicant the debt
   - Retain a sum equivalent to the fees and charges to which the officer is entitled

15.26 The application is made to the family court in Form N323 accompanied by a short statement. The procedure is governed by CPR 1998, Part 84[44]. The applications are rare in the family court, perhaps for obvious reasons, but there is no principled reason why such an order cannot be sought by an applicant creditor seeking to enforce a debt against an intransigent debtor who has disclosed no other more suitable (or practical) assets against which to enforce.

OTHER OPTIONS

Hadkinson orders

15.27 A *Hadkinson* order[45] is a type of interim remedy designed to incentivise compliance in circumstances where a party is in contempt of

42 If the proceedings are in the High Court, the court will issue a 'writ' directed to an enforcement officer (the Tipstaff) whereas the family court will issue a 'warrant' directed to an 'officer of the family court' (a bailiff) – Matrimonial and Family Proceedings Act 1984, s 31E(2).
43 See the Standard Order Template, Order 4.9 'Warrant of Control'.
44 Incorporated into the FPR 2010 by r 33.1(2).
45 Named after the case of *Hadkinson v Hadkinson* [1952] P 285, [1952] 2 TLR 416.

court. Such an order prevents the non-compliant respondent from participating further in proceedings (or limits their ability to do so) unless and until they are no longer in contempt.

15.28 The first step is to prove that the respondent is in contempt. It is important to note the following:

The contempt must be in relation to the same or related proceedings[46];

The contempt must be proved to the civil standard (balance of probabilities) not the criminal standard[47];

'Contempt' can include breach of an order, breach of an undertaking or contempt in the face of the court;

Non-payment of an order/undertaking is sufficient to establish contempt. Whether the contempt is wilful (including whether the respondent has the means to pay) is relevant to the subsequent discretionary exercise[48].

15.29 Once the contempt is established the court exercises a discretion. A *Hadkinson* order is draconian; it prevents a litigant from participating fully or at all in their proceedings contrary to their right to a fair trial[49] and is thus a 'remedy of last resort'[50]. The court must consider the following questions when deciding whether or not to exercise its discretion:

Is the contempt wilful (ie contumacious and continuing)?

Is there an impediment to the course of justice for so long as the contempt continues?

Is there any other effective means of securing compliance?

What conditions would be proportionate to impose on the respondent?

46 *DS v HR (Hadkinson Order)* [2019] EWHC 2425 (Fam), [2020] 1 FLR 945 and *Orenga de Gafforj v Orenga de Gafforj* [2018] EWCA Civ 2070, [2019] 1 FCR 73.

47 See **15.47–15.49** below as regards committal proceedings.

48 *Mubarak v Mubarik (No 2)* [2006] EWHC 1260 (Fam), [2007] 1 WLR 271, [2007] 1 FLR 722; and *Orenga de Gafforj v Orenga de Gafforj* [2018] EWCA Civ 2070, [2019] 1 FCR 73 at para [12].

49 ECHR, Art 6.

50 Bodey J in *M v M (Maintenance Pending Suit: Enforcement on Dismissal of Suit)* [2008] EWHC 2153 (Fam), [2009] 1 FLR 790 at para [52].

15.30 The authorities establish that it is highly unlikely that the court will debar a party from participating in a final hearing of a financial claim, as opposed to an interim hearing or an appeal[51].

Execution of documents

15.31 Section 39 of the Senior Courts Act 1981 (SCA 1981) provides that:

> '(1) where the High Court or family court has given or made a judgment or order directing a person to execute any conveyance, contract or other document … then, if that person –
>
> (a) neglects or refuses to comply with the judgment or order, or
>
> (b) cannot after reasonable inquiry be found
>
> that court may, on such terms and conditions, if any, as may be just, order that the conveyance or contract or other document shall be executed … by such person as the court may nominate for that purpose.'

15.32 The most obvious use of this provision is to enable the conveyance (sale, transfer etc) of land or other real property. In *Welch v Welch*[52] the court addressed the requisite stages to obtain an order under SCA 1981, s 39(1):

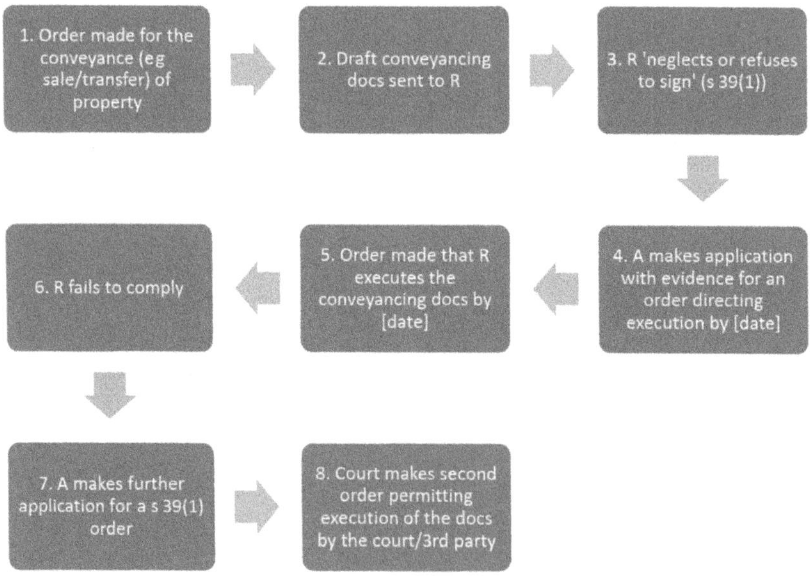

51 In *Young v Young* [2013] EWHC 3637 (Fam), [2014] 2 FCR 495, [2014] 2 FLR 786 Moor J refused to make a *Hadkinson* order preventing a contemnor husband from participating in the final hearing. In *LKH v Z* [2018] EWHC 2436 (Fam), [2018] 4 WLR 135, [2018] 3 FCR 553 Holman J also refused to debar the husband from engaging in the final hearing, as it was a 'very extreme course' and would prevent the court from discharging its inquisitorial function.

52 [2017] 3 FCR 405, per HHJ Hess.

15.33 As can be seen by the graphic above, the process can be convoluted and require two applications by the party seeking to enforce the conveyance in the face of breach, but it is a precondition of the court's jurisdiction under SCA 1981, s 39(1) that an order has been made 'directing a person to execute any conveyance, contract or other document.' So stage 5 of the graphic above is essential and cannot be avoided. There is some question as to whether stages 5 to 8 can be elided by making an *anticipatory* s 39(1) order which automatically bites only if the respondent fails to comply with the initial order to execute the documents. Such an order in default was made in *Welch* itself, but in circumstances where the judge concluded that the respondent wife had no intention of cooperating with his order and, even then, the judge acknowledged that the jurisdictional position in the authorities was far from clear[53]. In more recent authorities, the courts have refused to make such anticipatory orders and interpreted narrowly the statutory jurisdiction under SCA 1981, s 39(1)[54]:

Key citation: *Lindsay v O'Loughnane*[55]

> 'There is of course a temptation to make the order now including the default provision, if only in order to save the time and cost that would be associated with a further hearing if [the respondent] did not comply with it. That, however, would overlook the jurisdictional provision …'

There is thus a balance to be struck between: (i) the obvious cost and time efficiency of obtaining an anticipatory order; and (ii) the risk that such an order might be open to an appeal.

Freezing orders/injunctions

15.34 The jurisdiction to make orders under MCA 1973, s 37 (and its equivalent under CPA 2004, Sch 5, Pt 14) is not available to a party seeking to enforce an order made under CA 1989, Sch 1[56]. It is of note that there is no equivalent power afforded to the court under CA 1989, Sch 1 either to grant a freezing injunction, or to set aside a disposition carried out with the intention to defeat a financial claim.

53 *Welch v Welch* [2017] 3 FCR 405, HHJ Hess at paras 5–11, citing *Savage v Norton* [1908] 1 Ch 290.

54 See *Gee v Gee* [2020] EWHC 1842 (Ch), [2020] 7 WLUK 164 from para 26 and *Lindsay v O'Loughnane* [2022] EWHC 1829 (QB), [2022] Pens LR 13 at paras 56–65.

55 *Lindsay v O'Loughnane* [2022] EWHC 1829 (QB), [2022] 7 WLUK 213, [2022] Pens LR 13 at para [64].

56 That section provides the court with: (i) a pre-emptive injunctive power to prevent an anticipated disposal of property (a freezing injunction); and (ii) the power to set aside a 'reviewable disposition'. The powers under s 37 are available to enforce an order made for the benefit of a child under the Matrimonial Causes Act 1973, ss 22 to 24 itself.

15.35 The court has the power to grant a freezing injunction under SCA 1981, s 37[57]. This is a civil remedy (ie not specific to family proceedings), and there is no power to set aside a disposition under this provision. The following applies to this statutory jurisdiction[58]:

- Order can be made at any stage, including as part of enforcement proceedings
- Essential purpose of the order is to facilitate the enforcement of a judgment/order
- Order should do no more than is necessary to protect the claim
- Can be made against a third party where evidence that person/entity holds or controls the respondent's assets (*Chabra*)
- Order acts *in personam*

15.36 There are four conditions which must be satisfied before a court will grant injunctive relief in the form of a freezing injunction:

> Applicant has a 'good arguable case' for being granted (or has already been granted) a judgment or order for the payment of a sum of money that is or will be enforceable through the process of the court[59];
>
> Respondent holds assets against which a relevant judgment can or could be enforced[60];
>
> There is a sufficient 'risk of dissipation' by the respondent of his assets such that: (i) the judgment will go unsatisfied; or (ii) enforcement will be more difficult, unless he is restrained from dealing with his assets[61];
>
> It is 'just and convenient in all the circumstances of the case' to grant the order sought[62].

57 Applicable to the family court by virtue of SCA 1981, s 37(6).

58 See the Privy Council decision of *Broad Idea International Ltd v Convoy Collateral Ltd* [2021] UKPC 24, [2023] AC 389, [2022] 2 WLR 703 approved by the Court of Appeal in *Re G* [2022] EWCA Civ 1312, [2023] Fam 107, [2022] 3 WLR 1339 as representing 'the law of England and Wales as to the circumstances in which the Court may grant an injunction' (at para [61]). As to orders against third parties, see *TSB Private Bank International SA v Chabra* [1992] 1 WLR 231 and *Mercantile Group (Europe) AG v Aiyela* [1994] QB 366, [1993] 3 WLR 1116. The order acts in personam, ie against the respondent, and does not grant the applicant a proprietary right over the injuncted assets themselves.

59 In enforcement proceedings this will almost always be the case.

60 See *Ras al Khaimah Investment Authority v Bestfort Development LLP* [2017] EWCA Civ 1014, [2018] 1 WLR 1099.

61 The jurisdiction exists to prevent unjustified and deliberate dissipation of assets. If the dealing is in the respondent's ordinary course of business or is to meet his legitimate expenses (living expenses, legal fees debts etc) that cannot justify an order: Haddon-Cave LJ in *Lakatamia Shipping Company v Morimoto* [2019] EWCA Civ 2203, [2020] 1 CLC 562. The risk must be 'something which is more than fanciful': (*Les Ambassadeurs Club Ltd v Songvo Yu* [2021] EWCA Civ 1310, [2022] 4 WLR 1.

62 This test comprises of two parts: (i) the person protected by the injunction has an interest that merits protection; and (ii) there is a legal or equitable principle which justifies exercising the power to order

15.37 The court used its jurisdiction to grant freezing injunctions in *Re N (Payments for the Benefit of Child)*[63] and the subsequent *G v A* litigation[64] to aid enforcement of a settlement of property order against an intransigent respondent under CA 1989, Sch 1, considered at **15.40** ff below.

CHILDREN ACT 1989, SCH 1 TRUSTS: ENFORCEMENT AND INJUNCTIVE RELIEF

15.38 The capital orders available to a court to make housing provision for the benefit of a child have been discussed earlier in this book[65]. The most obvious and commonly used statutory route is CA 1989, Sch 1, under which the court can make a variety of orders for the benefit of a subject child[66]. In the absence of exceptional circumstances, when the court makes an order for housing provision under CA 1989, Sch 1 it will provide for the settlement of a property on trust for the duration of the child's educational minority at the conclusion of which the property will revert to the paying parent/party[67].

15.39 How does a party seek to enforce an order for the settlement of property under CA 1989, Sch 1 against an intransigent/non-compliant respondent? The answer is that it depends very much on: (a) the form of the non-compliance; and (b) the drafting of the court order and/or any accompanying deed of trust.

15.40 If the order provided for the respondent 'to settle on the applicant for the benefit of the child the sum of £X' which is to be used to purchase a property to house the child, but the respondent has subsequently failed to pay £X, the temptation would be for an applicant to apply to enforce the 'debt' against the respondent personally in the 'usual' way (eg charging order, third party debt order etc as discussed in the paragraphs above). However, care should be exercised: an order to settle property on trust is not an order for the respondent to pay a lump sum to the applicant, and a default does not create a judgment debt which can be enforced by way of a charging order, third party debt order, attachment of earnings order, or a warrant of control.

the respondent to do or not to do something: *Re G* [2022] EWCA Civ 1312, [2023] Fam 107, [2022] 3 WLR 1339 at [71].

63 *Re N (A Child) (Payments for the Benefit of a Child)* [2009] EWHC 11 (Fam), [2009] 1 WLR 1621, [2009] 1 FCR 606, [2009] 1 FLR 1442.

64 *G v A (No 1)* [2011] EWHC 2380 (Fam), [2012] 1 FLR 389; *G v A (No 2)* [2011] EWHC 968 (Fam), [2012] 1 FLR 402; *G v A (No 3)* [2011] EWHC 2377 (Fam), [2012] 1 FLR 415; *G v A (No 4)* [2011] 11 WLUK 836, [2012] 1 FLR 427.

65 **Chapter 10**.

66 **Chapter 10**, Part B, **10.4** ff.

67 See the discussion in **Chapter 10**, **10.12–10.14** and **10.24–10.27**.

15.41

Case Summary: Re N (Payments for the Benefit of Child)[68]

Facts:

A final order under CA 1989, Sch 1 included provision: (i) for F to settle on M for the benefit of their child the sum of £220,000, to be used to purchase a property (with a mortgage); and (ii) for F to pay £20,000 outright to M as regards moving and purchase costs. F did not pay either sum.

M applied to enforce and successfully obtained an interim charging order over a property in F's name for the full amount of £240,000.

F objected to the charging order being made final.

Held by Munby J:

Final charging order allowed in respect of the £20,000 outright sum, but discharged in respect of the £220,000.

There was no order to pay money to M, only to settle money, and as a result there was no 'debt' to enforce by way of a charging order.

The court instead granted an injunction over F's properties which restrained him from dealing with them pending satisfaction of the settlement of property order.

This case gave rise to the *G v A* litigation[69] discussed in the paragraphs below.

15.42 What is the solution to this enforcement problem? As can be seen from the case summary of *Re N*[70] above, the court can use its injunctive powers to encourage compliance and, as will be seen in the discussion below of the four judgments in *G v A* ('the *G v A* litigation')[71], the court can exercise its powers to enforce and alter the terms of the trust itself. However, such complexity can be avoided if the final order in CA 1989, Sch 1 proceedings is drafted properly.

68 *Re N (A Child) (Payments for the Benefit of a Child)* [2009] EWHC 11 (Fam), [2009] 1 WLR 1621, [2009] 1 FCR 606, [2009] 1 FLR 1442.

69 *G v A (No 1)* [2011] EWHC 2380 (Fam), [2012] 1 FLR 389; *G v A (No 2)* [2011] EWHC 968 (Fam), [2012] 1 FLR 402; *G v A (No 3)* [2011] EWHC 2377 (Fam), [2012] 1 FLR 415; *G v A (No 4)* [2011] 11 WLUK 836, [2012] 1 FLR 427.

70 *Re N (A Child) (Payments for the Benefit of a Child)* [2009] EWHC 11 (Fam), [2009] 1 WLR 1621, [2009] 1 FCR 606, [2009] 1 FLR 1442.

71 *G v A (No 1)* [2011] EWHC 2380 (Fam), [2012] 1 FLR 389; *G v A (No 2)* [2011] EWHC 968 (Fam), [2012] 1 FLR 402; *G v A (No 3)* [2011] EWHC 2377 (Fam), [2012] 1 FLR 415; *G v A (No 4)* [2011] 11 WLUK 836, [2012] 1 FLR 427.

Key citation: *G v A (No 1)*[72]

> '[42] … I venture to suggest that **an order properly drawn by the court is sufficient and indeed preferable method to define a trust in a case of this simplicity and in most [Schedule 1] cases where modest provision for a small house or flat is made**. I note that the well established and respected Resolution Precedents Handbook[73] now in its 8th edition in 2009 has precedent no 48 along just such lines.'

15.43 The Standard Orders Template Order 2.2[74] is titled Order under the Children Act 1989, Schedule 1. The wording of para 58, headed 'Provision of New Home – New Home on Trust' includes: **(i)** a lump sum order as between the respondent and applicant; **and (ii)** an order that the sum be settled on trust; **and (iii)** an order that this sum then be used to purchase a property held on trust. Such wording does not offend the prohibition against multiple property adjustment orders[75], and if the principle of that drafting is followed[76] then any failure by a respondent to pay the initial sum of money required to purchase a property on a CA 1989, Sch 1 trust ***can*** be enforced as a debt by the applicant against the respondent.

15.44 The court has additional wide-ranging powers to enforce its own order under CA 1989, Sch 1 and to make orders either enforcing or overriding the terms of a CA 1989, Sch 1 settlement of property order:

Key citations: the *G v A* litigation

> '[31] … It is a necessary foundation for the exercise of any power of the court to interpose a compulsive direction to enforce its order or possibly under TOLATA to have a firm sense of where obstruction to progress or assistance lies.'
>
> *G v A (No 1)*[77]

72 *G v A (No 1)* [2011] EWHC 2380 (Fam), [2012] 1 FLR 389 at [42] emphasis supplied. This was endorsed 'strongly' by Jackson J in *G v A (No 3)* [2011] EWHC 2377 (Fam), [2012] 1 FLR 415 at [35].

73 This has now been overtaken by the Standard Orders Template precedents endorsed by the President of the Family Division. See Order 2.2.

74 These precedents did not exist at the time of the *G v A* litigation referred to above.

75 See the discussion in **Chapter 10** at **10.5–10.11**.

76 Practitioners must be careful not to follow blindly the precedent wording of the Standard Orders Template orders but to ensure that the wording of any order is applicable and relevant to any particular case.

77 *G v A (No 1)* [2011] EWHC 2380 (Fam), [2012] 1 FLR 389.

> '[26] I find that the family court has not only the jurisdiction but the duty to consider any proper applications relating to the fulfilment of its order and to give whatever directions appear appropriate to give effect to it. Such directions may override the trust deed, which exists as an expression of the court's will and not as an obstruction to it.'
>
> *G v A (No 3)*[78]

15.45 In the *G v A* litigation, the court took increasingly extreme steps to encourage and enforce the respondent father's compliance with its order to settle £220,000 on trust on the mother to enable her to purchase a house for the child and her. Below is a summary of some of the orders it made, showing the range of its injunctive and directive powers[79]:

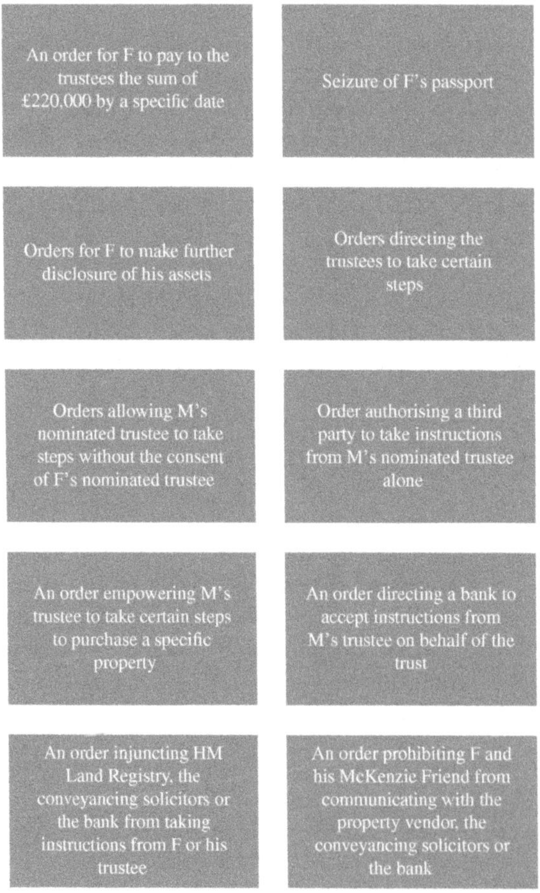

78 *G v A (No 3)* [2011] EWHC 2377 (Fam), [2012] 1 FLR 415. This was in response to a submission on behalf of the respondent father that the applicant mother was compelled to make a separate application in the Chancery Division to deal with the terms and operation of the CA 1989, Sch 1 trust.

79 See in particular *G v A (No 3)* [2011] EWHC 2377 (Fam), [2012] 1 FLR 415 at para [36]; and *G v A (No 4)* [2012]1 FLR 427 at para [11].

15.46 It should be noted that the circumstances of the *G v A* litigation involved massive delay and the litigation conduct by the father and his McKenzie Friend (and later his nominated trustee) was at the extreme end of the spectrum. As is repeated throughout the judgments, the powers exercised in that case will not be used lightly by the courts, and the facts and circumstances of a respondent's non-compliance (or those acting on his/her behalf) will have to justify such draconian orders[80].

COMMITTAL FOR CONTEMPT AND JUDGMENT SUMMONS

15.47 Where a respondent is **in breach of an order or an undertaking to pay money** the debt cannot be enforced under the court's general power to commit a person for contempt of court; it must be enforced by way of a judgment summons under the Debtors Act 1869 by a request in Form D62. If the respondent is **in breach of any other order or undertaking**, then that breach can be enforced by way of committal for contempt of court by application in Form FC600[81].

The most important difference between the two is that in respect of a judgment summons for failure to pay a sum of money, not only must it be established to the criminal standard of proof that the respondent is in breach of an order or an undertaking, but it must also be proved that:

> The defaulter has, or has had since the date of the order, the means to pay the sum in respect of which they are in default, and has refused or neglected, or refuses or neglects, to pay that sum[82].

15.48 The procedural requirements for each remedy are similar, although there are differences. Committal by way of judgment summons is covered by FPR 2010, Pt 33, Ch II. Committal for contempt of court is covered by FPR 2010, Pt 37[83]. Given that the possible implications of either application are the imprisonment of a defaulting respondent, procedural compliance is essential and a procedurally defective application may result in its dismissal.

80 By the end of the *G v A* litigation, the court had even gone so far as to direct that it could oversee the appointment of a new trustee on behalf of the father in the 'unusual circumstances' of the case, notwithstanding that Trusts of Land and Appointment of Trustees Act 1996, s 14 expressly excludes the power to appoint or remove trustees: *G v A (No 4)* [2012] 1 FLR 427 at para [15].

81 If the wrong application is made, it is almost certain to fail: *Zuk v Zuk* [2012] EWCA Civ 1871, [2013] 3 FCR 633, [2013] 2 FLR 1466.

82 Debtors Act 1869, s 5. See also Mostyn J in *Bhura v Bhura* [2012] EWHC 3633 (Fam), [2013] 3 FCR 142, [2013] 2 FLR 44.

83 The old FPR 2010, Pt 37 was replaced as of 1 October 2020 with the 'new' Part 37 and PD37A. The changes were not inconsiderable and it is essential to ensure that the up-to-date rules are followed in making an application.

15.49 The rules and legal principles applicable to committal (whether by way of judgment summons or contempt of court) are complex and require analysis outside of the scope of this necessarily summary chapter. In Chapters 3 and 4 of *1KBW on Enforcement in Financial Remedy Proceedings* the respective applications have been addressed in considerable detail, both as to the procedural requirements, the evidential requirements and as to the applicable legal principles. Practitioners interested in this topic are therefore referred to that work[84].

84 *1KBW on Enforcement in Financial Remedy Proceedings* (Bloomsbury Professional, 2023).

CHAPTER 16

Costs

Content at a glance:

Introduction

The rules

Procedure for costs applications

Managing costs

INTRODUCTION

16.1 Any litigation where lawyers are acting involves financial cost. This is becoming a significant topic of discussion in published judgments in financial provision cases, particularly in relation to the sometimes excessive spending on behalf of both parties.

16.2 This chapter will address the circumstances in which one party will be ordered to pay the other's costs, as well as how the parties and court are kept informed about costs throughout the proceedings.

THE RULES

16.3 The rules on costs in family proceedings are set out in the Family Procedure Rules 2010 ('FPR 2010'), Pt 28. These incorporate some of the relevant provisions of the Civil Procedure Rules 1998 ('CPR 1998') on costs into the FPR 2010.

16.4 Rule 28.3 of the FPR 2010 contains rules which pertain exclusively to 'financial remedy proceedings' as defined in that rule. The definition is narrower than the definition of financial remedy proceedings set out in FPR 2010, r 2.3(1). Crucially, for the purposes of FPR 2010, r 28.3, financial remedy proceedings do not include applications under the Children Act 1989 ('CA 1989'), Sch 1.

16.5 Applications which fall within the definition of financial remedy proceedings under FPR 2010, r 28.3 include:

Financial remedy proceedings under FPR 2010, r 28.3

(i) a financial order[1] except an order for maintenance pending suit, an order for maintenance pending outcome of proceedings, an interim periodical payments order, an order for payment in respect of legal services or any other form of interim order for the purposes of rule 9.7(1)(a), (b), (c) and (e);

(ii) an order under Matrimonial and Family Proceedings Act 1984 ('MFPA 1984'), Part 3;

(iii) an order under Civil Partnership Act 2004 ('CPA 2004'), Sch 7;

(iv) an order under Matrimonial Causes Act 1973 ('MCA 1973'), s 10(2);

(v) an order under CPA 2004, s 48(2).

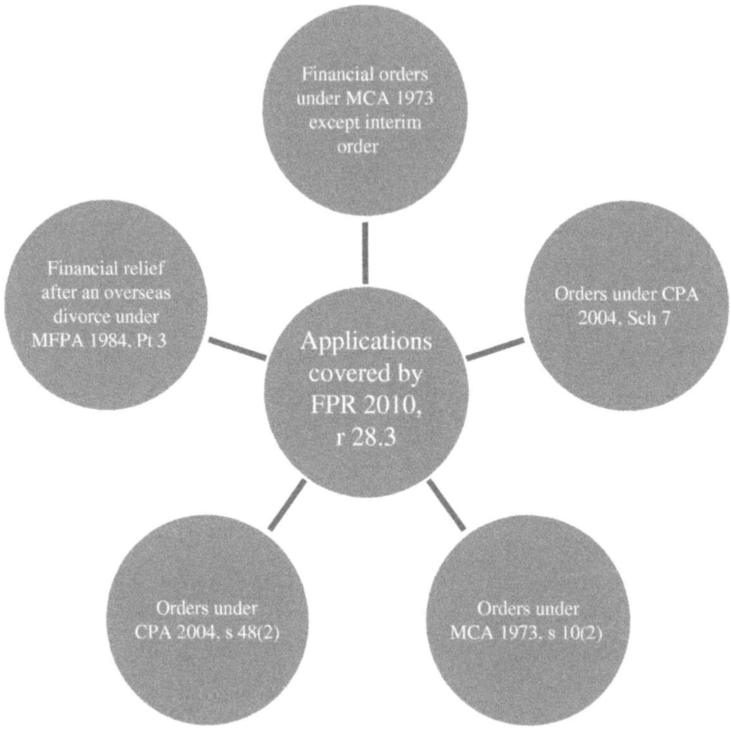

1 The term 'Financial order' is defined in FPR 2010, r 2.3. It means: (a) an avoidance of disposition order; (b) an order for maintenance pending suit; (c) an order for maintenance pending outcome of proceedings; (d) an order for periodical payments or lump sum provision under MCA 1973 (not s 27(6)) or CPA 2004; (e) a property adjustment order; (f) a variation order; (g) pension sharing and pension compensation orders; (h) legal services orders.

The effect of the rule is that applications for financial remedies for children brought under CA 1989 are subject to a different costs regime from those brought under MCA 1973 and CPA 2004.

The general rule

16.6 Rule 28.3 of the FPR 2010 contains a 'general rule' which is set out in FPR 2010, r 28.3(5)[2]. This general rule provides that:

> **The general rule as to costs (FPR 2010, r 28.3(5))**
>
> 'the court will not make an order requiring one party to pay the costs of another party.'

16.7 The general rule applies only to applications falling within the definition of financial remedy proceedings for the purposes of FPR 2010, r 28.3 (see **16.5** above).

16.8 By contrast with FPR 2010, r 2.3(1), orders for interim maintenance payments, orders for legal services payments and other interim orders are *excluded* from the definition of financial remedy proceedings under FPR 2010, r 28.3 and are therefore not subject to the general rule.

16.9 As is implied from the phrase 'general rule', it is not an absolute rule. The court retains the ability to make a costs order in the exercise of its discretion. The general rule is expressed as being subject to the provision in FPR 2010, r 28.3(6) that:

> **The *caveat* to the general rule as to costs (FPR 2010, r 28.3(6))**
>
> 'the court may make an order requiring one party to pay the costs of another party at any stage of the proceedings where it is appropriate to do so because of the conduct of a party in relation to the proceedings (whether before or during them)'.

16.10 The relevant factors to be considered when deciding what order as to costs (if any) to make are set out in FPR 2010, r 28.3(7). They include the following:

2 In civil proceedings governed by the CPR 1998, the general rule in CPR 1998, r 44.2(2)(a) is that the unsuccessful party will be ordered to pay the costs of the successful party. This is disapplied in family proceedings by virtue of FPR 2010, r 28.2.

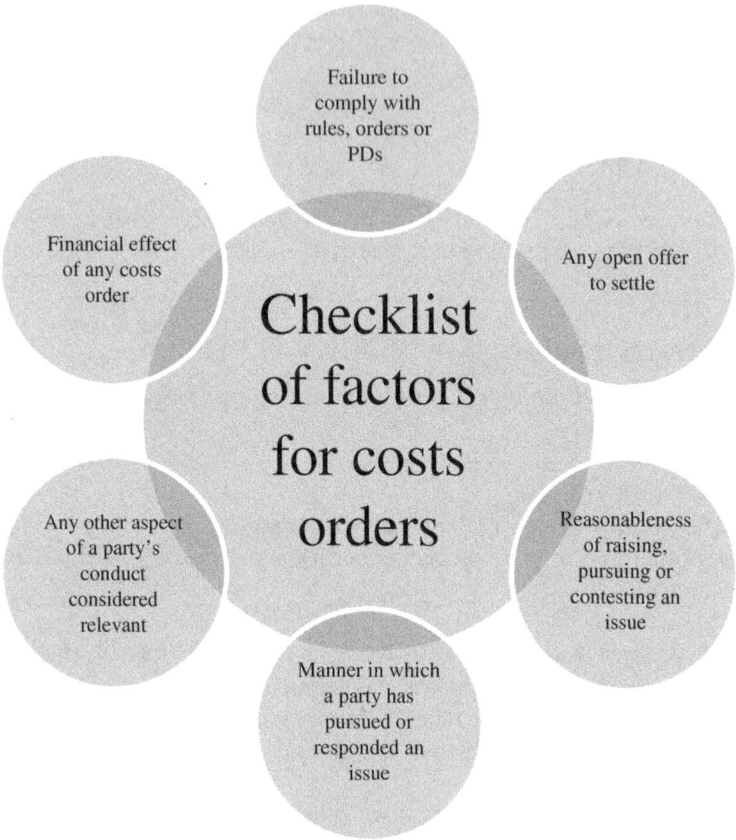

16.11 Significantly, as of 29 April 2024, FPR 2010, r 28.3(7) has been amended by the insertion of a new r 28.3(7)(aa). This requires the court, when considering issues as to costs, to have regard to any failure by a party – without good reason – to engage in non-court dispute resolution.

Failure to engage in ADR: FPR 2010, r 28.3(7)(aa)

(7) In deciding what order (if any) to make under paragraph (6), the court must have regard to –

(aa) any failure by a party, without good reason, to—

(i) attend a MIAM (as defined in rule 3.1); or

(ii) attend non-court dispute resolution;

…

16.12 The new r 28.3(7)(aa) echoes the approach that the court has recently been taking in respect of failures to negotiate openly and reasonably. The following cases are examples of the court expressing firm views about the impact of a refusal to negotiate either at all or reasonably.

E v L (Costs)[3]	'As I have said before, and will no doubt have cause to say again, if you do not negotiate openly, reasonably and responsibly you will suffer a penalty in costs.'
LM v DM (Costs Ruling)[4]	'Litigants must learn that they will suffer a cost penalty if they do not negotiate openly and reasonably.'
OG v AG[5]	'I hope that this decision will serve as a clear warning to all future litigants: if you do not negotiate reasonably you will be penalised in costs.'
Helliwell v Entwistle[6]	'Since the demise of *Calderbank* ... it is "cards on the table" and people have to negotiate sensibly.'

16.13 Whilst difficulties with disclosure may impact on a party's ability to make offers, once the picture is sufficiently clear it is likely that an open offer will be necessary so as to ensure that a costs order is safeguarded against. However, simply *making* an offer is not enough: such an offer must also be reasonable in order to offer genuine protection. For example, in *OG v AG*[7] the wife *had* made an open offer but it was considered not to be reasonable – Mostyn J described it as an 'unreasonable and untenable open negotiation stance'.

The 'clean sheet' principle

16.14 If the general rule is not applicable, the court starts with a 'clean sheet'[8] and has a wide discretion as to costs.

16.15 The clean sheet approach applies in family proceedings which are not covered by the definition of 'financial remedy proceedings' in FPR 2010, r 28.3(4)(b). A number of these will be particularly relevant to applications for financial provision for children:

3 [2021] EWHC 63 (Fam), [2022] 1 FLR 980, Mostyn J.
4 [2021] EWFC 28, [2021] 2 FCR 239, [2022] 1 FLR 393, Mostyn J.
5 [2020] EWFC 52, [2021] 2 FCR 187, [2021] 1 FLR 1105, Mostyn J.
6 [2024] EWHC 1298 (Fam), Francis J.
7 [2020] EWFC 52, [2021] 2 FCR 187, [2021] 1 FLR 1105.
8 Per Wilson LJ in *Baker v Rowe* [2009] EWCA Civ 1162, [2010] 1 FCR 413, [2010] 1 FLR 761.

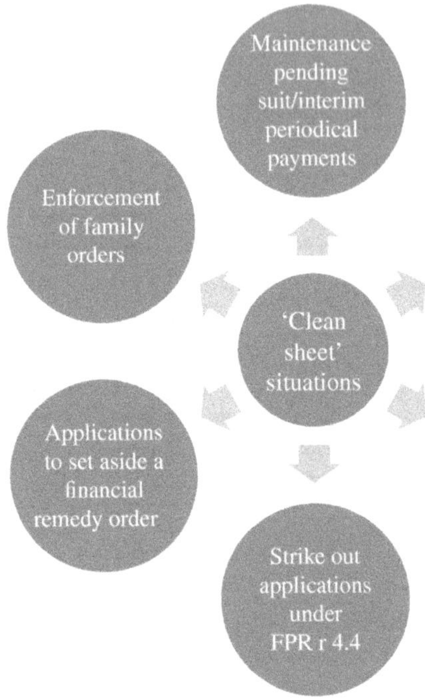

16.16 That the court has a 'clean sheet' in these applications does not mean there is no starting point. The starting point was considered by the Court of Appeal in 1991 in *Gojkovic v Gojkovic (No 2)*[9].

Key citation: *Gojkovic v Gojkovic (No 2)*[10]

Court of Appeal (Butler-Sloss LJ):

> 'there still remains the necessity for some starting-point. That starting-point, in my judgment, is that costs prima facie follow the event … but may be displaced much more easily than, and in circumstances which would not apply, in other Divisions of the High Court.'

16.17 The above quotation from *Gojkovic (No 2)* was approved by the Court of Appeal in *Solomon v Solomon*[11]. Accordingly, where the clean sheet approach applies, the starting point may be that the loser faces a costs

9 [1991] FCR 913, [1992] Fam 40, [1991] 3 WLR 621, [1991] 2 FLR 233.
10 [1991] FCR 913, [1992] Fam 40, [1991] 3 WLR 621, [1991] 2 FLR 233.
11 [2013] EWCA Civ 1095, although it is worth noting that this was an application for permission to appeal (which was refused) and so not a citable authority.

order being made against them (see, however, **16.20** below and *KS v ND*[12] where this proposition has been called into question in relation to CA 1989, Sch 1 proceedings).

16.18 The relevant factors for the court to consider in clean sheet cases come from CPR 1998, r 44.2(4) and (5)[13]. The court is required to have regard to all the circumstances, including:

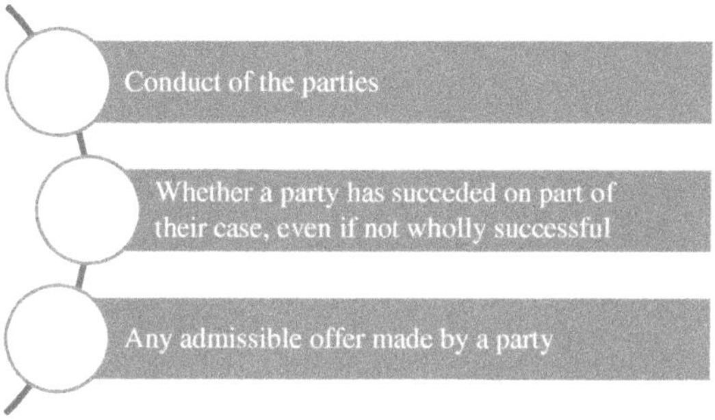

16.19 Conduct in this context is defined by CPR 1998, r 44.2(5) as including:

'(a) conduct before, as well as during, the proceedings and in particular the extent to which the parties followed … any relevant pre-action protocol;

(b) whether it was reasonable for a party to raise, pursue or contest a particular allegation or issue;

(c) the manner in which a party has pursued or defended its case or a particular allegation or issue;

(d) whether a claimant who has succeeded in the claim, in whole or in part, exaggerated its claim; and

(e) whether a party failed to comply with an order for alternative dispute resolution, or unreasonably failed to engage in alternative dispute resolution.'

Key differences between proceedings under MCA 1973 and CA 1989, Sch 1

16.20 The key difference between applications under MCA 1973 and CA 1989, Sch 1 is that the latter are excluded from the definition of financial remedy proceedings under FPR 28.3 and are therefore not subject to the

12 [2013] EWHC 464 (Fam), [2013] 2 FLR 698.

13 These rules are incorporated into the FPR 2010 by virtue of FPR 2010, r 28.2(1) although by virtue of FPR 2010, r 28.3(2) they do not apply to 'financial remedy proceedings' as defined in FPR 2010, r 28.3(4)(b).

'general rule' as to costs. That said, any *interim* applications within MCA 1973 applications will be subject to the 'clean sheet' approach; it is simply the costs at the conclusion of proceedings which will be treated differently.

STATUTE	COSTS REGIME
MCA 1973	GENERAL RULE
MCA 1973 (INTERIM)	CLEAN SHEET
CA 1989, SCH 1	CLEAN SHEET

16.21 There has been some doubt expressed as to whether the *Gojkovic* principle whereby prima facie 'costs follow the event' should apply to CA 1989, Sch 1 proceedings, where it can be said that the applicant is acting in what is effectively a representative capacity for the child[14].

Key citation: *KS v ND (Schedule 1: Appeal: Costs)*[15]

Mostyn J:

> 'An open question since the promulgation of Part 28 FPR 2010 on 6 April 2011 has been whether this principle of costs prima facie following the event has now been resurrected following the exception of these, and the other specified proceedings, from the general rule of no order as to costs now found in r 28.3. I consider it is certainly arguable that this principle should now apply in such proceedings when they are between husband and wife or between civil partners. However I am doubtful whether it should apply in Schedule 1 proceedings where the mother in effect makes her application in a representative capacity for the child. In Schedule 1 proceedings the court should in my opinion start with a 'clean sheet', as Wilson LJ (as he then was) put it in *Baker v Rowe* [2009] EWCA Civ 1162, [2010] 1 FLR 761.'

16.22 Although in *KS v ND*[16] Mostyn J expressed a preference for the approach adopted in *Baker v Rowe* over that which was formulated in *Gojkovic v Gojkovic (No 2)*[17], in reality there may be little difference between the two. In *Baker v Rowe*[18], Wilson LJ held that:

14 *KS v ND* [2013] EWHC 464 (Fam), [2013] 2 FLR 698.
15 [2013] EWHC 464 (Fam), [2013] 2 FLR 698.
16 [2013] EWHC 464 (Fam), [2013] 2 FLR 698.
17 [1992] Fam 40, [1991] 3 WLR 621, [1991] FCR 913, [1991] 2 FLR 233.
18 [2009] EWCA Civ 1162, [2010] 1 FCR 413, [2010] 1 FLR 761.

Key citation: *Baker v Rowe*[19]

Court of Appeal (Wilson LJ):

> 'Even where the judge starts with a clean sheet, the fact that one party has been unsuccessful, and must therefore usually be regarded as responsible for the generation of the successful party's costs, will often properly count as the decisive factor in the exercise of the judge's discretion.'

Calderbank offers

16.23 One particularly significant consequence of the incorporation into FPR 2010 of the relevant costs provisions of the CPR 1998 for applications which fall to be considered under the 'clean sheet' approach is the applicability and relevance of *Calderbank* offers[20].

16.24 A *Calderbank* offer is also known as one made 'without prejudice save as to costs', ie whilst it is protected against admissibility during a substantive trial it can be referred to within any costs arguments. The significance of such offers (or the absence thereof) was considered in *KS v ND (Schedule 1: Appeal: Costs)*[21].

Case summary: *KS v ND (Schedule 1: Appeal: Costs)*[22]

Facts:

M and F each cross-applied to vary a consent order under CA 1989, Sch 1, which continued to apply in relation to their 17 year old son. F sought a downwards variation of both his child maintenance payments and school fees payments; M sought an additional lump sum, an extension of the time period for child maintenance payments and an increase of those payments.

The district judge reduced the child maintenance, but extended it to the conclusion of tertiary education, incorporated a payment from F's bonus, ordered F to pay 76% of the school fees and provided no order for costs. M was granted permission to appeal on the school fees and costs decision only, and the parties were urged to settle.

19 [2009] EWCA Civ 1162, [2010] 1 FCR 413, [2010] 1 FLR 761.
20 From the case of *Calderbank v Calderbank* [1976] Fam 93, [1975] 3 WLR 586.
21 [2013] EWHC 464 (Fam), [2013] 2 FLR 698.
22 [2013] EWHC 464 (Fam), [2013] 2 FLR 698.

In advance of the appeal, F made a *Calderbank* offer to pay all of the school fees for the following year and a costs contribution of £4,500. M's proposal was for payment of all the school fees for the current and following year, 65% of her first instance costs and 80% of her appeal costs.

Held by Mostyn J:

Neither party had made *Calderbank* offers at first instance and the result was much closer to F's position than M's. Pre-proceedings conduct would only be relevant to costs where it had a direct causal connection to the later generation of costs.

Both parties' financial positions were 'calamitous' and so the claim that M would be adversely impacted by an order was equally applicable to F. M's appeal on costs was dismissed.

On appeal, the position is that prima facie costs should follow the event. Here, F had made a *Calderbank* offer which strengthened his case on costs considerably.

An order was made for M to pay £13,000 of F's costs, although as her position was 'dire' it would be deducted in 26 monthly instalments from the periodical payments.

16.25 In *M v F*[23], HHJ Booth (sitting as a judge of the High Court) dealt with a costs application following a final hearing of CA 1989, Sch 1 proceedings. When considering the factors to be written on the 'clean sheet' in such cases, along with directing himself to CPR 1998, r 44.2, the judge considered the following points to be of particular relevance in these types of cases.

23 [2016] EWHC B12 (Fam).

16.26 The economic impact of a costs order is relevant. This is likely to have a greater impact where the court is being invited to make a costs order against an applicant parent (usually the mother). However, that is not to say that such a party will always be protected from a costs order.

16.27 This can be seen from *KS v ND*[24] (above), where the court acknowledged the difficulties for the mother in paying the costs order and therefore allowed her to make payment by instalments but was not persuaded that the mother's financial difficulties should insulate her from an order. It is, however, worth noting that in that case the father was also heavily indebted and so the economically destructive impact of proceedings was significant for them both.

16.28

Case summary: *Re A (A Child: Financial Provision)*[25]

Facts:

The case concerned a six year old child, whose father was a very wealthy member of a Middle Eastern royal family. He had asserted the millionaire's defence. Though the parents had been religiously married, this was not recognised and so M had no financial claims in her own right. At trial, M was awarded a £3.5 million house, which would revert to F at the end of the child's tertiary education, in addition to periodical payments of £204,000 per annum, a school fees order, car allowance, ongoing house upkeep costs, a £25,000 redecoration fund and a £770,000 lump sum to clear her debts. Her legal fees, of almost £1 million, were also funded by F. M's application to vary the order was refused and she sought permission to appeal that refusal, and was granted an extension of time in relation to the original order. On appeal, M argued unsuccessfully that the millionaire's defence had no place in CA 1989, Sch 1 applications.

Held by Court of Appeal:

The court deplored M's application for variation as 'totally unmeritorious' and her manipulation of the rules to achieve an out-of-time appeal to the original order. M was ordered to pay a contribution of £25,000 towards F's costs, deducted from the periodical payments at the rate of £1,000 pm.

24 [2013] EWHC 464 (Fam), [2013] 2 FLR 698.
25 [2014] EWCA Civ 1577, [2015] Fam 277, [2015] 3 WLR 48, [2015] 2 FLR 625.

The court noted that M:

> 'must act responsibly in the stewardship of the moneys that are paid for [the child's] benefit. She is not entitled to assume that a court will countenance her unmerited applications by declining to order costs against her or ordering further lump sums to be paid by the father to make good the shortfall.'

16.29 By contrast, in *CA v DR*[26], Roberts J noted that outstanding costs owed by the caring parent risk simply creating another 'need' if they are not discharged in full. Despite the mother having pursued a carer's allowance claim which included provision for pension contributions (which was considered to go far beyond that which was required for the benefit of the child), the court noted that the gulf between the parties was such that court intervention was going to be required. The mother's outstanding costs liability was significant to her, but comparably insignificant in the context of the father's resources. The judge accordingly invited the father to agree to pay a lump sum to cover this, making clear that absent agreement she intended to include appropriate provision in her order.

16.30 *CA v DR*[27] highlights a difficulty sometimes faced by judges dealing with CA 1989, Sch 1 cases where there is a considerable disparity of wealth between the parties. Whilst it has been said that litigants cannot spend freely without regard to the consequences of doing so[28], without provision for a lump sum to meet any outstanding legal costs, there is a risk that what has been provided for the child will in fact be used to discharge legal fees on the part of the carer.

16.31 A somewhat novel approach was taken in *MT v OT (Financial Provision: Costs)*[29]. All of the costs had met by the father but the court considered it appropriate for the mother to bear *some* of the costs of her own litigation.

26 [2021] EWFC 21, [2021] 3 FCR 331.
27 [2021] EWFC 21, [2021] 3 FCR 331.
28 For example, Cobb J in *Re Z (No 2) (Schedule 1: Further Legal Costs Funding Order; Further Interim Financial Provision)* [2021] EWFC 72, [2022] 3 FCR 419 raised concerns about the mother's solicitors having billed £52,088 in excess of what had been permitted by an earlier funding order.
29 [2007] EWHC 838 (Fam), [2008] 2 FLR 1311.

Case summary: *MT v OT (Financial Provision: Costs)*[30]

Facts:

English financial remedy proceedings had been stayed between the parties pending the conclusion of Nigerian proceedings to decide whether they had been married under Nigerian law. M brought CA 1989, Sch 1 proceedings seeking financial provision for the couple's five year old twins.

F had conceded he was worth at least £40 million and had been ordered to make interim payments of around £130,000 pa, excluding provision for M's legal fees.

M sought 'lavish' financial support, including a property worth between £1.4–2 million, and presented a budget of £12,672 pm. She also argued that she should have a life interest in the property with the children having residual beneficial interests, and sought a lump sum to clear her debts of £281,000. F proposed M and children returning to Nigeria, or a property worth between £500,000–800,000, with a proposed budget of £4,172 pm.

Held by Charles J:

A property worth £900,000–975,000 should be purchased for the children, but should revert to F up to two years after the children finished tertiary education. In addition to school fees, interim rent and an allowance for special educational assistance for one child, M was to receive £6,500 pm inclusive of the carer's allowance.

In respect of costs, M should be left to bear one-third of the costs incurred by her on behalf of the children. This was to be funded by reducing the fund available for the purchase of the home by a sum equal to the one-third liability, such that the reduction was used to discharge the costs (without the father in fact 'paying' any greater sum). It was noted that this did not mean the children would not be adequately housed, but rather that the home would be in a slightly less pleasant location or street.

16.32 Although MCA 1973 claims are dealt with under the 'general rule', interim applications and hearings within those claims are not and will equally be subject to the 'clean sheet' approach.

30 [2007] EWHC 838 (Fam), [2008] 2 FLR 1311.

Case summary: *LM v DM (Costs Ruling)*[31]

Facts:

The wife obtained orders for maintenance pending suit, interim periodical payments for the children and for a legal services payment order. She applied for an order that the husband pay her costs, determined on written submissions.

Held by Mostyn J:

Interim applications such as this are governed by a 'soft costs-follow-the-event principle' and *Calderbank* offers are admissible, though neither party made such an offer in this case.

The obligation to negotiate openly and reasonably is of importance in interim applications, which should be pragmatically settled where – by definition – they are not final determinations.

Whilst the wife did not achieve as much by way of quantum as she sought, the result was much closer to her proposal and she was successful on issues of principle. However, she made no serious attempt to negotiate openly and reasonably, and appeared determined to 'fight'. As a result, she was awarded 50% of the costs the court otherwise would have made in her favour, to be assessed on the standard basis.

16.33 More generally, the frustration of courts at what is perceived to be (and, in fact, is) increasing disproportionality of costs in family proceedings means that costs orders are becoming more common where one party's conduct within proceedings has stymied or prevented settlement.

PROCEDURE FOR COSTS APPLICATIONS

16.34 If costs are sought at any hearing, a form N260 should be filed with the court and served on the other party not less than 24 hours before the relevant hearing, as required by the CPR 1998, PD44, para 9.5. This sets out the costs incurred, separated by category. A failure to serve a form N260 in sufficient time is not *necessarily* fatal to a costs claim, although it will be a factor considered by the court in deciding which order to make. Paragraph 9.6 of CPR 1998, PD44 highlights this point, although the late filing of or omission in filing a form N260 is relevant only if done 'without reasonable excuse'.

31 [2021] EWFC 28, [2021] 2 FCR 239, [2022] 1 FLR 393.

16.35 There are two types of assessment of costs: summary assessment; and detailed assessment. For relatively straightforward applications, and where a hearing has lasted a day or less, the summary assessment is generally appropriate[32]. This involves the trial judge simply determining the quantum of costs which should be paid by one party to the other on the basis of the form N260s provided.

16.36 Where a summary assessment is not appropriate, the assessment of costs will be adjourned to be carried out through a detailed assessment. The procedure for a detailed assessment is governed by CPR 1998, Part 47.

16.37 Costs can be awarded on two different bases: standard basis; and indemnity basis.

16.38 The standard basis is the norm where a costs order is merited, but there is nothing to take the case out of the ordinary. In those circumstances, the court will only allow costs that are proportionate, even if they were reasonably or necessarily incurred. Those costs which were unreasonably incurred or are unreasonable in amount will be disallowed. Doubts as to reasonableness and proportionality will be resolved in favour of the paying party. It is sometimes suggested that a standard assessment typically results in a reduction in costs of approximately 30%.

16.39 The indemnity basis is used to mark particularly poor conduct in litigation, and generally requires something significantly unreasonable or concerning in the paying party's conduct. Where an indemnity basis assessment takes place, costs are assessed without a focus on proportionality. Unreasonably incurred costs or those unreasonable in amount will be disallowed, but doubts will be resolved in favour of the receiving party. Unsurprisingly, this often results in a greater proportion of the overall costs being received by one party.

16.40 Ordinarily, payment of costs will be ordered to be made within 14 days.

16.41 The court can also be flexible in ordering the payment of costs. This is particularly so in cases involving provision for children, where the payment of a costs order may impact on the availability of that provision to support the children's upbringing.

16.42 In some cases, the court may make orders for costs but include provisions so that the costs do not have to be paid immediately in full.

32 This is set out in PD44 of the Civil Procedure Rules 2010 at para 9.2.

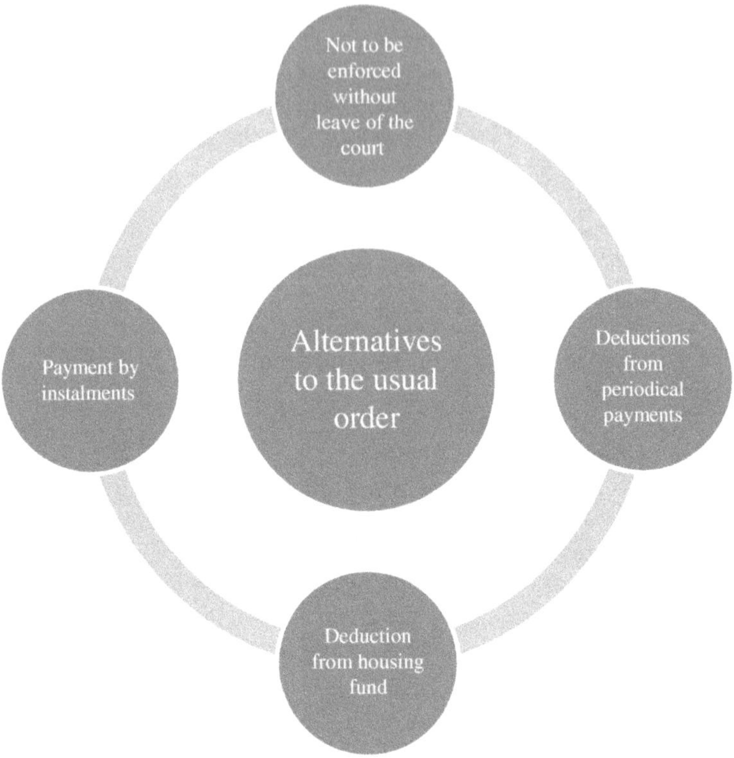

MANAGING COSTS

16.43 Case law is littered with criticism of litigants who have expended significant sums on costs, sometimes out of all proportion to the issues involved in the litigation. Such uncontrolled expenditure on costs has been the subject of increasingly strong judicial warning in recent years, with repeated comments that something must be done to control litigation spending. By way of illustration alone:

Crowther v Crowther[33]	'The only beneficiaries of this nihilistic litigation have been the specialist and high-quality lawyers. The main losers are probably the children who, quite apart from the emotional pain of seeing their parents involved in such bitter proceedings, will be deprived of monies which I am sure their parents would otherwise have wanted them to benefit from in due course.'

33 [2021] EWFC 88, [2022] 1 FCR 516, [2022] 2 FLR 243, Peel J.

Xanthopoulos v Rakshina[34]	'I have struggled to find the language that aptly describes the exorbitance of the litigious conduct of the parties in the case before me since it began on 21 September 2020 when the husband filed his petition. In the ensuing 18 months the parties have incurred costs in the extraordinary sum of **£5,401,503**. But that is not the end of the story. There are vast amounts of future costs in the pipeline.' 'It is difficult to know what to say or do when confronted with such extraordinary, self-harming conduct. Periodically the judges bemoan the heedless incurring by divorcing parties of huge costs.'
Goddard-Watts v Goddard-Watts[35]	'It is a tragedy that the parties have between them spent in legal costs in this round of the litigation alone (W:824k per Form H1: H:737k per Form H1) more by some way than the amount of my award. That will give rise to difficult questions when costs fall to be considered as they now will.'
Helliwell v Entwistle[36]	'again and again, the judges in this Division have to send out clear messages to those that are advising people in this field of work that you cannot just litigate on a blank cheque, or on the basis that someone else is going to underwrite your fees. £75,000 is an enormous amount of money to almost all people in this country and almost all people who come into this court. It is a lot of money to this husband, but it is not going to undermine the order that I made. It is not going to undermine the figures in my Judgment. I find that, applying the wide discretion afforded to me in relation to costs orders, it is fair as a representation of the way that the judges of this Division have to approach the issue of costs.'

16.44 Forms H have been mandatory in family litigation for some years. These require parties to set out the costs incurred in proceedings to date (inclusive of the hearing they have been prepared for). In July 2020, FPR 2010 r 9.27 was amended so as to require that the form H, used for hearings other than the final hearing, now sets out estimates for future hearings.

16.45 One day prior to the first appointment, a Form H must be filed and exchanged recording the costs incurred to that hearing together with an estimate of what will be spent up to and including an FDR if settlement is not reached. This must be repeated prior to the FDR appointment, save that the estimate of future costs must set out those expected to be incurred to the conclusion of the

34 [2022] EWFC 30, [2022] 2 FCR 712, [2023] 1 FLR 388, Mostyn J.
35 [2022] EWHC 711 (Fam), [2023] 1 FCR 65, Sir Jonathan Cohen.
36 [2024] EWHC 1298 (Fam), Francis J.

final hearing. A Form H1 is required prior to the final hearing, to include the costs up to the end of that hearing and including the implementation of any order.

16.46 In addition to this, the costs incurred and estimated must be recorded as a recital on the order made at the relevant hearing in accordance with FPR 2010, r 9.27(7). This enables both parties and the court to be aware of the growing costs and on the progress of those bills in the event settlement is not reached. The failure to provide a costs estimate must also be recorded if applicable.

APPENDIX 1

Tables from *James v Seymour*

For an explanation of the tables see the appendix to *James v Seymour* [2023] EWHC 844 (Fam).

CSSP = Child Support Starting Point; E = Earnings.

Table 1: CSSP per child, FORMULA UNADJUSTED (no shared care)

	Number of children		
E	**1**	**2**	**3**
156,000	15,300	10,200	8,400
175,000	17,000	11,300	9,300
195,000	18,800	12,500	10,300
215,000	20,600	13,700	11,300
235,000	22,400	14,900	12,300
255,000	24,200	16,100	13,300
275,000	26,000	17,300	14,300
295,000	27,800	18,500	15,300
315,000	29,600	19,700	16,300
335,000	31,400	20,900	17,300
355,000	33,200	22,100	18,300
375,000	35,000	23,300	19,300
395,000	36,800	24,500	20,300
415,000	38,600	25,700	21,300
435,000	40,400	26,900	22,300
455,000	42,200	28,100	23,300
475,000	44,000	29,300	24,300
495,000	45,800	30,500	25,300
515,000	47,600	31,700	26,300
535,000	49,400	32,900	27,300
555,000	51,200	34,100	28,300
575,000	53,000	35,300	29,300
595,000	54,800	36,500	30,300
615,000	56,600	37,700	31,300
635,000	58,400	38,900	32,300
650,000	59,700	39,800	33,100

Table 2: FORMULA ADJUSTED

		A CSSP per child no shared care			B CSSP per child: 1/7th shared care			C CSSP per child 2/7ths shared care			D CSSP per child 3/7ths shared care			E CSSP per child equal shared care		
	No. of children	**1**	**2**	**3**	**1**	**2**	**3**	**1**	**2**	**3**	**1**	**2**	**3**	**1**	**2**	**3**
Amount of E	**156,000**	15,300	10,200	8,400	13,100	8,700	7,200	10,900	7,300	6,000	8,700	5,800	4,800	7,300	4,400	3,100
	175,000	15,700	10,800	8,900	13,500	9,300	7,600	11,200	7,700	6,400	9,000	6,200	5,100	7,500	4,700	3,400
	195,000	16,200	11,400	9,500	13,900	9,800	8,100	11,600	8,100	6,800	9,300	6,500	5,400	7,700	5,000	3,700
	215,000	16,700	12,000	10,100	14,300	10,300	8,700	11,900	8,600	7,200	9,500	6,900	5,800	8,000	5,300	4,000
	235,000	17,200	12,600	10,700	14,700	10,800	9,200	12,300	9,000	7,600	9,800	7,200	6,100	8,200	5,600	4,300
	255,000	17,700	13,200	11,300	15,200	11,300	9,700	12,600	9,400	8,100	10,100	7,500	6,500	8,500	5,900	4,600
	275,000	18,100	13,800	11,900	15,500	11,800	10,200	12,900	9,900	8,500	10,300	7,900	6,800	8,700	6,200	4,900
	295,000	18,600	14,400	12,500	15,900	12,300	10,700	13,300	10,300	8,900	10,600	8,200	7,100	8,900	6,500	5,200
	315,000	19,100	15,000	13,100	16,400	12,900	11,200	13,600	10,700	9,400	10,900	8,600	7,500	9,200	6,800	5,500
	335,000	19,600	15,600	13,700	16,800	13,400	11,700	14,000	11,100	9,800	11,200	8,900	7,800	9,400	7,100	5,800
	355,000	20,100	16,200	14,300	17,200	13,900	12,300	14,400	11,600	10,200	11,500	9,300	8,200	9,700	7,400	6,100
	375,000	20,500	16,800	14,900	17,600	14,400	12,800	14,600	12,000	10,600	11,700	9,600	8,500	9,900	7,700	6,400
	395,000	21,000	17,400	15,500	18,000	14,900	13,300	15,000	12,400	11,100	12,000	9,900	8,900	10,100	8,000	6,700
	415,000	21,500	18,000	16,100	18,400	15,400	13,800	15,400	12,900	11,500	12,300	10,300	9,200	10,400	8,300	7,000
	435,000	22,000	18,600	16,700	18,900	15,900	14,300	15,700	13,300	11,900	12,600	10,600	9,500	10,600	8,600	7,300
	455,000	22,500	19,200	17,300	19,300	16,500	14,800	16,100	13,700	12,400	12,900	11,000	9,900	10,900	8,900	7,600
	475,000	22,900	19,800	17,900	19,600	17,000	15,300	16,400	14,100	12,800	13,100	11,300	10,200	11,100	9,200	7,900

Amount of £	No. of children	A CSSP per child no shared care			B CSSP per child: 1/7th shared care			C CSSP per child 2/7ths shared care			D CSSP per child 3/7ths shared care			E CSSP per child equal shared care		
		1	2	3	1	2	3	1	2	3	1	2	3	1	2	3
	495,000	23,400	20,400	18,500	20,100	17,500	15,900	16,700	14,600	13,200	13,400	11,700	10,600	11,300	9,500	8,200
	515,000	23,900	21,000	19,100	20,500	18,000	16,400	17,100	15,000	13,600	13,700	12,000	10,900	11,600	9,800	8,500
	535,000	24,400	21,600	19,700	20,900	18,500	16,900	17,400	15,400	14,100	13,900	12,300	11,300	11,800	10,100	8,800
	555,000	24,900	22,200	20,300	21,300	19,000	17,400	17,800	15,900	14,500	14,200	12,700	11,600	12,100	10,400	9,100
	575,000	25,300	22,800	20,900	21,700	19,500	17,900	18,100	16,300	14,900	14,500	13,000	11,900	12,300	10,700	9,400
	595,000	25,800	23,400	21,500	22,100	20,100	18,400	18,400	16,700	15,400	14,700	13,400	12,300	12,500	11,000	9,700
	615,000	26,300	24,000	22,100	22,500	20,600	18,900	18,800	17,100	15,800	15,000	13,700	12,600	12,800	11,300	10,000
	635,000	26,800	24,600	22,700	23,000	21,100	19,500	19,100	17,600	16,200	15,300	14,100	13,000	13,000	11,600	10,300
	650,000	27,100	25,000	23,200	23,200	21,400	19,900	19,400	17,900	16,600	15,500	14,300	13,300	13,200	11,800	10,500

APPENDIX 2

Children Act 1989

(1989 c 41)

SCHEDULE 1: FINANCIAL PROVISION FOR CHILDREN

Section 15(1)

1 Orders for financial relief against parents

(1) On an application made by a parent[, guardian or special guardian][1] of a child, or by any person [who is named in a child arrangements order as a person with whom a child is to live][2], the court [may make one or more of the orders mentioned in sub-paragraph (2).][3]

(a) ...[4]

(b) ...[4]

(2) The orders referred to in sub-paragraph (1) are –

(a) an order requiring either or both parents of a child –

(i) to make to the applicant for the benefit of the child; or

(ii) to make to the child himself,

such periodical payments, for such term, as may be specified in the order;

(b) an order requiring either or both parents of a child –

(i) to secure to the applicant for the benefit of the child; or

(ii) to secure to the child himself,

such periodical payments, for such term, as may be so specified;

(c) an order requiring either or both parents of a child –

(i) to pay to the applicant for the benefit of the child; or

(ii) to pay to the child himself,

such lump sum as may be so specified;

(d) an order requiring a settlement to be made for the benefit of the child, and to the satisfaction of the court, of property –

(i) to which either parent is entitled (either in possession or in reversion); and

(ii) which is specified in the order;

(e) an order requiring either or both parents of a child –

(i) to transfer to the applicant, for the benefit of the child; or

(ii) to transfer to the child himself,

such property to which the parent is, or the parents are, entitled (either in possession or in reversion) as may be specified in the order.

(3) The powers conferred by this paragraph may be exercised at any time.

(4) An order under sub-paragraph (2)(a) or (b) may be varied or discharged by a subsequent order made on the application of any person by or to whom payments were required to be made under the previous order.

(5) Where a court makes an order under this paragraph –

(a) it may at any time make a further such order under sub-paragraph (2)(a), (b) or (c) with respect to the child concerned if he has not reached the age of eighteen;

(b) it may not make more than one order under sub-paragraph (2)(d) or (e) against the same person in respect of the same child.

(6) On making, varying or discharging …[5] […[5] a special guardianship order][6][, or on making, varying or discharging provision in a child arrangements order with respect to the living arrangements of a child,][7] the court may exercise any of its powers under this Schedule even though no application has been made to it under this Schedule.

[(6A) For the purposes of sub-paragraph (6) provision in a child arrangements order is with respect to the living arrangements of a child if it regulates arrangements relating to –

(a) with whom the child is to live, or

(b) when the child is to live with any person.][7]

[(7) Where a child is a ward of court, the court may exercise any of its powers under this Schedule even though no application has been made to it.][8]

Amendments

1 Substituted by the Adoption and Children Act 2002, s 139(1), Sch 3, paras 54, 71(a)(i).

2 Substituted by the Children and Families Act 2014, s 12, Sch 2, paras 1, 40(1), (2)(a).

3 Substituted by the Crime and Courts Act 2013, s 17, Sch 11, paras 102, 112, 113(a).

4 Inserted by the Courts and Legal Services Act 1990, s 116, Sch 16, para 10(2).

5 Repealed by the Crime and Courts Act 2013, s 17, Sch 11, paras 102, 112, 113(b).

6 Repealed by the Children and Families Act 2014, s 12, Sch 2, paras 1, 40(1), (2)(b)(i).

7 Inserted by the Adoption and Children Act 2002, s 139(1), Sch 3, paras 54, 71(a)(ii).

8 Inserted by the Children and Families Act 2014, s 12, Sch 2, paras 1, 40(1), (2)(b)(ii), (c).

2 Orders for financial relief for persons over eighteen

(1) If, on an application by a person who has reached the age of eighteen, it appears to the court –

(a) that the applicant is, will be or (if an order were made under this paragraph) would be receiving instruction at an educational establishment or undergoing training for a trade, profession or vocation, whether or not while in gainful employment; or

(b) that there are special circumstances which justify the making of an order under this paragraph,

the court may make one or both of the orders mentioned in sub-paragraph (2).

(2) The orders are –

(a) an order requiring either or both of the applicant's parents to pay to the applicant such periodical payments, for such term, as may be specified in the order;

(b) an order requiring either or both of the applicant's parents to pay to the applicant such lump sum as may be so specified.

(3) An applicant may not be made under this paragraph by any person if, immediately before he reached the age of sixteen, a periodical payments order was in force with respect to him.

(4) No order shall be made under this paragraph at a time when the parents of the applicant are living with each other in the same household.

(5) An order under sub-paragraph (2)(a) may be varied or discharged by a subsequent order made on the application of any person by or to whom payments were required to be made under the previous order.

(6) In sub-paragraph (3) 'periodical payments order' means an order made under –

(a) this Schedule;

(b) …[1]

(c) section 23 or 27 of the Matrimonial Causes Act 1973;

(d) Part I of the Domestic Proceedings and Magistrates' Courts Act 1978, for the making or securing of periodical payments.

[(e) Part 1 or 9 of Schedule 5 to the Civil Partnership Act 2004 (financial relief in the High Court or a county court etc);

(f) Schedule 6 to the 2004 Act (financial relief in the magistrates' courts etc),][2]

(7) The powers conferred by this paragraph shall be exercisable at any time.

(8) Where the court makes an order under this paragraph it may from time to time while that order remains in force make a further such order.

Amendments

1 Repealed by the Child Support Act 1991, s 58(14).

2 Inserted by the Civil Partnership Act 2004, s 78(1), (2).

---

3 Duration of orders for financial relief

(1) The term to be specified in an order for periodical payments made under paragraph 1(2)(a) or (b) in favour of a child may begin with the date of the making of an application for the order in question or any later date [or a date ascertained in accordance with sub-paragraph (5) or (6)][1] but –

(a) shall not in the first instance extend beyond the child's seventeenth birthday unless the court thinks it right in the circumstances of the case to specify a later date; and

(b) shall not in any event extend beyond the child's eighteenth birthday.

(2) Paragraph (b) of sub-paragraph (1) shall not apply in the case of a child if it appears to the court that –

(a) the child is, or will be (if an order were made without complying with that paragraph) would be receiving instruction at an educational establishment or undergoing training for a trade, profession or vocation, whether or not while in gainful employment; or

(b) there are special circumstances which justify the making of an order without complying with that paragraph.

(3) An order for periodical payments made under paragraph 1(2)(a) or 2(2)(a) shall, notwithstanding anything in the order, cease to have effect on the death of the person liable to make payments under the order.

(4) Where an order is made under paragraph 1(2)(a) or (b) requiring periodical payments to be made or secured to the parent of a child, the order shall cease to have effect if –

(a) any parent making or securing the payments; and

(b) any parent to whom the payments are made or secured,

live together for a period of more than six months.

[(5) Where –

(a) a [maintenance calculation][2] ('the [current calculation][2]') is in force with respect to a child; and

(b) an application is made for an order under paragraph 1(2)(a) or (b) of this Schedule for periodical payments in favour of that child –

(i) in accordance with section 8 of the Child Support Act 1991; and

(ii) before the end of the period of 6 months beginning with the making of the [current calculation][2],

the term to be specified in any such order made on that application may be expressed to begin on, or at any time after, the earliest permitted date.

(6) For the purposes of subsection (5) above, 'the earliest permitted date' is whichever is the later of –

(a) the date 6 months before the application is made; or

(b) the date on which the [current calculation][2] took effect or, where successive [maintenance calculations][2] have been continuously in force with respect to a child, on which the first of [those calculations][2] took effect.

(7) Where –

(a) a [maintenance calculation][2] ceases to have effect …[3] by or under any provision of the Child Support Act 1991, and

(b) an application is made, before the end of the period of 6 months beginning with the relevant date, for an order for periodical payments under paragraph 1(2)(a) or (b) in favour of a child with respect to whom that [maintenance calculation][2] was in force immediately before it ceased to have effect …[3],

the term to be specified in any such order, or in any interim order under paragraph 9, made on that application may begin with the date on which that [maintenance calculation][2] ceased to have effect …[3], or any later date.

(8) In sub-paragraph (7)(b) –

(a) where the [maintenance calculation][2] ceased to have effect, the relevant date is the date on which it so ceased; …[3]

(b) …[3]][1]

Amendments

1 Inserted by the Maintenance Orders (Backdating) Order 1993, SI 1993/623, art 2, Sch 2, para 10, 11.

2 Substituted by the Child Support, Pensions and Social Security Act 2000, s 26, Sch 3, para 10(1), (2).

3 Repealed by the Child Support, Pensions and Social Security Act 2000, s 85, Sch 9, Pt I.

---

4 Matters to which court is to have regard in making orders for financial relief

(1) In deciding whether to exercise its powers under paragraph 1 or 2, and if so in what manner, the court shall have regard to all the circumstances including –

(a) the income, earning capacity, property and other financial resources which each person mentioned in sub-paragraph (4) has or is likely to have in the foreseeable future;

(b) the financial needs, obligations and responsibilities which each person mentioned in sub-paragraph (4) has or is likely to have in the foreseeable future;

(c) the financial needs of the child;

(d) the income, earning capacity (if any), property and other financial resources of the child;

(e) any physical or mental disability of the child;

(f) the manner in which the child was being, or was expected to be, educated or trained.

(2) In deciding whether to exercise its powers under paragraph 1 against a person who is not the mother or father of the child, and if so in what manner, the court shall in addition have regard to –

(a) whether that person had assumed responsibility for the maintenance of the child, and, if so, the extent to which and basis on which he assumed that responsibility and the length of the period during which he met that responsibility;

(b) whether he did so knowing that the child was not his child;

(c) the liability of any other person to maintain the child.

(3) Where the court makes an order under paragraph 1 against a person who is not the father of the child, it shall record in the order that the order is made on the basis that the person against whom the order is made is not the child's father.

(4) The persons mentioned in sub-paragraph (1) are –

(a) in relation to a decision whether to exercise its powers under paragraph 1, any parent of the child;

(b) in relation to a decision whether to exercise its powers under paragraph 2, the mother and father of the child;

(c) the applicant for the order;

(d) any other person in whose favour the court proposes to make the order.

[(5) In the case of a child who has a parent by virtue of section 42 or 43 of the Human Fertilisation and Embryology Act 2008, any reference in sub-paragraph (2), (3) or (4) to the child's father is a reference to the woman who is a parent of the child by virtue of that section.][1]

Amendments

1 Inserted by the Human Fertilisation and Embryology Act 2008, s 56, Sch 6, para 32(1), (2).

---

5 Provisions relating to lump sums

(1) Without prejudice to the generality of paragraph 1, an order under that paragraph for the payment of a lump sum may be made for the purpose of enabling any liabilities or expenses –

(a) incurred in connection with the birth of the child or in maintaining the child; and

(b) reasonably incurred before the making of the order,

to be met.

(2) …[1]

(3) The power of the court under paragraph 1 or 2 to vary or discharge an order for the making or securing of periodical payments by a parent shall include power to make an order under that provision for the payment of a lump sum by that parent.

(4) …[1]

(5) An order made under paragraph 1 or 2 for the payment of a lump sum may provide for the payment of that sum by instalments.

(6) Where the court provides for the payment of a lump sum by instalments the court, on an application made either by the person liable to pay or the person entitled to receive that sum, shall have power to vary that order by varying –

- (a) the number of instalments payable;
- (b) the amount of any instalment payable;
- (c) the date on which any instalment becomes payable.

[(7) The Lord Chief Justice may nominate a judicial office holder (as defined in section 109(4) of the Constitutional Reform Act 2005) to exercise his functions under this paragraph.][2]

Amendments

1 Repealed by the Crime and Courts Act 2013, s 17, Sch 11, paras 102, 112, 114.

2 Inserted by the Constitutional Reform Act 2005, s 15(1), Sch 4, paras 203, 209(1), (3).

6 Variation etc of orders for periodical payments

(1) In exercising its powers under paragraph 1 or 2 to vary or discharge an order for the making or securing of periodical payments the court shall have regard to all the circumstances of the case, including any change in any of the matters to which the court was required to have regard when making the order.

(2) The power of the court under paragraph 1 or 2 to vary an order for the making or securing of periodical payments shall include power to suspend any provision of the order temporarily and to revive any provision so suspended.

(3) Where on an application under paragraph 1 or 2 for the variation or discharge of an order for the making or securing of periodical payments the court varies the payments required to be made under that order, the court may provide that the payments as so varied shall be made from such date as the court may specify [except that, subject to sub-paragraph (9), the date shall not be][1] earlier than the date of the making of the application.

(4) An application for the variation of an order made under paragraph 1 for the making or securing of periodical payments to or for the benefit of a child may, if the child has reached the age of sixteen, be made by the child himself.

(5) Where an order for the making or securing of periodical payments made under paragraph 1 ceases to have effect on the date on which the child reaches

the age of sixteen, or at any time after that date but before or on the date on which he reaches the age of eighteen, the child may apply to the court which made the order for an order for its revival.

(6) If on such an application it appears to the court that –

(a) the child is, will be or (if an order were made under this sub-paragraph) would be receiving instruction at an educational establishment or undergoing training for a trade, profession or vocation, whether or not while in gainful employment; or

(b) there are special circumstances which justify the making of an order under this paragraph,

the court shall have power by order to revive the order from such date as the court may specify, not being earlier than the date of the making of the application.

(7) Any order which is revived by an order under sub-paragraph (5) may be varied or discharged under that provision, on the application of any person by whom or to whom payments are required to be made under the revived order.

(8) An order for the making or securing of periodical payments made under paragraph 1 may be varied or discharged, after the death of either parent, on the application of a guardian [or special guardian][2] of the child concerned.

[(9) Where –

(a) an order under paragraph 1(2)(a) or (b) for the making or securing of periodical payments in favour of more than one child ('the order') is in force;

(b) the order requires payments specified in it to be made to or for the benefit of more than one child without apportioning those payments between them;

(c) a [maintenance calculation][3] ('[the calculation][3]') is made with respect to one or more, but not all, of the children with respect to whom those payments are to be made; and

(d) an application is made, before the end of the period of 6 months beginning with the date on which [the calculation][3] was made, for the variation or discharge of the order,

the court may, in exercise of its powers under paragraph 1 to vary or discharge the order, direct that the variation or discharge shall take effect from the date on which [the calculation][3] took effect or any later date.][4]

Amendments

1 Substituted by the Maintenance Orders (Backdating) Order 1993, SI 1993/623, art 2, Sch 2, para 12.

2 Inserted by the Adoption and Children Act 2002, s 139(1), Sch 3, paras 54, 71(b).

3 Substituted by the Child Support, Pensions and Social Security Act 2000, s 26, Sch 3, para 10(1), (3).

4 Inserted by the Maintenance Orders (Backdating) Order 1993, SI 1993/623, art 2, Sch 2, para 13.

[6A Variation of orders for periodical payments etc made by magistrates' courts

(1) Subject to [sub-paragraph (7)][1], the power of [the family][1] court –

(a) under paragraph 1 or 2 to vary an order for the making of periodical payments, or

(b) under paragraph 5(6) to vary an order for the payment of a lump sum by instalments,

shall include power, if the court is satisfied that payment has not been made in accordance with the order, to exercise one of its powers under [section 1(4) and (4A) of the Maintenance Enforcement Act 1991][1].

(2) …[2]

(3) …[2]

(4) …[2]

(5) …[2]

(6) [Subsection (6) of section 1 of the Maintenance Enforcement Act 1991][1] (power of court to order that account be opened) shall apply for the purposes of [sub-paragraph (1)][1] as it applies for the purposes of that section.

(7) Before varying the order by exercising one of its powers under [section 1(4) and (4A) of the Maintenance Enforcement Act 1991][1], the court shall have regard to any representations made by the parties to the application.

(8) …[2]

(9) None of the powers of the court …[2] conferred by this paragraph shall be exercisable in relation to an order under this Schedule for the making of periodical payments, or for the payment of a lump sum by instalments, [unless at the time when the order was made the person required to make the payments was ordinarily resident in England and Wales.][1]

(10) …[2]][3]

Amendments

1 Substituted by the Crime and Courts Act 2013, s 17, Sch 11, paras 102, 112, 115(1)-(3), (5), (7)(b).

2 Repealed by the Crime and Courts Act 2013, s 17, Sch 11, paras 102, 112, 115(1), (4), (6), (7)(a).

3 Inserted by the Maintenance Enforcement Act 1991, s 6.

---

7 Variation of orders for secured periodical payments after death of parent

(1) Where the parent liable to make payments under a secured periodical payments order has died, the persons who may apply for the variation or discharge of the order shall include the personal representatives of the deceased parent.

(2) No application for the variation of the order shall, except with the permission of the court, be made after the end of the period of six months from the date on which representation in regard to the estate of that parent is first taken out.

(3) The personal representatives of a deceased person against whom a secured periodical payments order was made shall not be liable for having distributed any part of the estate of the deceased after the end of the period of six months referred to in sub-paragraph (2) on the ground that they ought to have taken into account the possibility that the court might permit an application for variation to be made after that period by the person entitled to payments under the order.

(4) Sub-paragraph (3) shall not prejudice any power to recover any part of the estate so distributed arising by virtue of the variation of an order in accordance with this paragraph.

(5) Where an application to vary a secured periodical payments order is made after the death of the parent liable to make payments under the order, the circumstances to which the court is required to have regard under paragraph 6(1) shall include the changed circumstances resulting from the death of the parent.

[(6) The following are to be left out of account when considering for the purposes of sub-paragraph (2) when representation was first taken out –

(a) a grant limited to settled land or to trust property,

(b) any other grant that does not permit any of the estate to be distributed,

(c) a grant limited to real estate or to personal estate, unless a grant limited to the remainder of the estate has previously been made or is made at the same time,

(d) a grant, or its equivalent, made outside the United Kingdom (but see sub-paragraph (6A)).

(6A) A grant sealed under section 2 of the Colonial Probates Act 1892 counts as a grant made in the United Kingdom for the purposes of sub-paragraph (6), but is to be taken as dated on the date of sealing.][1]

(7) In this paragraph 'secured periodical payments order' means an order for secured periodical payments under paragraph 1(2)(b).

Amendments

1 Substituted by the Inheritance and Trustees' Powers Act 2014, s 7, Sch 3, para 4(1), (2).

---

8 Financial relief under other enactments

(1) This paragraph applies where a [child arrangements order to which sub-paragraph (1A) applies][1] [or a special guardianship order][2] is made with respect to a child at a time when there is in force an order ('the financial relief order') made under any enactment other than this Act and requiring a person to contribute to the child's maintenance.

[(1A) This sub-paragraph applies to a child arrangements order if the arrangements regulated by the order consist of, or include, arrangements which relate to either or both of the following –

(a) with whom the child concerned is to live, and

(b) when the child is to live with any person.][3]

(2) Where this paragraph applies, the court may, on the application of –

(a) any person required by the financial relief order to contribute to the child's maintenance; or

(b) any person [who is named in a child arrangements order as a person with whom the child is to live or][3] in whose favour ...[4] [...[4] a special guardianship order][2] with respect to the child is in force,

make an order revoking the financial relief order, or varying it by altering the amount of any sum payable under that order or by substituting the applicant for the person to whom any such sum is otherwise payable under that order.

Amendments

1 Substituted by the Children and Families Act 2014, s 12, Sch 2, paras 1, 40(1), (3)(a).

2 Words inserted: Adoption and Children Act 2002, s 139(1), Sch 3, paras 54, 71(c).

3 Inserted by the Children and Families Act 2014, s 12, Sch 2, paras 1, 40(1), (3)(b), (c)(i).

4 Repealed by the Children and Families Act 2014, s 12, Sch 2, paras 1, 40(1), (3)(c)(ii).

---

9 Interim orders

(1) Where an application is made under paragraph 1 or 2 the court may, at any time before it disposes of the application, make an interim order –

(a) requiring either or both parents to make such periodical payments, at such times and for such term as the court thinks fit; and

(b) giving any direction which the court thinks fit.

(2) An interim order made under this paragraph may provide for payments to be made from such date as the court may specify [except that, subject to paragraph 3(5) and (6), the date shall not be][1] earlier than the date of the making of the application under paragraph 1 or 2.

(3) An interim order made under this paragraph shall cease to have effect when the application is disposed of or, if earlier, on the date specified for the purposes of this paragraph in the interim order.

(4) An interim order in which a date has been specified for the purposes of sub-paragraph (3) may be varied by substituting a later date.

Amendments

1 Substituted by the Maintenance Orders (Backdating) Order 1993, SI 1993/623, art 2, Sch 2, para 14.

---

10 Alteration of maintenance agreements

(1) In this paragraph and in paragraph 11 'maintenance agreement' means any agreement in writing made with respect to a child, whether before or after the commencement of this paragraph, which –

(a) is or was made between the father and mother of the child; and

(b) contains provision with respect to the making or securing of payments, or the disposition or use of any property, for the maintenance or education of the child,

and any such provisions are in this paragraph, and paragraph 11, referred to as 'financial arrangements'.

(2) [Subject to sub-paragraph (2A), where][1] a maintenance agreement is for the time being subsisting and each of the parties to the agreement is for the time being either domiciled or resident in England and Wales, then, either party may apply for an order under this paragraph.

[(2A) If an application or part of an application relates to a matter [in relation to which Article 18 of the 2007 Hague Convention applies, the court may not entertain the application or that part of it except where permitted by Article 18][2].

(2B) In sub-paragraph (2A), ['the 2007 Hague Convention' means the Convention on the International Recovery of Child Support and Other Forms of Family Maintenance concluded on 23 November 2007 at The Hague][2].][3]

(3) If the court to which the application is made is satisfied either –

(a) that, by reason of a change in the circumstances in the light of which any financial arrangements contained in the agreement were made (including a change foreseen by the parties when making the agreement), the agreement should be altered so as to make different financial arrangements; or

(b) that the agreement does not contain proper financial arrangements with respect to the child,

then that court may by order make such alterations in the agreement by varying or revoking any financial arrangements contained in it as may appear to it to be just having regard to all the circumstances.

(4) If the maintenance agreement is altered by an order under this paragraph, the agreement shall have effect thereafter as if the alteration had been made by agreement between the parties and for valuable consideration.

(5) Where a court decides to make an order under this paragraph altering the maintenance agreement –

(a) by inserting provision for the making or securing by one of the parties to the agreement of periodical payments for the maintenance of the child; or

(b) by increasing the rate of periodical payments required to be made or secured by one of the parties for the maintenance of the child,

then, in deciding the term for which under the agreement as altered by the order the payments or (as the case may be) the additional payments attributable to the increase are to be made or secured for the benefit of the child, the court shall apply the provisions of sub-paragraphs (1) and (2) of paragraph 3 as if the order were an order under paragraph 1(2)(a) or (b).

(6) …[4]

(7) For the avoidance of doubt it is hereby declared that nothing in this paragraph affects any power of a court before which any proceedings between the parties to a maintenance agreement are brought under any other enactment to make an order containing financial arrangements or any right of either party to apply for such an order in such proceedings.

[(8) In the case of a child who has a parent by virtue of section 42 or 43 of the Human Fertilisation and Embryology Act 2008, the reference in sub-paragraph (1)(a) to the child's father is a reference to the woman who is a parent of the child by virtue of that section.][5]

Amendments

1 Substituted by the Civil Jurisdiction and Judgments (Maintenance) Regulations 2011, SI 2011/1484, reg 9, Sch 7, para 12(1), (2)(a).

2 Substituted by the Jurisdiction and Judgments (Family) (Amendment etc.) (EU Exit) Regulations 2019, SI 2019/519, reg 7, Schedule, para 17(1), (2) (as substituted by the Jurisdiction, Judgments and Applicable Law (Amendment) (EU Exit) Regulations 2020, SI 2020/1574, reg 5(1), (3)(g)).

3 Inserted by the Civil Jurisdiction and Judgments (Maintenance) Regulations 2011, SI 2011/1484, reg 9, Sch 7, para 12(1), (2)(b).

4 Repealed by the Crime and Courts Act 2013, s 17, Sch 11, paras 102, 112, 116.

5 Inserted by the Human Fertilisation and Embryology Act 2008, s 56, Sch 6, para 32(1), (3).

11

(1) Where a maintenance agreement provides for the continuation, after the death of one of the parties, of payments for the maintenance of a child and that party dies domiciled in England and Wales, the surviving party or the personal representatives of the deceased party may apply to the High Court or [the family court][1] for an order under paragraph 10.

(2) If a maintenance agreement is altered by a court on an application under this paragraph, the agreement shall have effect thereafter as if the alteration had been made, immediately before the death, by agreement between the parties and for valuable consideration.

(3) An application under this paragraph shall not, except with leave of the High Court or [the family court][1], be made after the end of the period of six months beginning with the day on which representation in regard to the estate of the deceased is first taken out.

[(4) The following are to be left out of account when considering for the purposes of sub-paragraph (3) when representation was first taken out –

(a) a grant limited to settled land or to trust property,

(b) any other grant that does not permit any of the estate to be distributed,

(c) a grant limited to real estate or to personal estate, unless a grant limited to the remainder of the estate has previously been made or is made at the same time,

(d) a grant, or its equivalent, made outside the United Kingdom (but see sub-paragraph (4A)).

(4A) A grant sealed under section 2 of the Colonial Probates Act 1892 counts as a grant made in the United Kingdom for the purposes of sub-paragraph (4), but is to be taken as dated on the date of sealing.][2]

(5) …[3]

(6) The provisions of this paragraph shall not render the personal representatives of the deceased liable for having distributed any part of the estate of the deceased after the expiry of the period of six months referred to in sub-paragraph (3) on the ground that they ought to have taken into account the possibility that a court might grant leave for an application by virtue of this paragraph to be made by the surviving party after that period.

(7) Sub-paragraph (6) shall not prejudice any power to recover any part of the estate so distributed arising by virtue of the making of an order in pursuance of this paragraph.

Amendments

1 Substituted by the Crime and Courts Act 2013, s 17, Sch 11, paras 102, 112, 117(a), (b).

2 Substituted by the Inheritance and Trustees' Powers Act 2014, s 7, Sch 3, para 4(1), (3).

3 Repealed by the Crime and Courts Act 2013, s 17, Sch 11, paras 102, 112, 117(c).

---

12 Enforcement of orders for maintenance

(1) Any person for the time being under an obligation to make payments in pursuance of any order for the payment of money made by [the family court][1] under this Act shall give notice of any change of address to such person (if any) as may be specified in the order.

(2) Any person failing without reasonable excuse to give such a notice shall be guilty of an offence and liable on summary conviction to a fine not exceeding level 2 on the standard scale.

(3) …[2]

Amendments

1 Substituted by the Crime and Courts Act 2013, s 17, Sch 11, paras 102, 112, 118(a).

2 Repealed by the Crime and Courts Act 2013, s 17, Sch 11, paras 102, 112, 118(b).

---

13 Direction for settlement of instrument by conveyancing counsel

Where the High Court or [the family court][1] decides to make an order under this Act for the securing of periodical payments or for the transfer or settlement of property, it may direct that the matter be referred to one of the conveyancing counsel of the court to settle a proper instrument to be executed by all necessary parties.

Amendments

1 Substituted by the Crime and Courts Act 2013, s 17, Sch 11, paras 102, 112, 119.

[14 Jurisdiction ...[1]][2]

[[(1) The court has jurisdiction in relation to an application under paragraph 1 in respect of a child if any of the following persons are habitually resident or domiciled in England and Wales on the date of the application—

(a) a parent of the child;

(b) a guardian or special guardian of the child;

(c) a person who is named in a child arrangements order as a person with whom the child is to live;

(d) the child.

(2) The court has jurisdiction in relation to an application under paragraph 2 if the applicant or a parent against whom the order is sought or made is habitually resident or domiciled in England and Wales on the date of the application.][3]][4]

Amendments

1 Repealed by the Jurisdiction and Judgments (Family) (Amendment etc.) (EU Exit) Regulations 2019, SI 2019/519, reg 7, Schedule, para 17(1), (2A) (as inserted by the Jurisdiction and Judgments (Family) (Amendment etc.) (EU Exit) (No. 2) Regulations 2019, SI 2019/836, reg 2(1), (2)(a)).

2 Substituted by the International Recovery of Maintenance (Hague Convention 2007 etc) Regulations 2012, SI 2012/2814, reg 9, Sch 5, para 3.

3 Substituted by the Jurisdiction and Judgments (Family) (Amendment etc.) (EU Exit) Regulations 2019, SI 2019/519, reg 7, Schedule, para 17(1), (3) (as substituted by the Jurisdiction and Judgments (Family) (Amendment etc.) (EU Exit) (No. 2) Regulations 2019, SI 2019/836, reg 2(1), (2)(b)).

4 Substituted by the Civil Jurisdiction and Judgments (Maintenance) Regulations 2011, SI 2011/1484, reg 9, Sch 7, para 12(1), (3).

15 Local authority contribution to child's maintenance

(1) Where a child lives, or is to live, with a person as the result of a [child arrangements order][1], a local authority may make contributions to that person towards the cost of the accommodation and maintenance of the child.

(2) Sub-paragraph (1) does not apply where the person with whom the child lives, or is to live, is a parent of the child or the husband or wife [or civil partner][2] of a parent of the child.

Amendments

1 Substituted by the Children and Families Act 2014, s 12, Sch 2, paras 1, 40(1), (4).

2 Inserted by the Civil Partnership Act 2004, s 78(1), (3).

16 Interpretation

(1) In this Schedule 'child' includes, in any case where an application is made under paragraph 2 or 6 in relation to a person who has reached the age of eighteen, that person.

[(2) In this Schedule, except paragraphs 2 and 15, 'parent' includes –

(a) any party to a marriage (whether or not subsisting) in relation to whom the child concerned is a child of the family, and

(b) any civil partner in a civil partnership (whether or not subsisting) in relation to whom the child concerned is a child of the family;

and for this purpose any reference to either parent or both parents shall be read as a reference to any parent of his and to all of his parents.][1]

[(3) In this Schedule, '[maintenance calculation][2]' has the same meaning as it has in the Child Support Act 1991 by virtue of section 54 of that Act as read with any regulations in force under that section.][3]

Amendments

1 Substituted by the Civil Partnership Act 2004, s 78(1), (4).

2 Substituted by the Child Support, Pensions and Social Security Act 2000, s 26, Sch 3, para 10(1), (4).

3 Inserted by the Maintenance Orders (Backdating) Order 1993, SI 1993/623, art 2, Sch 2, para 15.

Index

[*all references are to paragraph number*]